The
REALLY USEFUL SCIENCE BOOK

Offering support to both trainee and practising teachers, the fourth edition of *The Really Useful Science Book* is the perfect tool for those who wish to extend their subject knowledge, enhance their teaching and create lessons which link directly to the National Curriculum. The easy-to-follow framework provides comprehensive science knowledge for Key Stages 1 and 2 and is fully updated with new material to inspire stimulating and engaging science lessons.

The book is divided into three sections: Biology, Chemistry and Physics. Each section integrates key scientific ideas and facts with innovative teaching methods and activity suggestions, and user-friendly language and illustrations help to explain key scientific concepts. With links to global learning, discussion of common misconceptions, and ideas for cross-curricular opportunities, each chapter connects knowledge to practice and informs creative and inspiring teaching.

The Really Useful Science Book is an invaluable reference resource for all classroom teachers who wish to develop the confidence to teach enquiry-based practical science with relevance to pupils and their global community.

Steve Farrow was Senior Lecturer in Science Education in the School of Education at Durham University, where he was also director of Primary ITT programmes.

Amy Strachan is Senior Lecturer in Primary Science Education at St Mary's University, Twickenham, UK. She has more than 10 years of experience as Head of Science in international, state and independent schools and has produced teacher materials for both the BBC and Oxfam.

The Really Useful Series

The
REALLY USEFUL SCIENCE BOOK

A Framework of Knowledge for Primary Teachers

Fourth Edition

Steve Farrow and Amy Strachan

Routledge
Taylor & Francis Group

LONDON AND NEW YORK

Fourth edition published 2018
by Routledge
2 Park Square, Milton Park, Abingdon, Oxon OX14 4RN

and by Routledge
711 Third Avenue, New York, NY 10017

Routledge is an imprint of the Taylor & Francis Group, an informa business

First edition published by Falmer Press 1996
Third edition published by Routledge 2006

British Library Cataloguing-in-Publication Data
A catalogue record for this book is available from the British Library

Library of Congress Cataloging-in-Publication Data
A catalog record for this book has been requested

ISBN: 978-1-138-19206-5 (hbk)
ISBN: 978-1-138-19208-9 (pbk)
ISBN: 978-1-315-64010-5 (ebk)

Typeset in Palatino and Gill Sans
by Florence Production Ltd, Stoodleigh, Devon, UK

Printed and bound by CPI Group (UK) Ltd, Croydon, CR0 4YY

Contents

Figures

SECTION ONE

Introduction

Introduction

THE NATURE AND PURPOSE OF THE BOOK: WHAT THE BOOK AIMS TO DO

This book has been written with primary teachers and teachers-in-training in mind, and its main purpose is to *support and extend teachers' own science knowledge*.

Notwithstanding all the changes that have taken place in primary education since the publication of the previous editions, the main aim of the book remains unchanged – to provide for primary classroom teachers and students, in a single volume, an outline of the key ideas that underpin the main branches of science.

The present, updated edition has been produced for two main reasons: First, the revision covers all changes seen in the National Curriculum (NC) reform in England for Key Stages 1 and 2. Second, the update has allowed for the inclusion of new material. Short chapter summaries in bite-size review pages will highlight opportunities for scientific discussions (views and attitudes), scientific enquiry (skills and investigation suggestions) and application (future developments). 'Teaching idea' boxes throughout the book include useful information linking knowledge to practice. These will include global learning links (e.g. food miles, recycling, technological advancements), common misconceptions (i.e. highlighting areas where there is frequent confusion in understanding) and cross-curricular opportunities (especially in mathematics). There will be short biographies of significant scientists highlighted in the Science National Curriculum (DfE, 2013), stating their importance in the development of our understanding to date. Finally, this edition will feature additional information on scientific enquiry, raising its significance in developing a more secure understanding of scientific phenomena and acquiring an appreciation for the beauty of discovery.

The new edition responds to the latest Teacher Standards used in England from 2012 (DfE, 2011), which replaced the *Professional Standards for Qualified Teacher Status* and the core professional standards published by the former Training and Development Agency for Schools. Teacher Standard 2 states: 'Promote good progress and outcomes by pupils'. This edition will use matrices to demonstrate how the curriculum can support progress of knowledge, understanding and skills in science. Teacher Standard 3 indicates the importance of 'demonstrating good subject and curriculum knowledge'. This book not only aims to support secure knowledge of related areas of science, but will aim to help foster and maintain pupils' interest in science and address common misunderstandings. Teacher Standard 8 requires teachers to 'fulfil wider responsibilities'. The 'In Practice' boxes sharing global learning links will demonstrate how science can support sustainable, environmentally and socially mindful, developments.

Although it is important to acknowledge the content of both schools' and ITT (initial teacher training) professional standards, the key ideas of science remain the key ideas, no matter which 'pieces' of science knowledge happen to be included in the current NC 'mosaic'. The aim is that the content included in this book, and the explanations given, will enable teachers and students to interpret more effectively the Science NC for the children in their charge, through the development of deeper understanding and greater confidence in their own science knowledge. There is now considerable evidence that increased subject knowledge can lead to increased confidence and to changes in the science learning opportunities presented to children – 'Now that I *know* more, I feel I'm a better teacher of science'.

WHAT THE BOOK *DOES NOT* DO

As the book is specifically devoted to the subject knowledge of science, there are two areas of science education that have deliberately not been addressed:

- Experimental and investigative science

Although this edition will highlight the importance of 'working scientifically' and the importance of different methods of scientific enquiry, there is no overt consideration of how different areas of science can be delivered through working-scientifically activities. However, many examples of investigations are provided that relate to the science knowledge under consideration. Wherever appropriate, 'classroom' versions of these investigations are indicated, and teachers may wish to include them in their own schemes of work. For more direct consideration of the implementation of working scientifically, readers are referred to other publications.

- The planning, organization and management of classroom science

The book does not address the issues inherent in the day-to-day provision of science education in primary classrooms. Once again, there are a number of excellent publications available that deal specifically with these issues.

THE STRUCTURE OF THE BOOK

The book contains three main sections, Biology, Chemistry and Physics.

At the beginning of each section, the Key Ideas are listed and are subsequently expanded in the following text. Concepts relating to the Key Ideas are presented as 'Concepts to support Key Stage 1' (or Key Stage 2, or both). The expectation is that the ideas presented will assist in teachers' understanding of the science involved and, hence, will support their own teaching of the various components of the Key Stage 1 and 2 programmes of study. Where concepts are presented that are not Key Stage 1 or 2 requirements for children, but may be helpful in terms of teachers' understanding of science, this distinction is made clear in the text.

At the end of each main section, there is a *National Curriculum progress matrix* demonstrating how the ideas build on each other. This allows the reader to relate each component of the programmes of study for Key Stages 1 and 2 to the Key Ideas and concepts presented and described in the book and may be useful as a quick reference guide for those seeking help with particular, specific aspects of NC-related science knowledge.

It is important to recognize that the book does not set out to provide material that can be used in the classroom in an unmodified form. It is not a book for children, but the hope is that it will be of value to teachers and students in supporting and extending their knowledge of science, so that what they provide in the way of science learning experiences for children will be grounded in a broader, more secure knowledge base and a deeper understanding of the subject knowledge context of the Science NC.

THE LANGUAGE OF SCIENCE

Throughout the book, the aim is to express scientific ideas in the most straightforward language possible, using examples from everyday experience. In each case, and at the appropriate place, the scientific terminology appropriate to the particular idea presented has been included in the explanation.

Where complex concepts are involved, scientific terminology becomes necessary for the accurate expression of ideas, as, in such cases, oversimplification could lead to distortion, omission and/or a potentially misleading explanation, and every effort has been made to avoid this. As highlighted in the NC (DfE, 2013), it is important for pupils to 'develop their scientific vocabulary and articulate scientific concepts clearly and precisely'.

It is hoped, therefore, that the self-avowed non-specialist will not be daunted, nor will those with a science background feel patronized, by the use of the language chosen (simple or scientific) for the expression and explanation of ideas.

Using accurate scientific language is essential for the development of children's scientific literacy. The progression of scientific vocabulary, consistent with the NC programmes of study, is therefore identified at the end of each section of this book. Development of scientific language will allow children to share their emerging scientific ideas with increasing confidence.

THE PROVISIONAL NATURE OF SCIENCE KNOWLEDGE

It is important to stress that science does *not* provide us, once and for all, with the *right* answers. What it can provide is a series of provisional explanations based on theory, observation and verification by experiment or investigation. In some cases, these explanations offer a degree of predictability so high that they can be generalized into 'laws' – the laws of motion, for example. In everyday terms, the laws of motion first propounded by Sir Isaac Newton can still offer us a useful explanation of the forces acting on moving objects – it is these laws that are described and explained in the subsection of this book that deals with forces.

Further theorization and experimentation, however, may bring new discoveries that increase our understanding of the way the world works and cause modifications to the explanations offered by science. Early in the last century, the 'frontiers' of Newtonian physics were extended by the theory of relativity proposed by Albert Einstein, and Einsteinian physics may well be supplanted in future by the attempt to provide a 'unified theory' that can explain the behaviour of all matter.

Scientific knowledge, then, is provisional and gives rise to current explanations of the nature of things – explanations that may only remain valid until further knowledge allows us to modify and improve them. In the writing of this book, every effort has been made to present the current, accepted thinking in science. Where alternative explanations or controversies exist (as with global warming, or 'cold' nuclear fusion, for example), these have been acknowledged and included. It is important, too, that we convey the nature of science through our teaching, together with the understanding that we do not have all the answers.

WORKING SCIENTIFICALLY

The NC (DfE, 2013) specifies that pupils should be taught to use practical scientific methods, processes and skills, through the teaching of the programme of study content. This is referred to as working scientifically and aims to develop children's independence in answering their own questions in science. It is essential that children learn about the nature, processes and methods of science. By working like scientists, children will develop the skills to answer the questions they raise. Not only does practical, hands-on learning aid the development of scientific skills, but it aims to nurture curiosity about the world and beyond.

Throughout this book, the famous scientists that are highlighted illustrate the common approaches to research and scientific methods and processes. It is important that children understand that they can be the scientists of the future, caring for and improving the planet on which we live. Exposing children to a variety of scientists, from those who work in laboratories to those who work out in the field, will demonstrate that ordinary people work in collaboration to make outstanding contributions to science.

Scientists use a range of enquiry approaches to answer their scientific questions. If these are modelled to children, they will help them to answer their own investigations, using the best approach to obtain relevant and accurate evidence. Critical thinking skills will also ensure that young people challenge ideas of other scientists, considering the reliability of evidence and alternative points of view.

Teachers must highlight the nature of science and celebrate uncertainty. It is fundamental that our future scientists realize that nobody has the answer to every question. Scientific enquiries may provide some answers, but should also generate further questions. The presence of a question box or question wall in classrooms can encourage the skill of raising questions and answering them in collaboration.

To provide some guidance on how these working-scientifically skills can be developed through the key stages, a progression of skills has been mapped out in a table format. This can be found in Table 1.1. Based on the NC Science programme of study guidance, the skills have been broken down into five key areas:

1   *thinking scientifically*: developing the ability to ask pertinent scientific questions and to have a perception of how they may be answered;
2   *planning scientifically*: considering the overarching plan of action to answer the question, the relevant variables and drawing on prior knowledge and experience to predict what might happen;
3   *working-scientifically approach*: beginning to develop a repertoire of key scientific enquiry approaches and to understand how they may be used to answer different scientific questions;
4   *observing, measuring and recording*: developing the refined skills to put the thinking and planning into action in a systematic way;
5   *communicating and reviewing*: ensuring that findings are shared, scientific enquiry is evaluated, and further exploration is considered.

PROGRESSION OF SCIENTIFIC VOCABULARY FOR WORKING SCIENTIFICALLY

The table below provides a useful progression of vocabulary that will support pupils to work scientifically and use appropriate equipment and skills (based on when the words are introduced in the NC programmes of study).

Year 1	Questions, answers, equipment, gather, measure, record, results, sort, group, test, explore, observe, compare, describe, similar/similarities, different/differences Egg timers, ruler, tape measure, metre stick, beaker, pipette, syringe
Year 2	Pictogram, tally chart, block diagram, Venn diagram, table, chart, order, observe changes over time, notice patterns, link, secondary sources Hand lenses, stopwatch
Year 3	Types of scientific enquiry, changes, identify, classify, order, comparative tests, fair tests, careful, accurate, observations, evidence, present, data/evidence/results, keys, bar charts, conclusions, prediction, support/not support Thermometers, data loggers, magnifying glass, microscope
Year 4	Increase, decrease, secondary sources, appearance
Years 5 & 6	Opinion/fact, variables, independent variable, dependent variable, controlled variable, accuracy, precision, degree of trust, classification keys, scatter graphs, line graphs, causal relationships, support/refute

Table 1.1 Mapping progression of working-scientifically skills

Early Years	Key Stage 1, (Years 1 and 2)	Lower Key Stage 2 (Years 3 and 4)	Upper Key Stage 2 (Years 5 and 6)	Deeper Learning / KS3
THINKING SCIENTIFICALLY				
Playing and exploring. Creating and thinking critically (having own ideas and making links)	Explore the world around them and raising own questions.	Exploring, talking about, testing and developing ideas about everyday phenomena and the relationships between living things and familiar environments. Develop ideas about functions, relationships and interactions. Ask own questions about what they observe.	Exploring and talking about ideas. Asking own questions about scientific phenomena. Analysing functions, relationships and interactions more systematically. Use science experiences to explore ideas and raise different kinds of questions.	Ask questions and develop a line of enquiry based on observations of the real world, alongside prior knowledge and experience.
PLANNING SCIENTIFICALLY				
Mostly whole-class planning		Facilitated independent and group planning	Independent and group planning	
Respond to teacher's questions	With help, plan and perform simple tests	Begin to make own decisions about the most appropriate type of scientific enquiry they might use to answer questions	Select and plan the most appropriate type of scientific enquiry to use to answer scientific questions;	Select, plan and carry out the most appropriate types of scientific enquiries to test predictions, including identifying independent, dependent and control variables

Table 1.1 *continued*

Early Years	Key Stage 1 (Years 1 and 2)	Lower Key Stage 2 (Years 3 and 4)	Upper Key Stage 2 (Years 5 and 6)	Deeper Learning / KS3
WORKING-SCIENTIFICALLY APPROACH (pattern-seeking, observing over time, grouping and classifying, comparative and fair testing, scientific research)				
	Experience different types of scientific enquiries, including practical activities. Begin to recognise ways in which they might answer scientific questions.	Make some decisions about which types of scientific enquiry are likely to be the best ways of answering questions, including observing changes over time, noticing patterns, grouping and classifying things, carrying out simple compara-tive and fair tests and finding things out using secondary sources of information.	Select the most appropriate ways to answer science questions using different types of scientific enquiry, including observing changes over different periods of time, noticing patterns, grouping and classifying things, carrying out comparative and fair tests and finding things out using a wide range of secondary sources of information.	Use appropriate techniques, apparatus, and materials during fieldwork and laboratory work, paying attention to health and safety.
OBSERVING, MEASURING AND RECORDING				
Look closely at similarities, differences, patterns and change.	Use simple measurements and equipment (for example, hand lenses, egg timers) to gather data, carry out simple tests and record simple data.	Begin to look for naturally occurring patterns and relationships and decide what data to collect to identify them. With support, make decisions about what observations to make, how long to make them for and the type of simple equipment that might be used. Begin to use new equipment, such as data loggers, appropriately. Collect data from own observations and measure-ments, using notes, simple tables and standard units.	Make own decisions about what observations to make, what measurements to use and how long to make them for, and whether to repeat them. Choose the most appropriate equipment to make measure-ments and explain how to use it accurately. Decide how to record data from a choice of familiar approaches. Look for different causal relation-ships in data and identify evidence that refutes or supports their ideas.	Understand and use SI (International system) units. Use and derive simple equations and carry out appropriate calculations. Undertake basic data analysis including simple statistical techniques

Table 1.1 *continued*

Early Years	Key Stage 1 (Years 1 and 2)	Lower Key Stage 2 (Years 3 and 4)	Upper Key Stage 2 (Years 5 and 6)	Deeper Learning / KS3
		Help to make decisions about how to record and analyse data. Record findings using simple scientific language, drawings, labelled diagrams, keys, bar charts, and tables.		
COMMUNICATING AND REVIEWING				
	With help, record and communicate findings in a range of ways and begin to use simple scientific language. Talk about what has been found out and how it was found out.	Look for changes, patterns, similarities and differences in data in order to draw simple conclusions and answer questions. With support, identify new questions arising from the data, making predictions for new values within or beyond the data collected, and find ways of improving what has already been done. Recognise when and how secondary sources might help to answer questions that cannot be answered through practical investigations. Use relevant scientific language to discuss ideas and communicate findings in ways that are appropriate for different audiences.	Draw conclusions based on data and observations. Use evidence to justify ideas, and use scientific knowledge and understanding to explain findings. Use results to identify when further tests and observations might be needed. Recognise which secondary sources will be most useful to research ideas and begin to separate opinion from fact. Use relevant scientific language and illustrations to discuss, communicate and justify scientific ideas and talk about how scientific ideas have developed over time.	Interpret observations and data, including identifying patterns and using observations, measurements and data to draw conclusions Present reasoned explanations, including explaining data in relation to predictions and hypotheses Evaluate data, showing awareness of potential sources of random and systematic error. Identify further questions arising from their results.

Figure 1.1 An image of working scientifically

A NOTE ON UNITS

Throughout the book, the attempt has been made to express units in the most easily understandable form. So, for example, the units of density have been cited as *grams per cubic centimetre* and have been expressed in terms of g/cm^3, rather than in terms of the more conventional $g\ cm^{-3}$. Similarly, *acceleration* is expressed in terms of *metres per second per second*, written as m/s^2, rather than as $m\ s^{-2}$.

FURTHER READING

Supporting teaching, planning and assessment

ASE. (2010) *The Language of Measurement: Terminology Used in School Science Investigations.* Hatfield, UK: Association of Science Education.

Cooke, V. and Howard, C. (2014) *Practical Ideas for Teaching Primary Science.* Northwich, UK: Critical Publishing.

Cross, A. and Board, J. (2014) *Creative Ways to Teach Primary Science.* Maidenhead, UK: McGraw-Hill Education.

Davies, D., Collier, C., Earle, S., Howe, A. and McMahon, K. (2014) *Approaches to Science Assessment in English Primary Schools: Interim Findings from the Teacher Assessment in Primary Science (TAPS) Project.* Bristol, UK: Primary Science Teaching Trust.

Harlen, W. and Qualter, A. (2015) *The Teaching of Science in Primary Schools*. London: Routledge.

Naylor, S., Koegh, B. and Goldsworthy, A. (2004) *Active Assessment*. Sandbach, UK: Millgate House.

Weavers, G. (2008) *Made You Look, Made You Think, Made You Talk – Science Activities for Kids*. Sandbach, UK: Millgate House.

Supporting working scientifically

Goldsworthy, A. and Ponchaud, B. (2007) *Science Enquiry Games*. Sandbach, UK: Millgate House.

Smith, K. (2016) *Working Scientifically: A Guide for Primary Science*. London: Routledge.

Turner, J. (2012) *'It's Not Fair': ASE Primary Science*. Sandbach, UK: Millgate House.

Supporting practical science

Association of Science Education. (2011) *Be Safe*, 4th edn. Hatfield, UK: Association of Science Education.

References

DfE. (2011) Teacher standards. Department for Education. Available at: www.gov.uk/government/publications/teachers-standards (accessed 9 April 2017).

DfE. (2013) National curriculum in England: Primary curriculum. Department for Education. Available at: www.gov.uk/government/publications/national-curriculum-in-england-primary-curriculum (accessed 9 April 2017).

SECTION TWO

Biology

SOME KEY IDEAS IN BIOLOGY

2.1 *The characteristics of living things: All living things have a number of characteristics in common*

2.2 *Life processes: These characteristics are the observable outcomes of the processes that sustain and renew life*

2.3 *Optimum conditions for survival*

2.4 *The variety of life: There is a large variety of life forms on Earth*

2.5 *Adaptation to environment: Animals and plants tend to adapt to their environments (natural selection)*

2.6 *The transfer of energy: Life is sustained through the transfer of energy (from the sun to the tissues of living organisms)*

Figure 2.0 Life on Earth

The characteristics of living things

All living things have a number of characteristics in common.

CONCEPTS TO SUPPORT KEY STAGE 1

How do we know that things are alive? Young children have been known to describe a car as being alive because it can move, or a calculator, because numbers appear when you switch it on and press the buttons. A group of 5-year-olds once explained that big boulders grew from little ones – a perfectly understandable 5-year-old conclusion, as they had seen plants grow from seeds, and they knew that small, young people grew into bigger, older people!

It takes time and experience with a variety of living and non-living material to begin to develop the notion of 'alive' and the understanding that all living things have a number of characteristics in common. It may be helpful to remember that, although some 'inanimate' objects may exhibit some of these characteristics, only living things exhibit them all.

The characteristics of living things

Living things, including humans, have the ability to: *feed, respire, excrete, grow, respond to stimuli, move* and *reproduce.*

It is worth remembering, however, that these characteristics provide us only with an operational definition – they tell us what living things *can do*, not what they *are*. In some cases, this can be a source of real confusion for primary pupils. Living things are not doing all of these things simultaneously. Many of these characteristics are not directly observable – pupils cannot see a tree 'feeding' itself for example; not all living organisms move, nor do all of them reproduce. A mule, for instance, though very much alive, is an infertile hybrid resulting from the mating of a horse and a donkey.

To add to the confusion, some organisms, at some stages of their life cycles, show no signs of life at all. Plant seeds are good examples of organisms in such a state, which is known as *suspended animation*. What has happened is that the seed has dried out – typically, seeds contain less than 10 per cent water, compared with 80–90 per cent in the parent plant. This desiccation slows down the rate at which chemical reactions take place in the seed, allowing it to survive periods of relatively hostile conditions – drought, for example, or the onset of winter.

So, the answer to the question 'Is a seed alive?' is 'We do not know' – at least, not until we have restored normal growing conditions to see if the seed germinates.

An example of suspended animation from the animal kingdom would be the desiccated egg cysts of brine shrimps (sold commercially as 'sea monkeys'). These cysts appear to be completely inert and can withstand years of desiccation, only to 'come to life' when rehydrated in the correct saline conditions. Perhaps the most crucial idea relating to living organisms is that they are all capable of *self-maintenance* and can respond, within limits, to changes in their environment. Such responses limit the effect of change on an organism and help it to maintain an internal environment at or near optimum. The mechanisms by which such responses occur will be explained in Key Idea 2.2: Life processes.

CONCEPT CONFUSION

Children may find it challenging to recognize some living things owing to their lack of movement – for example trees, coral and lichen. It may also be difficult to distinguish between things that were once alive and things that were never alive. One strategy is to ask children where something came from. For example, wood was once part of a tree, and so we can say it was once living, whereas a rock or stone was part of the Earth's crust, and so we can say it was never living. Fossils add another layer of complexity, as they are mineral 'casts' of something that was once alive.

CONCEPTS TO SUPPORT KEY STAGE 2

The characteristics of living things (feeding, excretion, respiration, growth, response to stimuli, movement and reproduction), outlined above, are all processes that occur as a result of the specialization of cells in the plants and animals concerned.

It is possible to visualize the processes on a 'micro-to-macro' scale (Figure 2.1):

- life processes at the most fundamental level involve the synthesis, breakdown and recombination of inorganic and organic *molecules*;
- these molecules are broken down, reassembled and incorporated into the individual units of life – the *cells*;
- cells of a similar kind, having similar functions, are grouped together as *tissues*;
- tissues are grouped together in *organs*; and
- organs that contribute to major bodily functions are grouped in *organ systems*.

Cells and tissues

All living organisms are made up of *cells*. Cells are the microscopic 'packets' of living matter that make up the complete organism. In some cases, the organism itself consists of a single cell (see Key Idea 2.4: The variety of life), but all higher plants and animals are composed of millions (or even billions) of cells, many of which are specialized to perform specific functions. But, no matter how simple or complex the organism is, the cells of which it is made have a number of characteristics in common with all other cells:

- they will have arisen from pre-existing cells (by some form of cell division);
- they will be the reaction sites for all the metabolic processes that take place in the organism.

In addition, almost all cells (red blood cells are an exception):

- contain a *nucleus* that is composed mainly of the chemicals (nucleic acids) that control the functioning of the cell.

These nucleic acids (the most famous of which is deoxyribonucleic acid – DNA) carry the 'blueprint' or 'toolbox' for the functioning of each cell and enable the assembly of the various organic chemicals that allow the cell to function.

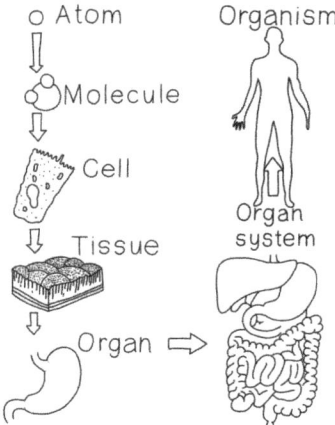

Figure 2.1 Processes on a micro-to-macro scale

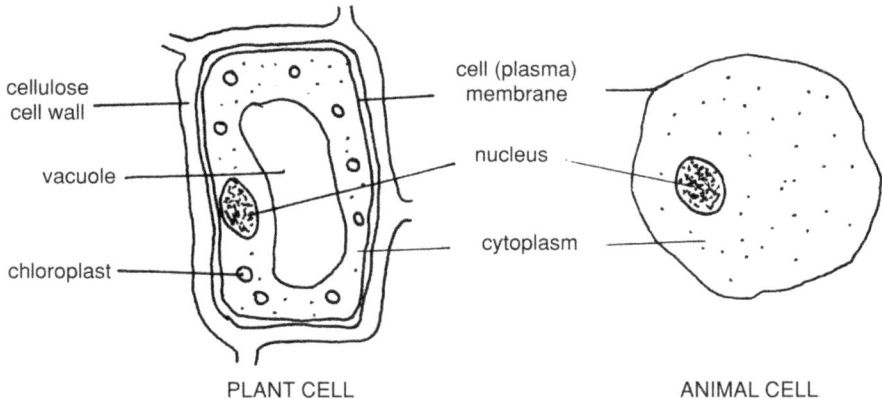

Figure 2.2 Plant and animal cells

Figure 2.2 is a diagram of generalized plant and animal cells. Differences in cellular structure are listed in Key Idea 2.2: Differences between plants and animals.

Many types of cell are specialized to perform specific functions and are grouped together in *tissues*. In some tissues, the constituent cells are able to transmit impulses (nerve cells), or are able to slide across one another (muscle cells). Some are able to engulf bacteria (white blood cells), or are sensitive to light (retinal cells).

Organs and organ systems

The organs and organ systems can be grouped according to their functions, and one convenient grouping for mammals is as follows:

System name	Functions	Mammalian organs
Nutrition system, cardio-vascular system, musculo-skeletal system, nervous system, reproductive system	Feeding, digestion, egestion, circulation, respiration, excretion, support, movement, sensitivity, coordination, reproduction	Gut, liver, pancreas, heart, lungs, kidneys, skeleton, muscles, tendons, ligaments, brain, sense organs, sexual organs

In the next section (Key Idea 2.2), these systems will be described, with particular reference to humans and, where appropriate, to flowering plants.

KEY IDEA 2.1 SUMMARY

Evidence suggests that life on planet Earth has existed for about 3.7 billion years. Scientists have observed living things in a systematic way to identify their commonalities and the conditions that are essential to support life. Inspiring children to identify and explore living things is an important foundation of all areas of biology.

Discussion points

- What makes something alive?
- How would we identify life that may appear very different, if we were to travel to a distant planet?

Working scientifically

- *Observing and comparing* the things humans can do with things other animals can do, using photographs of familiar vertebrates and invertebrates, can stimulate rich discussion.
- *Sorting and classifying* living, once-living and non-living things: Children could use photographs, images cut out of magazines and newspapers, or real objects.
- Outdoor learning and nature walks can help children *observe* living things in their natural habitats.

Application

Scientists carefully study what living things have in common and what conditions are essential to support life. When discovering more about the conditions on other planets, such as Mars, scientists can begin to predict whether they could also sustain life.

An appreciation of living things and the essential conditions for life helps children understand the importance of conservation and environmental sustainability.

Cross-curricular links

- *Maths*: Children could make tally charts or create simple graphs to present the number of living, once-living and non-living things in their classroom or local area.
- *Literacy*: Creating poems to describe what particular living things can do is a fun way to highlight their characteristics.
- *Art*: Children could use sketch books when in the local park to draw and label living things and non-living things.

Health and safety

- When observing and sorting living and non-living things, children need to be reminded not to put their hands near their mouths and to wash them once they have finished. Consult the ASE *Be Safe* guide (4th edn) for further guidance.

Assessment for learning

Children may be asked to draw a living thing of their choice, identifying five things that tell us why they know it is alive. They may also be challenged to raise questions about other things they would like to find out about the living thing, to further learning.

KEY IDEA 2.2

Life processes

These characteristics are the observable outcomes of the processes that sustain and renew life.

CONCEPTS TO SUPPORT KEY STAGE I

Life is sustained as a result of complicated chemical reactions that happen continuously in the cells and tissues of each animal or plant. The basic chemicals that secure this process (which is known as metabolism) are supplied to the cells through the feeding process.

Feeding

Green plants are unique in the living world in that they are able to make their own food. They do this by using the energy from sunlight to make organic molecules (carbohydrates) from simple molecules such as carbon dioxide and water. This process is known as photosynthesis and is the basic support system for life on Earth (see Key Idea 2.6: Energy transfer).

Animals are not able to synthesize carbohydrates, and so they need to feed either on plants (when they are known as herbivores), on other animals (carnivores), or both (omnivores).

However the food is derived, it is used to 'fuel' the life support systems of the individual plant or animal – the systems that ensure continued survival. In animals, the food is broken down by a process known as digestion, where the useful components of the food are broken down physically and chemically, absorbed into the blood and finally taken in solution to the tissues where the processes of life take place.

CONCEPT CONFUSION

It is important that teachers highlight that food is needed for two processes: growth and respiration. It is commonly thought that feeding only provides fuel, but it also provides nutrients for growth, defence and repair.

Elimination of waste (excretion)

Living things are able to eliminate from their tissues the components of food that are of no value (e.g. the *egestion* of faeces in animals) and the by-products of metabolism that are toxic (e.g. the *excretion* of carbon dioxide and urea).

Respiration

The food produced by plants, or eaten by animals, is broken down so that it can be used to provide energy to support the life processes of the organism. Energy is released by the breakdown of organic molecules (usually in the presence of oxygen), and the process is known as respiration.

Respiration consists of up to three processes:

1   *breathing*: the supply of oxygen to the surfaces for gaseous interchange;
2   *gaseous interchange*: the diffusion of oxygen into the organism and of carbon dioxide out;
3   *cellular respiration*: chemical reactions in the cells that result in the transfer of energy.

Some organisms are able to respire in the absence of oxygen (anaerobic respiration), but the process is much less efficient than aerobic respiration.

CONCEPT CONFUSION

Plants do not just take in carbon dioxide and get rid of oxygen in the process of photosynthesis. Like animals and micro-organisms, they respire and use energy to grow and reproduce. This often happens at night when they are not photosynthesizing.

Growth

Some of the food produced by plants, or eaten by animals, is used in the production of cells – the organism increases in size. Plants tend to grow throughout their lives, adding new tissue as time progresses. Animals tend to grow until they reach maturity, when tissue growth gives way to replacement.

A salutary thought is that old age ensues when replacement fails to keep pace with wear and tear, and death occurs when all metabolism ceases.

FACT POINT

- The oldest known tree, a Great Basin bristlecone pine, has lived for more than 5,000 years.
- The largest flower species in the world is the *Rafflesia arnoldii*, which grows to a diameter of about 1 metre.

Response to stimuli (sensitivity)

Organisms are able to react and respond to stimuli. Animals are able to respond to some or all of: light, heat, sound, touch and the chemical indicators of taste and smell. Plants respond to light and gravity (some respond to touch, e.g. mimosa, venus flytrap).

Movement

Animals are able to move by conscious decision and to travel using limbs or all of their bodies. Plants tend to grow towards favourable stimuli – for example, light.

Reproduction

Fertile organisms are able to produce offspring of their own kind through sexual reproduction. Asexual or vegetative reproduction (cloning) results in offspring that are genetically identical to the parent organism.

Differences between plants and animals

Using the list of characteristics of living things, it is possible to draw up a table showing the main differences between plants and animals:

	Plants	Animals
Feeding	Food synthesized from inorganic molecules	Eat plants or other animals
Respiration	Energy stored as starch	Energy stored as glycogen
Elimination of waste	Oxygen and CO_2, leaf fall	CO_2, urine, defecation
Growth	Branching, continues to death	Compact, continues to maturity
Response to stimuli	Slow (growth), no obvious nervous system	Rapid, through nervous system and sense organs
Movement	Anchored, rigid cell walls	Mobile, skeleton and muscles
Reproduction	Frequently, asexual embryos as seeds	Infrequently, asexual embryos in eggs or live-born
Cellular structure	Rigid cellulose cell wall, chloroplasts present in green plants	Thin cell membrane

WORKING SCIENTIFICALLY

Children can be challenged to group and classify living and non-living things using their own criteria, encouraging them to justify their decisions.

TEACHING IDEA

Using old pots, plants, bundles of twigs, pine cones, bamboo canes, bricks and any other objects in which invertebrates may be able to shelter, you could make a bug hotel in your playground. This will allow children to observe living organisms and the conditions they prefer.

CONCEPTS TO SUPPORT KEY STAGE 2

TEACHING IDEA

Children may have misconceptions about the location of organs in the human body. They may be supported by using models or drawing around each other and working with their teacher to locate and label different organs. This could make an interactive wall display, on which children may be encouraged to raise questions about different organs using post-it notes.

Nutrition systems (feeding, digestion, egestion)

A major difference between living and non-living things is that living organisms are able to replace, from outside themselves, energy lost in the maintenance of life. In order to do this, they must supply themselves with energy-rich organic compounds that can be used to 'fuel' the processes of life, and they do this by feeding.

All life depends, directly or indirectly, on the most fundamental life process of all – the ability of green plants to make food from simple inorganic molecules – photosynthesis.

Plant nutrition – photosynthesis

Photosynthesis is a two-stage process. The first, or light, stage, involves the transfer of energy from sunlight to the molecules of chlorophyll (the green pigment) in the leaves of a plant.

The units of light energy, the photons, transferred through the chlorophyll, enter a chemical pathway and combine with hydrogen ions from water in the plant. At the end of the light stage, the hydrogen has combined with other energy carriers in the cells, and oxygen (from the water) is produced as a waste product and is released to the atmosphere through the tissues of the plant (see Figure 2.3).

The second stage of photosynthesis does not need light, but can be affected by temperature. Essentially what happens is that the hydrogen from the light stage, via the energy-carrying molecules, combines with carbon dioxide, absorbed from the atmosphere by the plant, to produce glucose, and eventually starch, which is the main energy-rich compound in green plants.

The chemical formula for the process is as follows:

$$6CO_2 + 6H_2O \xrightarrow{\text{sun's energy, through chlorophyll}} C_6H_{12}O_6 + 6O_2$$

carbon dioxide + water $\longrightarrow$ glucose oxygen

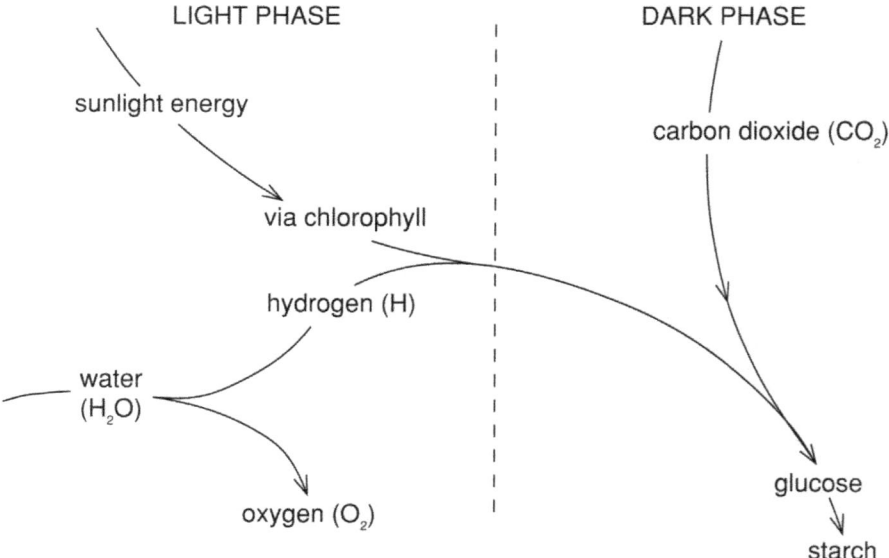

Figure 2.3 The process of photosynthesis

Animal nutrition – digestion

Animals are not able to synthesize energy-rich compounds, and so they feed on plants or on other animals (or both), in order to secure a supply for themselves. The body has developed a series of processes that cause physical and chemical breakdown of the food, absorption of the required components, and elimination of waste material, as follows:

- physical processes – chewing, swallowing, churning in stomach;
- chemical processes – breakdown by enzymes;
- absorption of food into bloodstream;
- reabsorption of water from waste – faeces;
- elimination of faeces from anus.

The physical process of chewing allows the food to be broken down into smaller pieces. The front, incisor teeth act as shears to 'chop' the food, and the rear, molar, teeth help to grind the food to a pulp (Figure 2.4). The overall effect is to increase the surface area of the swallowed food, so that the digestive enzymes can act with greater efficiency.

The physical process continues after the food leaves the mouth, as swallowing regulates the amount and frequency of food reaching the stomach. The muscles of the gullet (oesophagus) wall contract once the food has passed and help to push it into the stomach (a process known as peristalsis), and the contractions of the muscular stomach wall 'churn' the food to allow better mixing with the digestive enzymes.

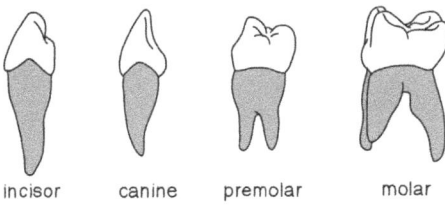

incisor   canine   premolar   molar

Figure 2.4 The types of teeth

The basic function of the chemical process of digestion is to break down the food molecules into units that are soluble and small enough to be absorbed into the body through the gut wall. The digestion of the various components of the food is assisted by specific enzymes, which are biological catalysts. Enzymes speed up the rate of chemical reactions and are 'added' to the ingested food at various places during its journey through the gut.

To start with, the salivary glands in the mouth secrete saliva, which is a mixture of mucus, to lubricate the food and make it easier to swallow, and amylase, an enzyme that helps the breakdown of starch in the food.

Once the food is in the stomach, glands in the stomach wall secrete gastric juice, a mixture of hydrochloric acid and pepsin, an enzyme that helps to break down proteins into peptides. When the food passes out of the stomach into the duodenum, bile (produced by the liver and stored in the gall bladder) is added. This has the function of emulsifying the fat from the food into small droplets. From the pancreas come a mixture of enzymes that enter the duodenum and help with the breakdown of starch and glycogen to sugars, fats to glycerol and fatty acids, and proteins to peptides.

As the food passes from the duodenum to the ileum, millions of tiny finger-like processes in the gut wall, the villi, absorb into the bloodstream the soluble molecules that are the products of digestion – sugars are digested as glucose, fats as glycerol and fatty acids, and peptides as amino acids (the building blocks of proteins).

What passes from the ileum to the colon is a mixture of undigested food and water. During its passage through the colon, water is absorbed into the bloodstream, so that the remaining material becomes more solid, forming faeces, which pass out of the body through the anus (see Figure 2.5 for a diagram of the human digestive system).

TEACHING IDEA

You can model the process of digestion using everyday household items:

1   Start with bread, oats, a banana and perhaps some sweetcorn. Use a pair of scissors to represent incisors and a potato masher to represent molars. Break up and mash the foods in a bowl (representing the mouth) and add some liquid (this can be coffee or juice).

2   Pour the contents of the bowl into a transparent food bag (the stomach), along with some red and green food dye (bile and hydrochloric acid), and use a squeezing motion to mix up the contents.

3   Next, pour the mixture into a leg of a pair of tights (the small intestine), demonstrating how nutrients are able to pass through into the bloodstream.

4   Squeeze out any remaining liquid using a tea towel (the large intestine) and then cut a hole in the toe of the tight leg (anus), to reveal the excreted faeces!

The cardio-vascular system (circulation and respiration)

The human cardio-vascular system has a number of components. These include the heart (a pump), the lungs (for oxygen supply), a network of branching blood vessels (arteries, veins and capillaries) that allows blood to reach every part of the body, and the blood itself (a vehicle for the transport of dissolved oxygen and food substances, and the waste products of metabolism).

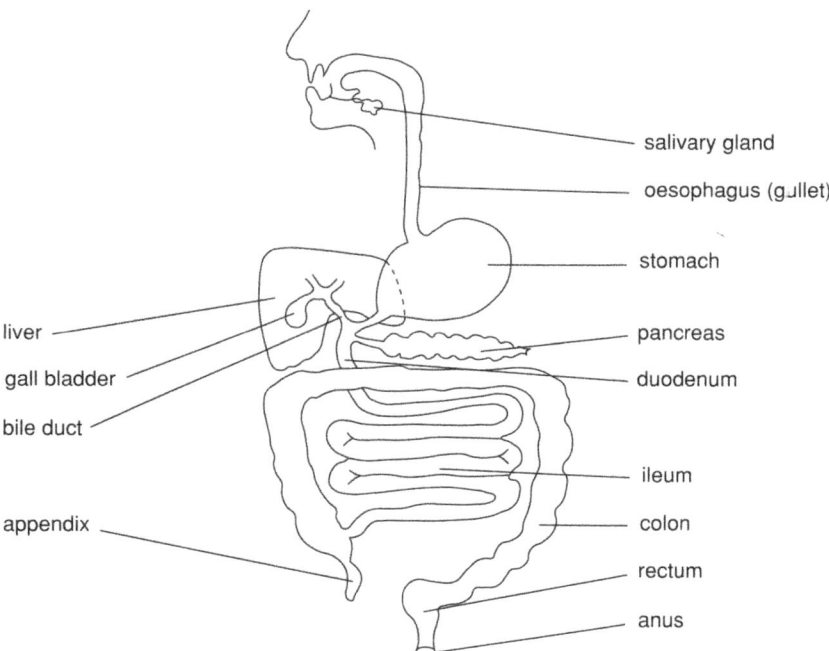

Figure 2.5 The human digestive system

FACT POINT

Gravity is not needed for food to reach the stomach. The muscles in the oesophagus constrict and relax in a wave-like manner called peristalsis, pushing the food down into the stomach. So, even if you were to eat while standing on your head, the food would still be able to get to your stomach.

The small intestine is about 7 m long and about 2.5 cm in diameter. Spread out, the surface area of the small intestine is about 250 m² and would cover the area of a tennis court.

Blood

In examining the constituent parts of blood, it is possible to list the various functions of the system as a whole:

- *Plasma (a straw-coloured liquid)* transports dissolved food (glucose, fatty acids and amino acids) and mineral salts, waste products (carbon dioxide and urea) and hormones; it contains antibodies and protein used in clotting (fibrinogen).
- *Red blood cells (erythrocytes)* are shaped like flattened discs and have no nucleus, and they are produced in red bone marrow. They transport oxygen in solution round the body. Haemoglobin is the oxygen-carrying pigment.
- *White blood cells (leucocytes)* are of two types:
  1 phagocytes, which kill bacteria by engulfing them and are produced in red bone marrow;
  2 lymphocytes, which produce antibodies that dissolve into the plasma and kill invading bacteria, and are produced in the lymph nodes.
- *Platelets (thrombocytes)* are fragments of blood cells that help blood to clot and wounds to heal and are produced in red bone marrow.

Famous scientist factbox

Name	Marie M. Daly (1921–2003), Queens, New York Chemist
Link to NC	Year 6 Animals including humans: – identify and name the main parts of the human circulatory system and describe the functions of the heart, blood vessels and blood; – recognize the impact of diet, exercise, drugs and lifestyle on the way their bodies function
Famous for	Marie M. Daly is best known for being the first African American woman to receive a PhD in chemistry in the United States
Working scientifically	Daly's hard work and fascination with the human body's inner workings motivated her to observe, identify and conduct fair test experiments to discover how chemicals affected different parts of the body
Impact on society	Daly's work helped us understand how proteins are constructed in the body She worked on the causes of heart attacks She developed a new understanding of how foods and diet can affect the health of the heart and the circulatory system. As a result, we are more informed about the relationship between diet and healthy lifestyles today

To summarize, the blood acts as:

- a *transport* system for oxygen, nutrients and waste;
- a *defence* system against invasion by bacteria and other antigens;
- a *sealing* system against wounds;
- a *regulation* system for body temperature and water and chemical balance.

Circulation (see Figure 2.6)

The circulation of the blood around the body is basically a double system, with the heart acting as the double pump that drives it. The sequence is as follows:
In Phase 1:

- *de-oxygenated blood* from the tissues arrives at the right upper chamber (atrium) of the heart;
- the atrium contracts, sending the blood into the right lower chamber, or ventricle;
- the right ventricle contracts, sending the de-oxygenated blood to the lungs, via the pulmonary artery (the only artery to carry de-oxygenated, i.e. venous, blood);

FACT POINT

The heart is about the size of a clenched fist, situated on the centre-left of the chest. Muscles in the heart are bigger on the left as they have to pump blood all the way around the body (the muscles on the right only have to pump blood to the lungs). The heart beats about 115,000 times in one day and about 42 million times in a year.

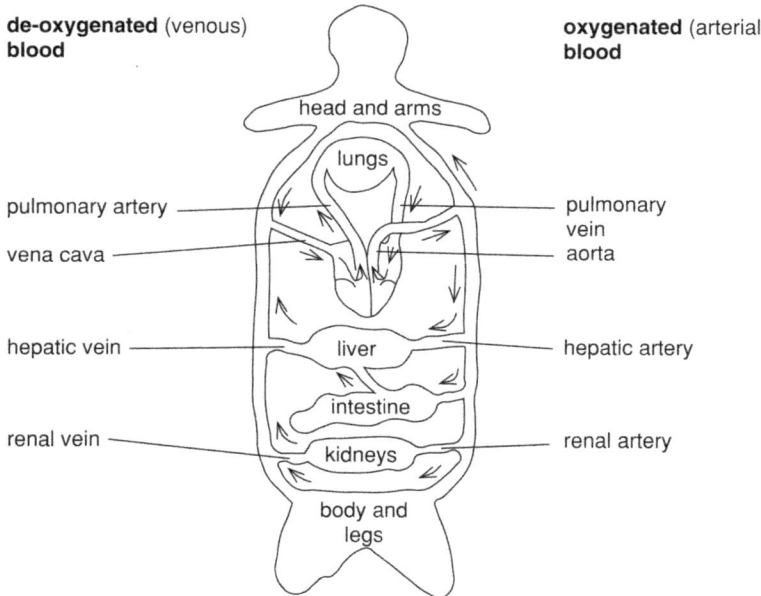

de-oxygenated (venous) **blood**

oxygenated (arterial) **blood**

Figure 2.6 The circulation of the blood

- in the microscopic blood vessels that supply the lung surface, carbon dioxide diffuses out of solution from the blood plasma, and oxygen diffuses from the lungs, combining with the haemoglobin in the blood platelets to form oxyhaemoglobin – *the blood has been oxygenated*;

In Phase 2:

- the oxygenated blood returns from the lungs (via the pulmonary vein) to the left atrium;
- the left atrium contracts, sending the oxygenated blood to the left ventricle;
- the left ventricle contracts, *sending oxygenated blood round the body* via the aorta, and to the head via the carotid artery.

In practice, both atria contract at the same time, rapidly followed by the ventricles, so that the two circulations, one to the lungs, the other to the rest of the body, are running simultaneously. Non-return valves between the atria and the ventricles ensure that the blood always flows in the same direction. The left ventricular (systolic) contraction, which forces oxygenated blood round the body, can be felt from outside the body as the 'pulse' and is a direct measure of the speed of blood circulation. Heart rate is controlled naturally by specialized tissues within the atrium walls, or artificially by the implantation of a 'pacemaker', which delivers small, regular electrical impulses to the heart muscle, helping to stabilize the heart rate.

A variety of factors can influence heart rate:

- *increased exercise*, leading to oxygen debt, will cause the rate to rise to compensate;
- certain *hormones*, notably *adrenaline*, the 'fight or flight' hormone, can increase heart rate in order to allow the individual to react quickly and with great energy to particular situations;
- *cooling of the outer body* can cause a compensatory increase in heart rate, for example in winter;
- *alcohol* stimulates an increase in heart rate.

The oxygenated blood is carried away from the heart in arteries. These are capable of withstanding high pressure and have strong, elastic walls. As they divide into smaller and smaller vessels, they eventually become capillaries. These are very small tubes with walls only one cell thick, thus presenting the smallest barrier to the diffusion of oxygen and waste products into and out of the cells that they supply. Capillaries eventually combine to form veins, which are thin-walled vessels carrying de-oxygenated blood towards the heart at low pressure. Veins contain a system of flaps or non-return valves that prevent blood from flowing back towards the tissues.

The organs that remove some of the waste products of metabolism are the kidneys. They are particularly concerned with the elimination of urea, which has a high nitrogen content and is formed from the breakdown of proteins. As blood is pumped through the kidneys, excess water and urea diffuse as urine into the kidney tubules. These coalesce to form collecting ducts, and, eventually, via the ureters, urine is carried to the bladder, whence it is emptied to the outside by the relaxation of a muscular ring (sphincter) at the head of the urethra.

Respiration

Respiration takes place in every living cell, in every living organism. It is a sequence of processes that basically results in the oxidation of glucose molecules to form carbon dioxide and water, with an accompanying transfer of energy. The most efficient form of respiration takes place in the presence of oxygen and is known as *aerobic* respiration.

In order for aerobic respiration to take place, all organisms need a regular supply of oxygen, a medium for gaseous exchange and a supply of glucose (either manufactured or consumed). Up to three processes are involved:

Breathing

Breathing (or ventilation) is the mechanism by which all land animals ensure that a regular supply of oxygen is delivered to the body. This is achieved by the inhalation of air into the lungs. In humans, the muscles between the ribs, the intercostal muscles, contract to lift the ribs upwards and outwards. At the same time, the sheet of muscle at the base of the rib cage, the diaphragm, is pulled downwards by contraction. The net effect of these two movements is to increase the size of the chest (or thoracic) cavity, thus lowering the pressure and causing air to flood into the lungs. Conversely, when the diaphragm and intercostal muscles relax, the thoracic cavity contracts, pressure increases, and air is forced out of the lungs. Humans ventilate their lungs about twelve times per minute when at rest, exchanging about 0.5 litres of air as they do so. After exercise, this rate can increase to 60 breaths per minute, exchanging 2–3 litres at each inhalation.

In aquatic animals such as fish, the supply of oxygen is ensured by the passage of water, containing dissolved oxygen, across the gills.

Plants do not need a mechanism for breathing, as air can diffuse directly into plant tissues through pores (stomata) in leaves and other tissues.

FACT POINT   ⓘ

On average, an adult can hold their breath for 30–60 seconds. This limitation is more about the build-up of blood-acidifying carbon dioxide rather than the lack of oxygen.

However, free divers (people who dive underwater without specialist breathing apparatus) use different techniques to allow them to hold their breath for long times. Stig Severinsen, from Denmark, currently holds the Guinness World Record for the longest free dive – in 2010, he held his breath underwater for 22 minutes.

Gaseous exchange

Air enters the lungs through the windpipe or trachea (see Figure 2.7). This is a tube of tissue, strengthened with cartilage rings to prevent it from collapsing. The trachea divides into two bronchi (one to each lung), and the bronchi divide into smaller bronchioles. At the end of each bronchiole are bunches of very small air sacs called alveoli, each one less than 1 mm in diameter. The alveoli have walls that are one cell thick and they are covered with a network of extremely fine capillary blood vessels. The effect of this arrangement is to create a large surface area over which diffusion can take place – it has been estimated that the surface area of a pair of human lungs is equivalent to that of a tennis court!

The alveoli have a moist lining, and the closeness of the surrounding capillaries allows diffusion of gases in solution to take place at the surface of the lungs. Oxygen diffuses from the lungs into the red blood cells (platelets) in the capillaries, and carbon dioxide, a waste product of respiration, diffuses from the blood plasma into the lungs. The diffusion gradient is maintained by the continual replenishment of the oxygen supply (by breathing) and the removal to the tissues of the oxygen absorbed by the red blood cells (by circulation).

Inhaled air contains about 20 per cent oxygen and 0.03 per cent carbon dioxide; exhaled air contains about 16 per cent oxygen and 4 per cent carbon dioxide.

Cellular or tissue respiration

Cellular respiration is the set of chemical reactions that take place in the cells of the organism. It usually takes place in the presence of oxygen. The basic formula for aerobic respiration is:

$$\underset{\text{glucose}}{C_6H_{12}O_6} + \underset{\text{oxygen}}{6O_2} \longrightarrow \underset{\text{carbon dioxide}}{6CO_2} + \underset{\text{water}}{6H_2O} + \textbf{energy transfer}$$

This reaction is, apparently, a reversal of that of photosynthesis (see above), where carbon dioxide and water are combined, using energy derived from sunlight, to produce glucose molecules, with oxygen as a 'waste' product.

The reaction is not, however, a direct reversal. In the first phase of respiration, glucose is converted into pyruvic acid. This can then be respired aerobically, in the presence of oxygen, to liberate a relatively large amount of energy (as in the above equation), or can be respired less efficiently, in the absence of oxygen (anaerobically), to produce different waste products.

In the plant kingdom, the *anaerobic* respiration of yeast cells results in the production of ethanol (alcohol), a reaction at the heart of the brewing industry, and carbon dioxide, which forms the basis of the baking industry. In animals, anaerobic respiration of pyruvic acid

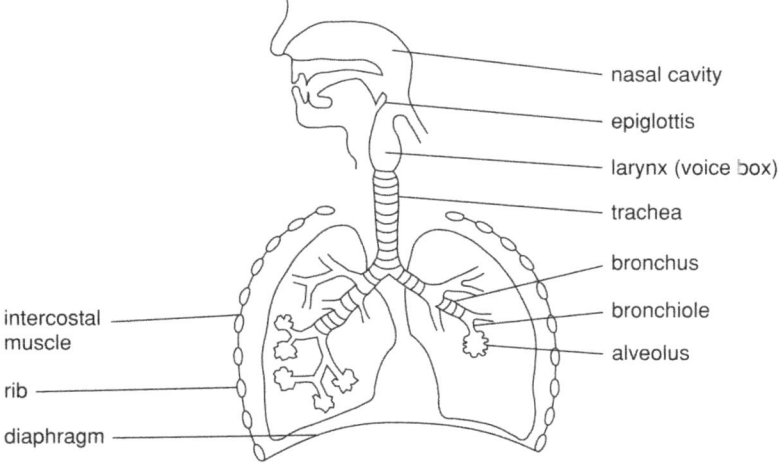

Figure 2.7 The human thoracic cavity

produces lactic acid. This can occur in humans when oxygen demand exceeds supply – for example, during strenuous physical exercise such as sprinting. The lactic acid produced by anaerobic respiration in humans is also the cause of 'stiff muscles' after unaccustomed exercise.

About 60 per cent of the energy released by aerobic respiration is in the form of heat. This helps to maintain the body temperature of warm-blooded animals (mammals and birds). The remaining energy can be used for growth and repair, as some of the by-products of the oxidation process can be used in the production of other 'building blocks', such as amino acids and fatty acids, or for muscular movement – for example, locomotion or the maintenance of heartbeat and breathing.

The musculo-skeletal system (support and movement)

As plants and animals have evolved larger forms, systems of support have become necessary.

Support in plants

Plants tend to grow upwards in the competition for light (the largest trees are over 100 m tall), and they have evolved two main support systems:

1   *Water (hydrostatic) pressure*: Plant cells absorb water until they are inflated (turgid). The cell walls are strengthened with cellulose, and this prevents the cells from bursting. The overall effect of this process is to 'stiffen' the plant tissue. A useful mental model of turgid plant cells is to imagine typical supermarket 1-litre cardboard containers full of fruit juice. A stack of such containers would not collapse, as it would gain support from the liquid inside each 'cell'.
2   *Woody tissue*: Some plants (mainly trees and shrubs) derive support from cells whose walls are thickened with *lignin*. The cells are thus mechanically strengthened and make no energy demands on the plant.

Support in animals – the skeleton

TEACHING IDEA

To help remember the three main functions of the skeleton, the mnemonic SPaM can be used:

Support, Protection and Movement

Similarly, animals developed support systems as increasing size and range of activity brought larger forces to bear on the body forms that evolved.

Some animals without backbones (invertebrates) have evolved *exoskeletons*. These are rigid external coverings that offer protection to their owners and also provide large internal surfaces for the attachment of muscles. The arthropods provide excellent examples of animals with exoskeletons – crabs, lobsters and insects, for instance.

FACT POINT

The exoskeleton (a thick shell) of a crab is made of chitin. Chitin is the second most abundant natural carbohydrate on earth, after cellulose.

The five groups of vertebrate animals (fish, amphibians, reptiles, birds and mammals) have developed internal skeletons (*endoskeletons*) based on a remarkably similar pattern, which demonstrates their common evolutionary ancestry. All have skulls and backbones containing brains and spinal cords, and land animals also have four limbs (again, structured on similar patterns) attached to the backbone via two limb girdles. One group – the sharks, dogfish and rays – have skeletons made of cartilage, but all the other vertebrates have bony skeletons. Figure 2.8 shows the main parts of the human skeleton.

The tissues that constitute the skeleton in humans are bone, cartilage and ligaments.

Bone is a hard, strong, slightly flexible tissue made of calcium phosphate. This is secreted by bone cells arranged in cylindrical layers (for strength), which are connected to a network of fibres that give the bone its flexibility. Blood vessels and nerves run through canals in the structure of the bones. The bones of the skeleton provide a strong, rigid support for the body. The flexibility necessary in the skeleton in order for movement to take place is provided by joints, which act as articulations between individual bones.

FACT POINT

Bones are built to endure a lot of force. Weight for weight, they are five times stronger than steel. However, tooth enamel, another part of the skeletal system, is even harder. Its strength is a result of its high concentration of minerals.

Cartilage is an elastic, rubbery protein that covers the ends of bones at joints. It can act as a smooth, load-bearing surface in a joint – for example, the semi-lunar cartilage in the knee joint – and also as a shock absorber between bones – for example, the 'discs' of cartilage between the vertebrae of the spine. The most obvious piece of cartilage, which can be 'felt', is the end of your nose!

Ligaments are strong, elastic groups of fibres that bind the bones tightly together at joints and help to prevent them from dislocating. The joints themselves are enclosed by a synovial

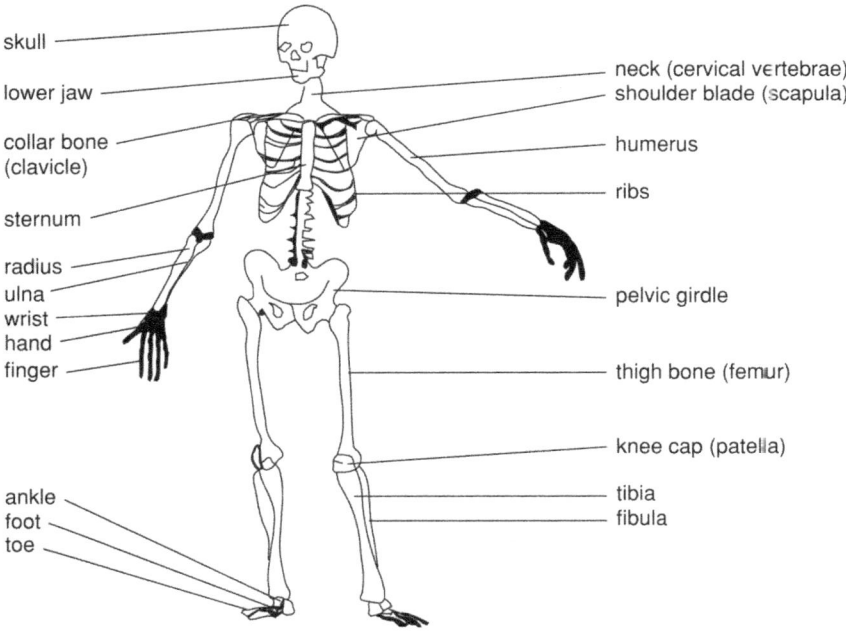

Figure 2.8 The main parts of the human skeleton

Famous scientist factbox

Name	Marie Curie (1867–1934), Poland, France Chemist and physicist
Link to NC	Year 3 – Animals, including humans (investigating skeletons)
Famous for	First women to be awarded a Nobel Prize in Physics for her work on radiation Also awarded a Nobel Prize in Chemistry for discovering two elements, polonium and radium In World War I, Marie learned that X-rays could be used to diagnose injured soldiers
Working scientifically	Classification: Marie and her husband discovered two new elements for the periodic table: polonium and radium Fair testing and experimentation: She worked for many hours in a science lab investigating the properties of the new elements
Impact on society	Her work on radiation helped scientists to realize that radiology could be used to cure cancer

membrane that secretes synovial fluid, which lubricates the joint. Over-use of a joint can cause the over-production of synovial fluid, causing painful swelling at the joint – for example, in tennis elbow.

Movement in animals

Animals can move in a variety of ways: by swimming (fish, marine mammals, seals), crawling (lizards, toads), sliding (snakes), walking (humans), hopping (perching birds, kangaroos), running (gazelles, cheetahs) or flying (birds, bats).

FACT POINT

An animal's movement helps it survive. Its movement helps an animal find food, shelter and protection within its habitat. An animal's skeletal system has evolved efficiently. For example, unlike the jaw of a mammal, built for instinctive force, a snake's jaw is fixed with tendons, muscles and ligaments, giving the jaw flexibility, allowing it to open nearly 180° and eat its dinner whole!

In addition to the skeletal tissues above, two further tissues are involved in movement.

Muscles are tissues made up of fibres (mainly of protein) that are able to contract and so shorten their length. It is believed that this shortening is achieved by the muscle filaments sliding between one another, rather than by the actual contraction of individual fibres.

Muscles that are involved in movement are examples of voluntary muscles, that is, they are under conscious control. Although muscles can contract and shorten, they cannot lengthen again. They must be stretched back to full length by the pull of an opposing or antagonistic muscle. So, the muscles that control movement are found in opposing pairs.

A good example of this arrangement can be found in the human arm. The biceps muscle on the inside of the upper arm is a flexor muscle. When it contracts, it pulls on the fore-arm and moves it towards the shoulder, bending the arm. At the same time, the opposing

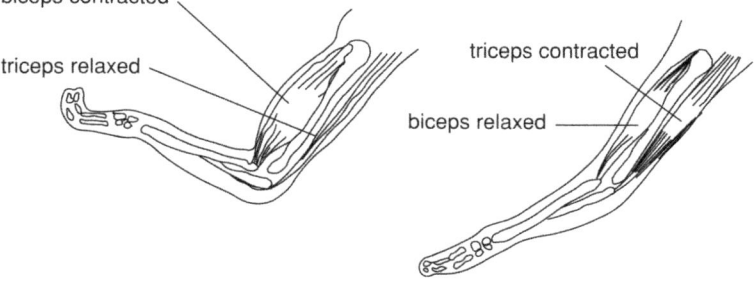

Figure 2.9 The muscles and movement of the human arm

muscle, the triceps, on the outside of the upper arm, relaxes to allow the biceps to contract. When the triceps (an extensor muscle) contracts, it shortens and 'pulls' the arm straight, at the same time returning the biceps to its original, uncontracted length (see Figure 2.9).

Similarly, the shin and calf muscles of the lower leg allow the foot to be 'waggled' up and down.

Some muscles cause internal movements in the body and are involuntary, that is, they normally operate automatically and are not under conscious control. Two examples of involuntary muscles already described are the heart and the diaphragm (see previous section).

FACT POINT

The tongue is the only muscle in the human body that works without any support from the skeleton and is known as a muscular hydrostat. It is incredibly flexible and allows us to talk and eat, and it never gets tired!

Tendons are strips of strong, inelastic tissue that attach muscles to bones. The inelasticity allows the 'pull' of the contracting muscle to act directly on the bone and so cause movement of some kind.

Muscles are able to cause movement because the bones articulate together at the joints. There are two basic types of joint:

- *fixed* and immobile joints, where plates of bone are tightly interlocked like the pieces of a jigsaw; these joints are known as sutures – for example, the bones of the cranium (skull);
- *movable* joints, of which there are three types:
  - *ball-and-socket* joints, which can move in more than one plane;
  - *hinge* joints, which can move in a single plane; and
  - *sliding* joints, which have a limited rotary movement.

All of these joint types can be found in the limbs of humans, which have ball-and-socket joints at the shoulder and hip, hinge joints at the elbow and knee, and sliding joints at the wrist and ankle (see Figure 2.10).

Movement can take place because of a sequence of events:

- *energy* is supplied by the *contraction* and shortening of muscles;
- the muscular contraction allows *bones* to *move* relative to each other;
- the *movement* of the bones *exerts* a *force* on the load-bearing surface in contact with the environment; for example, the tail of a fish 'presses' against the water, the hoof of a horse grips the ground, the wing of a bird 'pushes' the air.

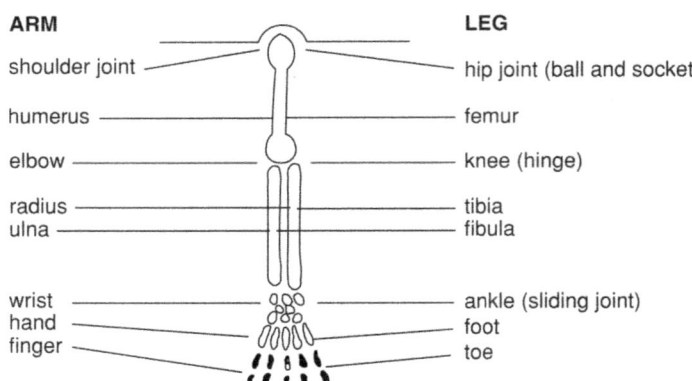

Figure 2.10 The joints in human limbs

The nervous system (sensitivity, coordination)

In order to survive, plants and animals need to be able to respond to the variety of conditions presented by the environment in which they live. These conditions may be long term and therefore demand a long-term response (e.g. bears respond to the onset of winter by hibernating), or may be sudden and potentially life-threatening (e.g. bears will fight or move away when attacked by another, larger animal).

Animals are able to respond to the stimuli presented by the environment because they have a number of specialized organs for sensing the environment in which they live and by which they are affected, and a system of specialized tissues – the nervous system – capable of receiving, relaying, analysing and responding to 'messages' about that environment.

Human sense organs

The specialist organs, or sensors, that allow mammals (including humans) to monitor the state of their environment are:

- the *eyes*, which respond to *light* and allow humans to see colour, shape and movement;
- the *ears*, which respond to *sound and gravity* and allow people to hear and to be aware of 'where they are in space' – hence, the ability to remain balanced;
- the *tongue*, which responds to *chemicals* in solution and which can distinguish bitter, sweet, salty and sour tastes;
- the *nose*, which responds to airborne *chemicals* as smells; and
- *skin sensors*, which respond to touch (*pressure*), *heat* and *cold*.

The eye

It is perhaps important to remember that the eye is a specialized organ for the collection and focusing of light. The 'seeing' is done when the signals received by light-sensitive cells in the eye are relayed as impulses by the optic nerve for interpretation by the brain.

The human eye (see Figure 2.11) is a fluid-filled sac housed in a bony socket. The front surface of the eye, the *cornea*, is protected by *eyelids*, which can 'blink' or stay closed to keep out dust, smoke or other irritating substances, and by fluid (tears), which lubricates the eyeball and also helps to wash out any solid or liquid irritants. The cornea also acts as an external lens and helps to focus light into the eye. Behind the cornea lies the *iris*, which gives the eye its 'colour' and which can enlarge or make smaller the hole (*pupil*) that admits light

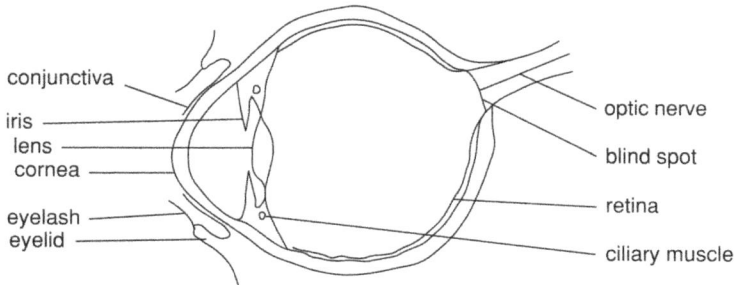

Figure 2.11 The human eye

to the eye. It is easy to watch the pupil size change as light intensity varies, for example, by alternately shading the eyes and then looking towards a light; torchlight is sufficient – *never use direct sunlight*.

Behind the iris is the *lens*, the shape of which can be changed by the contraction or relaxation of a ring of muscle (*ciliary muscle*) that surrounds it. When the ciliary muscle is relaxed, the ligaments that suspend the lens are stretched and it becomes thin and able to focus on distant objects. When the ciliary muscle contracts, the strain on the *suspensory ligaments* is lessened, and the lens becomes fatter and can focus on near objects. Finally, the lens inverts the image of the 'seen' object on to the *retina* – a thin layer of light-sensitive cells on the back of the eye. Impulses from these cells, some of which detect 'black and white' and others of which detect 'colour', travel along the *optic nerve* to the brain (Figure 2.12).

FACT POINT

The eye lens grows continuously during life by the addition of new cells inside the surrounding case, like layers of an onion. This growth helps us understand why people get cataracts (a clouding of the lens in the eye leading to a decrease in vision) when they are older.

The ear

The ear has two basic functions: hearing and sensing changes of position (hence, balance).

The outer ear (*pinna*) collects sound waves as vibrations in the air (see Key Idea 4.1: Sound) and channels them down the ear canal to the *eardrum*. Behind the eardrum are three small

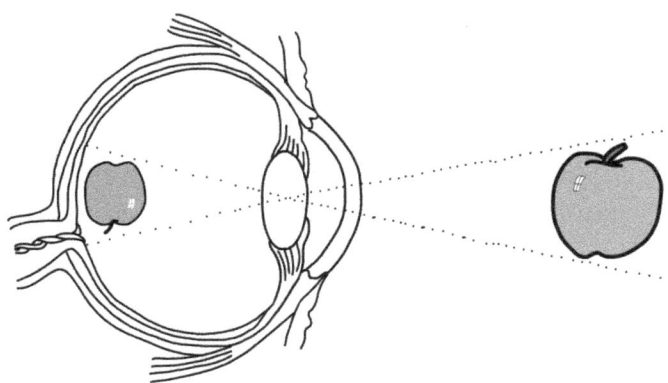

Figure 2.12 A diagram showing how we see

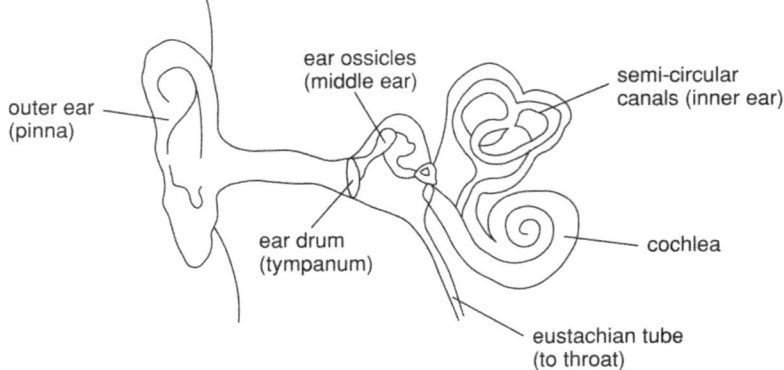

Figure 2.13 The human ear

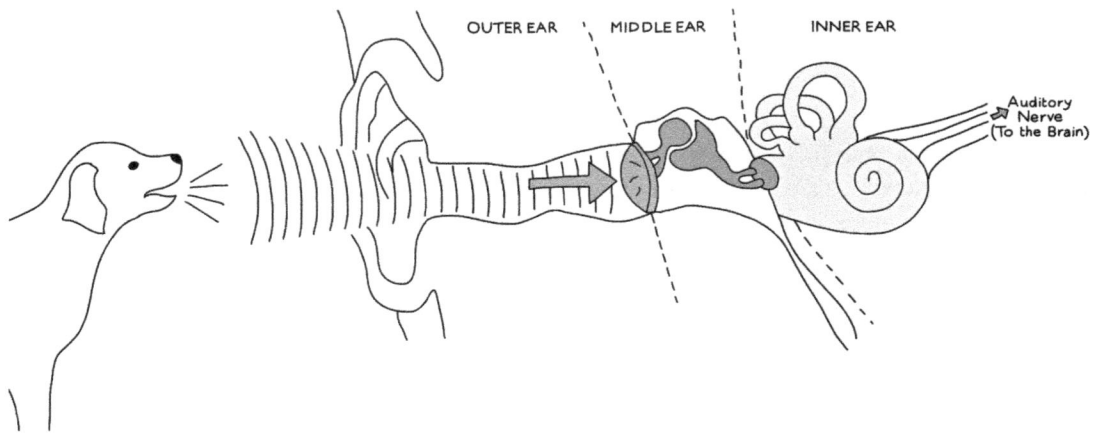

Figure 2.14 A flow diagram illustrating how we hear

bones, the ear *ossicles*, which vibrate as the eardrum resonates with the incoming sound waves. This vibration is passed on to a fluid-filled spiral tube (the *cochlea*), where sensitive hair cells pick up the vibrations and send impulses along the *auditory nerve* to the brain. The upper part of the inner ear forms three *semicircular canals*, which are arranged in three planes. They, too, are fluid-filled, and, because the fluid tends to 'stay put' (as a result of inertia) when the canals move with the body, sensitive *ampullae* in the canals can detect movement in any direction, and impulses sent to the brain allow it to 'decide' what actions will be necessary to maintain balance (see Figures 2.13 and 2.14).

Taste and smell

Taste and smell are closely linked, relying as they do on groups of sensory cells in the mouth and nose cavities. The taste buds on the tongue are able to sense bitter, sweet, sour and salty flavours (Figure 2.15). As the mouth and nose cavities are linked, the sense of smell also adds to our appreciation of a full range of flavours. This is noticeable when the nasal passages are blocked, for example by a head cold. Not only is the sense of smell impeded, the sense of taste is also diminished, and food seems 'flavourless'.

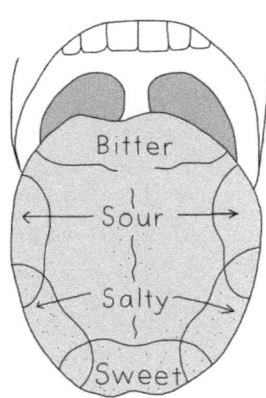

Figure 2.15 The tongue

The skin (touch, temperature)

Sensory nerve endings in the middle layer of the skin (dermis) enable us to feel pressure and temperature. So, in addition to 'feeling' the touch of an object on the skin, we are able to tell whether it is hot or cold. If pressure on the skin is large, pain sensors in the upper layer of the skin (the epidermis) send impulses to the brain, and avoiding action can be taken (see Figure 2.16).

In addition to this sensory capacity, the skin also has the following functions:

Protection

- The skin is waterproof, so it prevents water entry to, or loss from, the body.
- It prevents the entry of harmful bacteria and viruses.
- It produces the pigment melanin, which protects the body from the harmful ultraviolet (UV) component of sunlight.

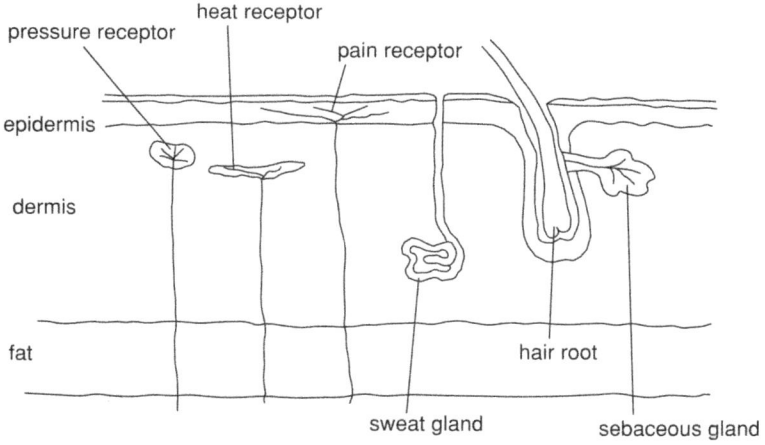

Figure 2.16 A section of human skin

Excretion

Some urea and salts are lost in sweating.

Temperature regulation

- In mammals, hair traps layers of warm air.
- Sweating assists heat loss by the evaporation of perspiration from the skin surface.
- Surface capillaries can open in warm weather (vaso-dilation) to flush the skin surface with blood, assisting cooling, or close in cold weather (vaso-constriction), restricting blood flow and conserving heat.
- The fat layer under the skin provides heat insulation.

Plant responses to environmental stimuli

Plants respond in three main ways to the environments in which they grow:

1   They *grow towards light*: the shoots of green plants grow towards the sunlight they need for photosynthesis (positive phototropism);
2   The *roots* of plants *grow* downwards *towards gravity* (positive geotropism). This helps to stabilize the plants and helps them to reach sources of groundwater; the *shoots* of plants *grow* upwards *away from gravity* (negative geotropism), thus helping with the search for light (Figure 2.17).
3   They *respond to changes in day length* (photoperiodism). A blue pigment (phytochrome) in plant leaves reacts as day length increases, producing a hormone (florigen) that triggers flower formation.

Coordination and control

It is important for an animal to give a coordinated response to information received about the state and nature of the surrounding environment. A random response is inefficient and may be ineffective, if not fatal.

There are two basic body systems for coordination and control: the *nervous system* and the *endocrine* or *hormone system*.

The nervous system

At its most basic, the nervous system represents a communication system that connects environmental sensors (the sense organs) to effectors (muscles and glands) by means of a

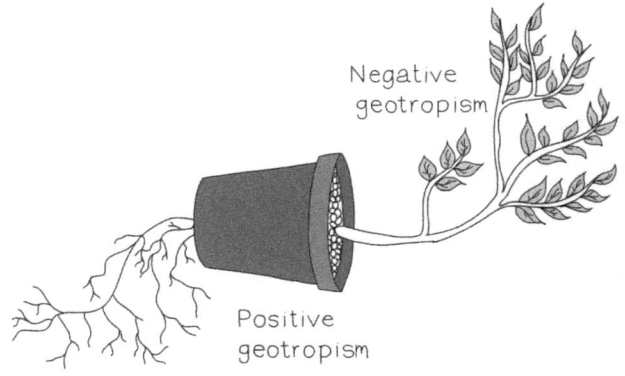

Figure 2.17 Geotropism in Darwin's work

switchboard or relay system (the spinal cord) and a computer (the brain). The system allows for very rapid coordination and control of actions and responses.

The brain and spinal cord form the *central nervous system* (CNS), and the network of nerve cells linking the CNS with receptors (in the sense organs) and effectors (the muscles, glands etc.) all over the body is known as the *peripheral nervous system* (PNS).

Nerve cells, or neurones, occur in bundles known as nerve fibres. These are long, narrow cells that are specialized to allow for the one-way passage of impulses similar to those of an electrical current. The impulses are caused by changes in the concentration of sodium (chemical symbol: Na) and potassium (K) ions in the neurones and can travel at up to 120 m/s. Unlike the wires in an electrical circuit, neurones in the nervous system do not make direct contact with other neurones but are separated by small gaps (or synapses). When a nerve impulse reaches a synapse, it causes the secretion of a transmitter substance that allows the passage of the impulse across the synapse, so triggering an impulse in the next neurone along the line.

An example of the basic stimulus–response sequence for conscious action is as follows:

- information from the environment is received by sensory cells in the body – for example, hair cells in the cochlea of the inner ear (see above) are stimulated by vibration;
- an impulse, triggered by the sensory cells, passes along the sensory neurones to the spinal cord;
- relay neurones in the spinal cord carry the impulse to pyramidal neurones in the brain;
- the pyramidal neurones, with many connections to others, allow the brain to decode and 'perceive' the stimulus (e.g. a doorbell ringing) and 'decide on' a course of action;
- the pyramidal neurones pass on the impulse to motor neurones, which activate muscles;
- movement begins to 'answer the door' (Figure 2.19).

If the stimulus is of an urgent, painful or life-threatening nature – an object moving rapidly towards the eye, for example – the relay neurones in the spinal cord would route the impulse direct to motor neurones, speeding up the response time, and an automatic, or reflex, action would result – the eyelids would quickly close – the 'blink' reflex (see Figure 2.18).

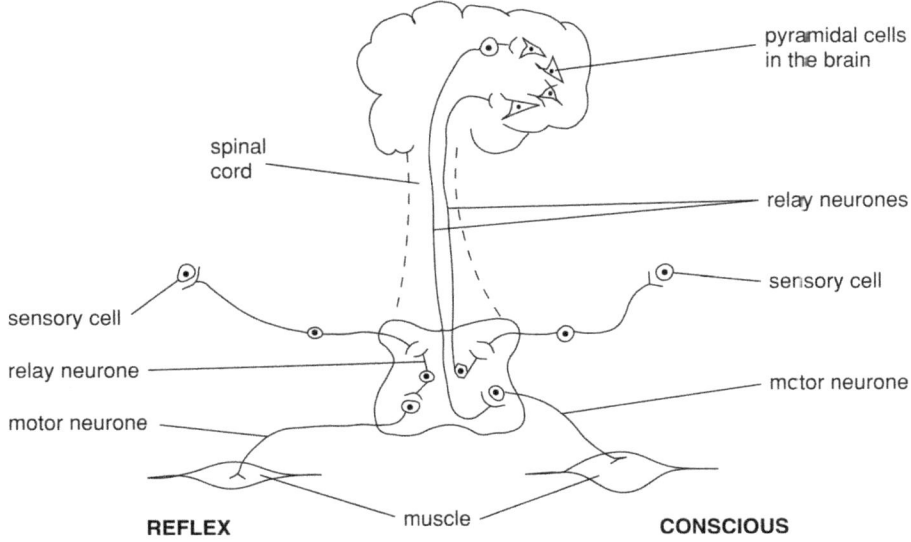

Figure 2.18 Conscious and reflex action pathways

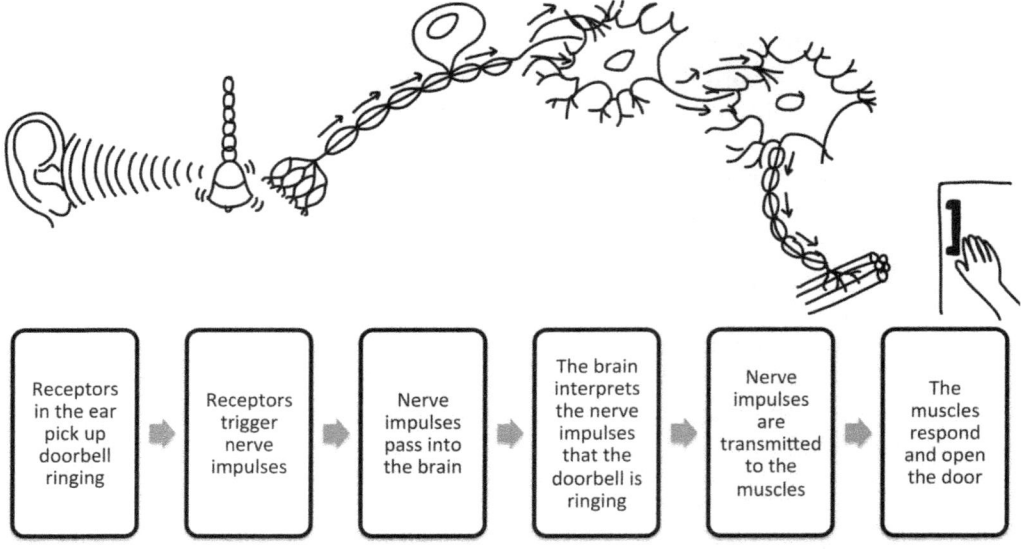

Figure 2.19 Flow diagram to show stimulus–response sequence

Self-maintenance

In addition to the examples of conscious responses described above, living organisms also possess systems that respond to change in their internal environment, thus allowing self-maintenance to occur. Such systems function as *negative feedback* or *detection–correction* mechanisms. There are hundreds, if not thousands, of such mechanisms in humans, and almost all of them operate outside our conscious control. Indeed, we are often aware of them only when they malfunction, or if the change to which they are responding is outside the range normally tolerated by the system as a whole.

DISCUSSION POINT

Why do people breathe into a brown paper bag if they are hyperventilating?

Healthy breathing happens with a balance between breathing in oxygen and breathing out carbon dioxide. When you hyperventilate, the body does not have long enough to retain carbon dioxide and use the oxygen it has. Breathing into a brown paper bag allows the person to 'rebreathe' their exhaled carbon dioxide, bringing the balance of oxygen and carbon dioxide back to normal.

Negative feedback (detection–correction) mechanisms

Imagine standing outdoors on a winter day, dressed in shorts and a T-shirt. How would our bodies react to the cold? Blood from the surface layers of the body, cooled by contact with the surrounding cold air, is 'sensed' by the temperature control centre in the brain as being below the optimum temperature (about 37°C). This sensing of the temperature is the 'detection' component of the system. Without any conscious effort on our part, the 'correction' component then begins to take effect, reversing the downward trend and minimizing any possible harmful effects: we begin to shiver, generating heat internally; our skin rises in 'goose bumps', as the hairs on our body surface rise to trap layers of still air; and we go 'blue with cold', as our surface capillaries contract, concentrating our blood into the body core. All of these reactions are designed to reverse the cooling process and maintain our normal body temperature. If our exposure to low temperatures is prolonged, we may consciously augment the detection–correction mechanism by putting on layers of protective clothing or by 'buffing' our arms to generate further internal heat.

Conversely, in warm weather, if we become too hot, the increase in blood temperature is detected by the brain, and a different set of effectors come into action – we begin to perspire, cooling our body surface as the perspiration evaporates; we 'flush' as our surface capillaries dilate, allowing more blood near to the body surface to radiate its heat away from the core. If high temperatures persist, we may augment the detection–correction mechanism by seeking out shade or by jumping into water!

Another example of a detection–correction mechanism involves the response of the eye to changes in light intensity. If external lighting conditions are too bright for our eyes, this is detected by the brain, and the pupil of the eye becomes smaller, restricting the amount of light entering the eye. If conditions are too dim, the pupil enlarges to allow more light into the eye. The overall effect of pupil size changing in response to changing external light intensity is the maintenance of the light intensity *inside the eye* at or near the optimum value.

These are just two examples from countless detection–correction mechanisms operating in humans. In each case, the system detects a change from the optimum and then initiates action to reverse the change and to limit its possible harmful effects. The body systems are responding to stimuli without our being aware of what is happening, and each system has evolved to allow us to self-maintain at or near optimum conditions for our survival. Other examples of such mechanisms would include: water balance in the body, blood glucose and CO_2 levels, dynamic balance when walking or running, and so on.

FACT POINT

How do sunglasses work?

Good sunglasses work in four ways:

1 They protect eyes from UV rays in sunlight, preventing damage to the cornea and retina.
2 They protect eyes from glare.
3 They protect eyes from intense light, preventing squinting and retina damage.
4 They can eliminate specific frequencies of light that can blur vision.

The endocrine or hormone system

In contrast to the nervous system, where rapidly transmitted impulses tend to result in rapid, relatively short-term responses, hormones are 'chemical messengers' that are secreted in glands and released into the bloodstream. Hormonal 'messages' therefore travel more slowly (at the speed of the blood circulation), and, hence, their actions tend to take effect more slowly and be longer lasting.

A summary of human hormones, production sites and effects is shown in the table.

Hormone	Gland	Effect
Growth hormone	Pituitary gland (base of brain)	Increases growth in young, maintains size in adult
Thyroid stimulating hormone	Pituitary	Acts on thyroid, thereby controlling metabolic rate
Prolactin	Pituitary	Mammary gland development, milk production
Thyroid gland (throat)	Controls cellular energy release (metabolism)	Thyroxine
Pancreas	Absorption of glucose from blood into storage; deficiency causes diabetes	Insulin
Adrenal glands (near kidneys)	Raises blood sugar levels, preparing the body for action (the 'fight or flight' hormone)	Adrenaline
Ovaries	Controls female sexual development and menstrual cycle	Oestrogen
Testes	Controls male sexual development and sperm production	Testosterone

Reproductive systems

Asexual reproduction

Asexual reproduction occurs when an organism reproduces a genetically identical copy (clone) of itself. It is a process that is common in simple animals and many plants and can take the following forms:

- *Fission*: the original organism splits into two equal parts, each of which grows to form new individuals; fission is a method commonly used by bacteria, resulting in exponential growth potential as one individual becomes two, two become four, and so on.
- *Budding*: the parent produces an outgrowth that detaches and develops into a new individual – for example, yeast cells.
- *Spore formation*: the parent produces single-celled bodies that detach and disperse themselves and can grow into new individuals under suitable conditions – an excellent method of surviving adverse environmental conditions or for increasing the distribution of the species. Examples include bacteria and simple plants.
- *Vegetative reproduction (propagation)*: part of a plant can develop into a new individual, eventually becoming detached and independent. Examples are the overground runners of strawberry plants, the underground rhizomes of marram or bracken, the tubers of potatoes and the bulbs of daffodils and onions.

The advantages of asexual reproduction are that it can take place with a single individual and can produce identical copies of a particularly favoured strain. In addition, asexual reproduction can allow for rapid population expansion, both in terms of numbers and distribution. Areas of grassland of up to 400 m^2 are known to be covered by clones of a single individual.

The disadvantages of asexual reproduction are:

- that it limits the genetic variability, and hence the evolutionary potential, of a population, as it does not involve the mixing of genetic material from different individuals;
- that a population composed of genetically identical individuals would be more vulnerable to disease than one with the genetic variability generated by sexual reproduction.

Sexual reproduction

Sexual reproduction takes place in all higher animals and plants, although it is possible for plants to revert to vegetative reproduction if environmental conditions are not suitable. Many plant populations survive by a mixture of asexual and sexual reproduction.

The key biological feature of sexual reproduction is that specialized cells (gametes) from a male and a female individual of the same species fuse to form a zygote cell, which then develops to form a new individual.

The importance of DNA

The nature of a particular plant or animal is a result of the overall functioning of the cells of which it is made. These cells in turn are controlled by the assembly of chemicals that allow metabolic reactions to take place within the cells. What governs the assembly of the various chemicals needed by the cell is the 'code' provided by the long chain molecules of *deoxyribonucleic acid* (DNA) contained in the nucleus of each cell.

Basically, DNA molecules consist of a sequence of bases arranged in two interwoven spirals – the famous 'double-helix' structure of the Watson–Crick hypothesis. At intervals along the molecules, specific sequences of bases (known as *genes*) 'code' for the assembly of amino acids. These in turn allow for the assembly of the proteins that form the enzymes that govern the metabolic functioning of the cells, tissue and organs of the organism concerned. The DNA molecules are arranged along a discrete number of *chromosomes* (characteristic of each species – the human chromosome number is forty-six, arranged as twenty-three pairs) within the nucleus of each cell. So, the nuclear DNA in *every* cell of each plant or animal contains the genetic 'blueprint' or 'toolkit' for the *entire* organism – 30,000 genes in the case of the human genome.

Perhaps the most remarkable attribute of the DNA molecule (and some argue that this is at the heart of life itself) is its ability to replicate itself. During normal cell division, for example when an organism is growing, the two spirals of the DNA molecules are able to 'unwind', each making a 'copy' of the original double helix. The two resulting daughter cells are thus identical copies of the original parent cell.

This is not the case when sexual reproduction occurs. During the division of the germ cells that produce the gametes, the components of each chromosomal pair separate, so that

FACT POINT

Twins vs siblings

Identical twins happen if a single egg is fertilized and then splits in half to make two embryos. The embryos possess identical genetic information, and so the twins share exactly the same DNA and, consequently, look the same. Siblings, on the other hand, will have a distinctive mixture of traits from their parents, and so may have similar features, but will not look the same.

each gamete contains half the normal number of chromosomes for the species. When the gametes (one contributed by each parent) fuse, the genetic material re-combines, the normal chromosome number is restored, and the new individual has received one half of its 'genetic code' from each of its parents.

In humans, the female gametes (egg cells or ova) are produced in the ovaries, usually singly and at approximately 28-day intervals (under hormonal control). Each ovum, containing half the number of chromosomes of all other cells in the body, is released (at ovulation) and begins a journey down the Fallopian tube (oviduct) see Figure 2.20.

When sexual intercourse (copulation) takes place, sperm, produced in large numbers by the male testes, are released from the erect male penis by reflex muscular spasm during orgasm, into the female vagina. Sperm begin to swim towards the oviducts, where fertilization may take place if copulation has occurred within 3 days or so of ovulation.

Fertilization involves the surrounding of the ovum by sperm and the eventual entry into the ovum of the head of a single sperm. The head of the sperm also contains half the chromosomal material of all other body cells, and the fusing of the sperm head with the nucleus of the ovum restores the full chromosomal complement to the fertilized egg (zygote).

As the zygote continues its journey down the oviduct towards the uterus, cell division begins, and, after about 1 week, the developing embryo arrives in the uterus as a hollow ball of cells (blastocyst), and implantation occurs into the wall of the uterus.

Finger-like villi grow into the uterus wall to form the placenta, and it is here that the exchange of food and waste products takes place by diffusion between the blood vessels of the mother and the embryo. There is no direct connection of the two blood supplies.

The embryo becomes surrounded by a fluid-filled protective membrane (the amnion) that supports it and cushions it from shock. It continues to develop and, after 2 months, is a recognizably human foetus. Nine months after fertilization, at the end of the period of internal development (or gestation), the baby is born.

The muscular wall of the uterus begins to contract regularly and forces the baby down the widened uterus–cervix–vagina – the 'birth canal'. The contractions become more frequent and powerful, eventually bursting the amnion and releasing its fluid to the outside. The most difficult part of the birth (from the point of view of the mother) is the passage of the baby's head through the birth canal. This is effected by the continuing (involuntary) muscular contractions of the wall of the uterus, assisted by the mother 'pushing'. Once the head of the baby has emerged from the birth canal (most babies are born head first), the remainder of the birth is usually easier.

After the birth, the cord connecting the baby to the placenta (the umbilical cord) is ligatured and cut, and, some minutes later, after further contractions, the placenta is expelled from the mother's uterus.

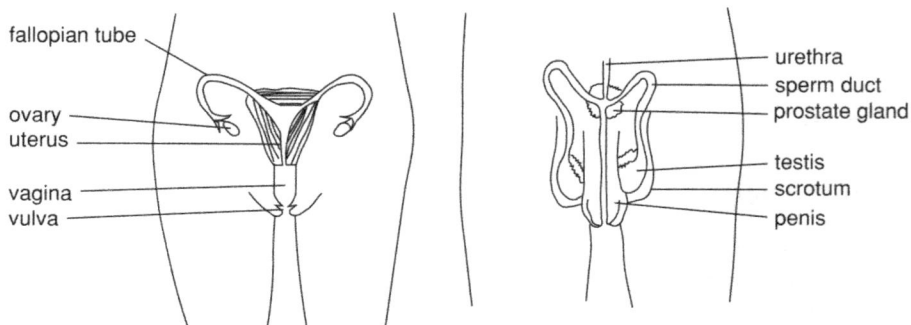

Figure 2.20 Human sexual organs

Puberty

Humans are not able to reproduce until they are sexually mature. Development towards that maturity is triggered by male and female sex hormones and is signalled by the onset of puberty.

In girls aged 10–12 years this causes:

- the development of secondary sexual characteristics (breasts, pubic and armpit hair);
- the onset of ovulation and menstruation;
- widening of hips.

In boys aged 12–14 years, it causes:

- the development of secondary sexual characteristics (voice breaks, pubic and armpit hair);
- the onset of sperm production.

The menstrual cycle

The female menstrual cycle is, in the absence of fertilization, a 28-day cycle of egg production and release (ovulation), and the breakdown and expulsion from the body of the remains of the wall of the uterus (menstruation).

During the first 2 weeks of the menstrual cycle, the female sex hormone oestrogen, produced by the ovaries, causes thickening of the uterine wall and stimulation of the pituitary gland to produce luteinizing hormone, which causes ovulation. If fertilization and implantation occur, another hormone, progesterone, is produced that stops any further production of ova during pregnancy. If fertilization does not occur, or if implantation fails, the ovum dies, and the uterus wall begins to break down.

The expulsion of the remains of the uterine wall and the accompanying 4–7 days of bleeding is known as the 'period' of menstruation. After menstruation, oestrogen promotes the repair of the uterine wall, and a further hormone – follicle stimulating hormone (FSH) – causes the development of the ovum to be released at the next ovulation.

TEACHING IDEA

It is important to teach the changes of the human body (puberty) consistently with the school's sex education policy. Teaching about puberty before children experience it is necessary to ensure that pupils' physical, emotional and learning needs are met, and that they have the correct information about how to take care of their bodies and keep themselves safe.

Sexual reproduction in flowering plants

As plants grow towards maturity, they produce flower buds, which eventually develop into flowers (see Figure 2.21). These are, in effect, a series of modified leaves, each set of which is specialized to perform a specific function. In general terms, a flower would consist of:

- an *outer ring of sepals* (the calyx), which protects the contents of the flower bud during development;
- an inner *ring of petals* (the corolla), which may be coloured and scented and which attracts and provides nectar for visiting insects;

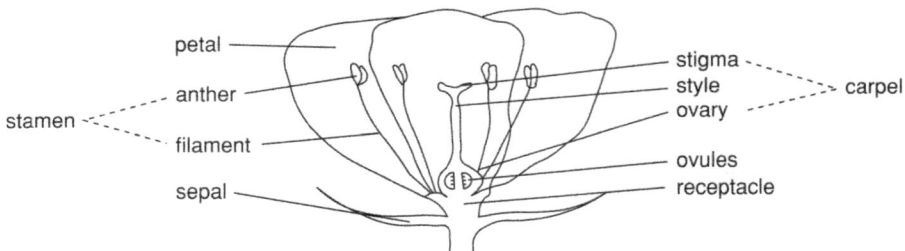

Figure 2.21 The parts of a flower

- a *ring of stamens* (the male parts of the flower), each comprising a stalk (filament) and a pollen sac (anther);
- a *central carpel* (the female part of the flower), comprising an ovary at its base and a style or stalk that supports a stigma (a surface specialized for the receipt and germination of pollen).

This arrangement allows for self-pollination – that is, the transfer of pollen from the anthers to the stigma, either in the same flower or to another flower on the same plant. Modifications include the ripening of anthers and ovaries at different times, so that self-pollination is avoided, the presence of only male (or only female) parts on individual flowers, or the presence of only male (or female) flowers on individual plants, thus requiring cross-pollination for successful sexual reproduction. Some plants have 'fail-safe' mechanisms that guarantee self-fertilization if cross-pollination does not occur – for example, as flowers wither in late season, the anthers bend to touch the stigma, so ensuring pollination.

The sequence of events in the life cycle of a flowering plant may proceed as follows:

Germination

The seed swells as it absorbs water. The root and then the shoot emerge.

WORKING SCIENTIFICALLY

To highlight the difference between germination and plant growth, it is important that children explore the conditions seeds and seedlings need to grow effectively (water, sunlight, warmth and different types of soil). They should discover that seeds do not need light to germinate, but seedlings need light to grow.

Growth to flowering

The plant grows by branching. Flower buds emerge, and flowers open.

Pollination

- Pollen grains mature in the anthers, which split on ripening, releasing pollen to the outside.
- The pollen grains are transported, either by insects that have visited the flower to collect nectar, or by the wind, to the stigma of a flower of the same species (each plant produces species-specific pollen).
- A number of pollen grains germinate on the stigma, and, within minutes, pollen tubes begin to grow towards the ovary. The pollen tubes eventually reach the ovary and

penetrate the embryo sac. The nuclei from the pollen grains fuse with egg cells (ova), and fertilization has taken place.

Development of seeds and fruit

- Each fertilized ovum develops into a seed containing a shoot (plumule), a root (radicle) and one (monocotyledons) or two (dicotyledons) seed leaves.
- The ovary containing fertilized seeds develops into a fruit. The seeds may be borne internally, as in apples and tomatoes, or externally, as in blackberries and strawberries, where the 'fruit' is the swollen base (or receptacle) of the flower bud.

Dispersal

The seed pod dries out and splits. Seeds are shaken out and fall to the ground, where they, in turn, may germinate under suitable conditions.

Dispersal

The advantage of sexual reproduction, and particularly fertilization by cross-pollination, is the potential increase in variability (and therefore survival chances) that it provides.

In order to maximize the impact of this variability, and to minimize direct competition for scarce resources, plants have developed a number of ways in which their seeds can be dispersed and, hence, the range and distribution of the species increased (see Figure 2.22).

Examples of different dispersal mechanisms include:

- 'bouncers and rollers' – acorns, horse chestnuts;
- 'parachutes' – dandelions, thistles;
- 'helicopters' – sycamore, ash;
- 'pepper pots' – poppies;
- 'edibles' – blackberries, strawberries, apples;
- 'hookers and stickers' – burdock, goose grass (cleavers), herb bennet (wood avens);
- 'splitters' – wallflowers, lupins, laburnum.

In addition to dispersal as a method for increasing range and distribution, seeds also allow plants to survive hostile environmental conditions, as they may lie dormant for long periods of time – for example, during drought or extreme cold – before germinating when conditions have improved and survival chances are better.

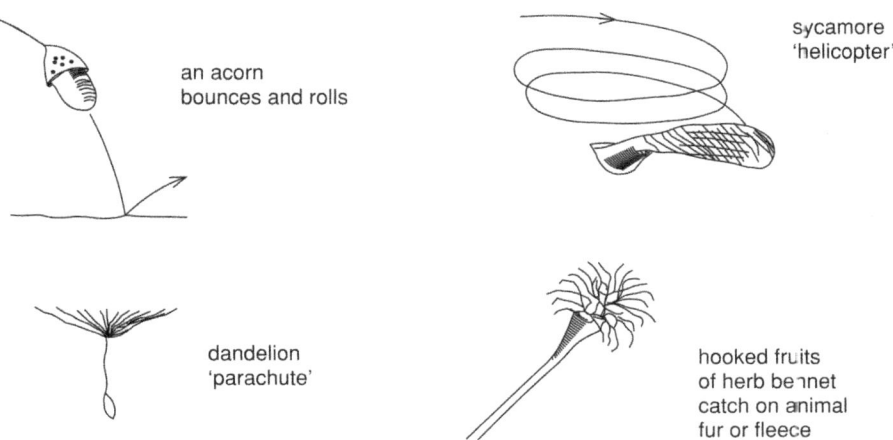

Figure 2.22 Examples of seed dispersal mechanisms

KEY IDEA 2.2 SUMMARY

Understanding of plant and animal systems highlights how life is sustained and renewed. Animals are unable to manufacture their food in the same way that plants do. As a result, life and existence are determined by their ability to obtain the food they need.

Discussion points

- *How do we grow, and why do we stop growing?* Once the body has grown to a point that it can reproduce, the purpose for growth is complete, and so our genetic program tells us to stop growing.
- What limits the size of different animals and plants? What would it be like if worms were the same size as humans?
- *Why doesn't our heart get tired?* The heart does not get tired because it is made of cardiac muscles. These contain lots of mitochondria, which are structures that can take lots of energy from food, so that it does not fatigue.

Working scientifically

- *Fair testing*: An investigation to test the effects of exercise on heart rate supports understanding of the heart and circulation system. Children can make *predictions* about their heart rate at rest, during different exercises and after exercise. This can also be done with breathing rate to gain a deeper understanding of respiration.
- *Pattern-seeking*: Taste and smell can be investigated during *pattern-seeking* enquiries – for example, finding out which crisp flavour children prefer, or whether crisps taste the same with or without the aid of smell.

Cross-curricular links

- *Maths*: Measuring and recording can be conducted in lots of ways. Simple experiments to measure and compare children's lung capacity, measure pulse rates and record rates of germination and plant growth are all ways to encourage data handling in context.
- *Physical education*: Making links between life processes and sport helps children to learn about exercise and the body. In PE, children can be encouraged to think about how muscles are used in different sports and the effects of exercise on the heart, lungs and muscles.
- *PSHE*: Children may develop a deeper understanding of human development by researching and discussing physical changes as humans grow older. The issue of growing older can be embraced by exploring how children can help elderly relatives and the local community.

Future application

Scientists are constantly gaining an even deeper understanding of different processes that happen in the human body, as well as in other organisms. Not only can this help fight illness and increase longevity, but it can assist athletes during training and improve performance.

Health and safety

- When investigating children's pulse rate, keep exercise to the same level as in normal PE sessions. Any equipment used must be robust and well maintained.
- Beware of using stairs for exercising. Children should be taught to hold the handrail.

- When conducting experiments to identify the relationship between exercise and pulse rates, it is also important to identify any children with asthma, ensuring their inhalers are close by.
- When smelling things, put them in a container covered with muslin or a lid with small holes so that substances cannot be ingested by mistake (ASE, *Be Safe*, 4th edition).

Assessment for learning

Floorbooks: Children may wish to record their initial ideas about life processes or how parts of the body work in a floorbook (typically, an A3/A2 scrapbook of developing ideas, sketches, photos, annotations, post-it notes and questions to show a development of ideas). At the end of a lesson or topic, they can revisit how their understanding has developed. This can include adding additional labels to diagrams, as well as interesting facts and future questions about living things.

KEY IDEA 2.3

Optimum conditions for survival

CONCEPTS TO SUPPORT KEY STAGE I

For animals and plants in hostile environments, survival may simply be a matter of 'hanging on', or of being able to tolerate conditions that other organisms cannot (e.g. desert, salt marsh). For most organisms, however, it is possible to identify optimum conditions in which they will flourish.

Healthy plants

For successful establishment and growth to reproduction, plants need:

- A 'safe site' for germination: plants need a place where a seed can settle, preferably in well-drained, well-aerated soil, with space to grow and with little likelihood of being blown or washed away. Much of the autumn 'seed rain' dies without ever reaching a safe site. Either there is no space available, or the seeds are washed or blown away, or collected and eaten by predators.
- Water availability: plants need water in order to synthesize food, as a medium for metabolic reactions and internal transport, and for support (this can be seen when a plant begins to wilt if it is not watered regularly). Most of this water comes from the soil and reaches the plant tissues through the root system. A small amount is absorbed directly from the leaves.
- Carbon dioxide (for photosynthesis) and oxygen (for respiration): both of these substances enter the plant by diffusion through small pores (or stomata), usually on the underside of the leaves.
- Nutrients (minerals from the soil): iron and magnesium salts are used in the production of chlorophyll; nitrates and sulphates are used in protein and DNA production; phosphates are used in 'energy-carrier' molecules (ATP); and calcium is laid down in the middle layer between plant cell walls.
- Sunlight (after germination): sunlight is essential for photosynthesis and is the source of energy that sustains life on Earth.
- Space to grow: all plants in a natural environment are competing for available moisture, nutrients, etc. Those that have the largest spaces into which to grow will usually be the

---

FACT POINT

Can you grow plants in space?

Without soil, growing plants is still possible, if the roots are in nutrient- and mineral-rich water. This is called *hydroponics* and has been used for growing plants on the International Space Station (ISS).

most successful. This principle can be very easily demonstrated by sowing different numbers of seeds into same-size pots of soil and then observing the difference in size of the germinated plants.

- *Warmth*: the chemical reactions that occur in the cells of plants will 'work' better at higher natural temperatures. That is why growth is so luxuriant in equatorial forests, and why gardeners 'force' the growth of plants in glasshouses. Plant growth generally stops when the temperature falls below 6°C or rises above 40°C.

- *A system of pollination*: in order for a plant to set seed, pollen from the male parts of a flower needs to reach the female parts of a flower so that the gamete cells can fuse. Some plants rely on insects for pollination. Insects visit the flowers to collect nectar and, in doing so, brush against the pollen-bearing structures of the plant. When visiting another plant in search of nectar, some of the pollen is brushed off on to the female parts of the new flower, and pollination has taken place. Other plants rely on the wind 'shaking' the pollen out of male flowers and carrying it to female flowers of the same species.

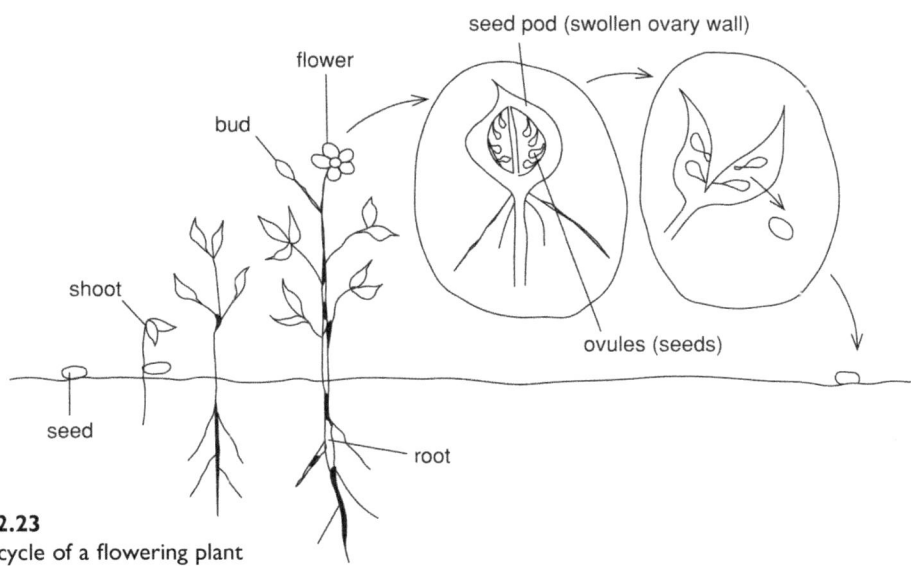

Figure 2.23
The life cycle of a flowering plant

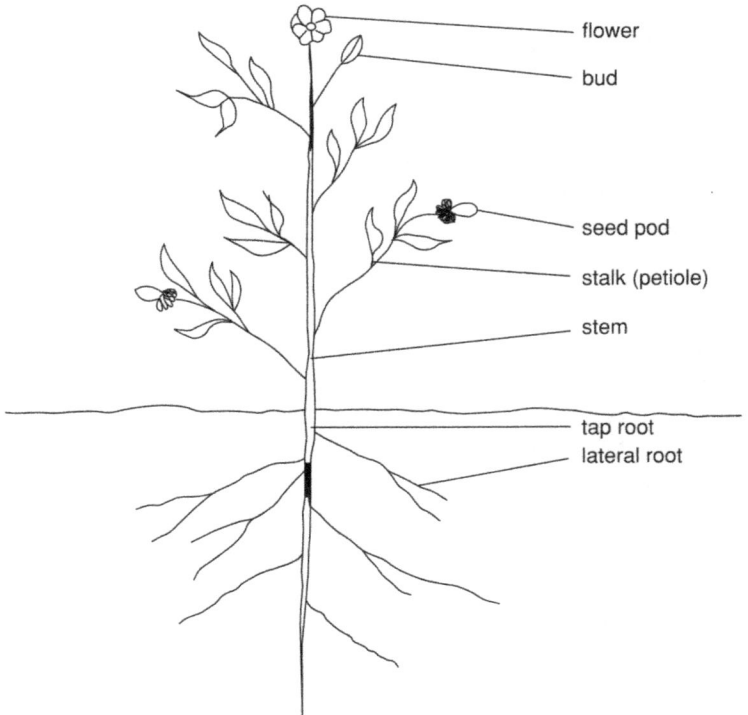

Figure 2.24 The main parts of a flowering plant

Healthy animals

In order to survive, grow and stay healthy, animals need the following:

Food

Animals cannot make their own food, and so they have to eat plants or other animals. For healthy living, a balanced diet is necessary and should contain carbohydrates and fats (for energy), proteins (for body building) and vitamins and minerals (for maintenance). The table shows some food types, examples and functions.

The main parts of a balanced diet will consist of carbohydrates, fats and proteins. Vitamins and minerals are needed in very small quantities, but their absence will often have a serious effect on health and well-being. The importance of a balanced diet is now better understood, as are the dangers of overeating. Eating 'more than is necessary' to sustain health can lead to obesity (being overweight) and is an increasing problem in children and young adults. Eating too much of one kind of food (particularly fatty and sugary food) can increase the likelihood of a person suffering from heart disease, high blood pressure or strokes (cerebral – brain – haemorrhage).

Water

It has been estimated that human beings consist of 70 per cent water. We need water for the processes of metabolism that go on inside the cells in our bodies; for the internal transport of metabolic products; and for the movement (diffusion) into our bodies of the oxygen for respiration, and out of our bodies of waste and carbon dioxide. In addition to the water that is part of our food (cabbage and bananas are about 90 per cent water; meat is about 60 per cent), we need to drink the equivalent of 1.5 litres of water a day in order to survive.

Type of food	Examples	Functions
Carbohydrate	Glucose, starch	Energy supply, plant cell walls, 'building blocks' of other molecules
Fats	Animal fat, oils in plants	Energy supply (double the 'energy per gram' of carbohydrates), insulation
Proteins	Muscle, tendons, enzymes and hormones used in metabolism, haemoglobin	Movement, insulin used to control blood sugar levels (oxygen carrier)
Vitamins	A (retinol) from vegetables, liver oils	Helps night vision
	B_1 (thiamine) from wholemeal bread	Builds strong muscles
	B_2 (riboflavin) from milk and eggs	Helps respiration
	B_{12} (cobolamine) from meat, salmon	Helps make red blood cells
	C (ascorbic acid) from citrus fruit and fresh vegetables	Strengthens skin, helps heal wounds
	D (calciferol) from butter and egg yolk	Assists calcium and phosphate deposition in bones
Minerals	Ca (calcium) and P (phosphorus) from cheese and milk	Bones and teeth are 66 per cent calcium phosphate
	Fe (iron) from liver, meat and beans	Part of haemoglobin (oxygen carrier)
	Na (sodium) salt	Helps nerves and muscles to work properly
	I (iodine) from sea foods and table salt	Makes the hormone thyroxine, which helps to control metabolism

FUTURE APPLICATION

Around the world, not all human populations are able to access good sanitation and adequate water supplies, leading to disease. For example, cholera is a water-borne disease found in areas of war, civil unrest and famine. Providing access to safe drinking water, sanitation and hygiene can help people around the world prevent diseases such as cholera, typhoid and dysentery.

Oxygen

Air, which is a mixture of gases, contains about 20 per cent oxygen. Almost all animals (and certainly all vertebrate animals) use oxygen in respiration. Oxygen is carried into the bodies of land animals in the air that is breathed into the lungs. On the damp surfaces of the lungs are very fine blood vessels (capillaries), where the oxygen from the air dissolves into the blood. At the same time, carbon dioxide, which is a waste product of respiration, comes out of solution in the blood and is exhaled from the lungs. The dissolved oxygen in the blood is then transported all round the body, where it can be used for cellular respiration – the 'oxidation' of energy-rich molecules such as glycogen or fats to produce energy, carbon dioxide and water.

Warmth

Two of the groups of vertebrate animals (birds and mammals) are 'warm-blooded', that is, they maintain a constant body temperature. This characteristic has allowed the two groups to colonize almost every area of the Earth, as the processes of life are not controlled by outside temperatures, although they may be influenced by them. Outside the tropics, most animals have evolved some system to retain body heat and so ensure a stability of temperature that will allow them to survive. The body covering is significant here: feathers for birds and hair or fur for land mammals. Other adaptations include the slowing down of the body systems during cold weather (hibernation in mammals) and migration to warmer places during the worst of the winter weather.

Safe site

Animals also need safe sites, to lessen the chances of attack by predators and for undisturbed breeding. Again, birds and mammals are groups that pay particular attention to the rearing of young, and one reason for this is that they produce far fewer offspring than do the 'cold-blooded' vertebrate groups – fish lay eggs in thousands, and amphibians and reptiles in hundreds. In order to rear young beyond the stage of dependency, they need a sheltered, safe site over a period of weeks or months. In many (most) animal species, the female is responsible for rearing the young, and this is one reason why female animals are often well camouflaged, so that they are less likely to be noticed by predators during the breeding phases of their lives.

A further salutary thought is that the activities of people have often been responsible for denying animals the 'safe sites' they need to breed successfully, whether through ploughing, building on, or changing in some other way, the animals' original habitat.

The idea of safe sites can also be extended to people, who are just as much in need of security as any other group. For people, and particularly young people, this implies a safe home environment and enough knowledge to deal with the parts of their environment over which they have no control. This knowledge may include procedures for road safety, how to deal with approaches from strangers, and so on.

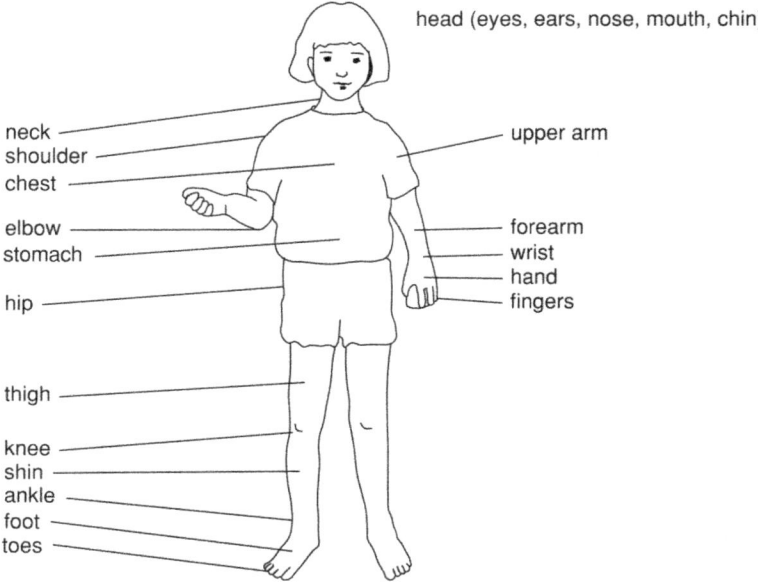

Figure 2.25 The main external parts of the human body

Exercise and rest

Animals in the wild are continuously exercising – frequently, they are hunting or being hunted! As humans, our lifestyle choices have a major impact on our health and well-being. In order to allow the body to grow and be healthy, it is important that people take regular exercise too. This ensures that the heart and lungs are strengthened, and that all the 'moving parts' are in working order. Exercise also frequently results in a feeling of well-being, although excessive or obsessive commitment to an exercise regime can be harmful, both physically and mentally.

An important part of healthy living is the requirement of the body for rest. It is not possible to 'keep going' for ever, and the human system needs to rest and recover on a daily basis. Most people need about 8 hours sleep per night, and young people probably need more. Lack of sleep causes inattentiveness and irritability (which primary teacher has not noticed that during a morning session?), and, although it is not appropriate to 'moralize' about how children should live their home lives, it may be worth pointing out the noticeable effects that lack of sleep can cause.

FUTURE APPLICATION

Modelling healthy choices is an important aspect of the PSHE and wider school curriculum. There are lots of ways schools can promote a healthy attitude and approach to exercise and sleep: early morning jogging clubs, breakfast clubs, walking-to-school challenges and sports clubs. This is important for children to lead healthy lifestyles.

CONCEPTS TO SUPPORT KEY STAGE 2

A number of factors are involved in the establishment and maintenance of human health and well-being. Some of these factors relate to the defence systems of the body, and others are under conscious control.

The defence systems of the body

The human body is continuously at risk of invasion by potentially harmful agents. Some of these are inanimate and take the form of atmospheric or water pollutants. Historical examples would include coal dust from mining, soot from coal fires (a substantial cause of the 1952 London 'smog', which caused more than 2,000 deaths from bronchial disease) and asbestos fibres, which were a primary cause of lung disease. Although these potential dangers have largely been removed (by the Clean Air Act and by health and safety legislation), modern examples would include the exhaust gases from motor vehicles (which may be the cause of a twofold increase in the incidence of childhood asthma over the past 20 years) and increased levels of heavy metals, such as lead, absorbed into human systems. Contentiously, we are told that there is no apparent connection between locally higher incidences of childhood leukaemia and closeness to sites that emit ionizing radiation (nuclear power stations, for example).

The second group of agents are those living organisms that can 'invade' the body, and these are mainly viruses, bacteria and parasites. Lifestyle and personal habits play a part in the prevention of infection by such organisms, and these are considered below (see 'Conscious action that can promote health'). In addition to conscious action to maintain health, the body has its own defence systems that can prevent or deal with invasion and infection, and these are now described.

External resistance to invasion

The 'first line of defence' for the body is the skin (see Key Idea 2.2). The skin forms a physical barrier that prevents the direct entry of pollutants or infectious organisms. Second, there are a number of other devices used by the body to contain invasion. These include:

- 'filter' systems such as nasal hairs, which prevent or slow down the inhalation of airborne particles;
- mucous membranes – again, for example, those in the nasal cavity, which secrete sticky mucus to trap airborne particles or bacteria (although it may be an unpleasant topic for discussion, both of these examples can be used to show the importance of blowing the nose to remove such matter, rather than sniffing and swallowing into the stomach);
- specialized areas of cells (ciliated epithelium) with a surface of very small hairs (cilia), which can 'waft' unwanted particles in a certain direction; an example of such tissue is the ciliated epithelium at the top of the trachea or windpipe: dirt particles and bacteria that are trapped by mucus are swept by the cilia towards the throat, where they are either swallowed or coughed up, in either case removing the risk to the lungs;
- the conjunctiva, the surface membranes of the eye, sense dirt and dust particles or other foreign bodies and trigger the production of tears to 'flood out' the irritants.

Responses following invasion

The *innate* or *natural immune response* – immediately following infection – is for groups of cells in the body to act to limit the damage that can be done by the invading organism. The action can take the form of engulfment (e.g. by phagocytes) or destruction or inactivation by chemicals produced by a variety of different cell types.

The adaptive immune response is a process triggered when an invading organism 'escapes' the innate immune response. It involves the processing and recognition of the invading organism (the antigen) and the production of soluble factors (antibodies) that will lead eventually to its elimination.

The adaptive immune response has been successfully exploited in the production and action of vaccines. If dead or inactive infectious organisms (in the form of a vaccine) are injected into a human, the adaptive immune response will cause antibody-producing 'memory cells' to be formed. These cells will 'recognize' and resist the effect of any live forms of the injected organism that may invade the body at a later date.

The immune response is not always successful in combating disease. One of the most urgent modern examples is the apparent inability of the human system to deal with the human immunodeficiency virus (HIV), which causes AIDS (acquired immune deficiency syndrome). Basically, HIV acts to destroy the cells in the body that are able to resist infection, leading to a decreasing ability to mount immune responses. Eventually, the immune system of the body is unable to deal with infections, and the individual may suffer from a combination of illnesses. It is at this stage that the sufferer is said to have AIDS, a condition for which there is no known cure.

The virus is known to be transmitted through unprotected sexual contact (particularly between homosexual and bisexual men), the administration of infected blood or blood products, exposure to blood-containing needles and syringes, or through the placental wall of a mother to an unborn child.

Conscious action that can promote health

In addition to the defence work that our bodies do on our behalf, there are a number of areas relating to health over which we have a degree of control. We can decide on various aspects of our lifestyle and can develop personal habits that can affect our health; although the extent to which a teacher should promote aspects of lifestyle that relate to health is arguable, it is important for people to know the possible implications of any health-related decisions they may make. Areas of consideration are shown in the table.

Diet	Prevention of infection	Lifestyle
Types and balance of food eaten, regularity of feeding	Washing of self and clothing; oral hygiene; toilet routines; use of handkerchief if suffering from cold; food hygiene	Attention to personal fitness; exercise regime; rest and sleep patterns; awareness of the dangers of substance abuse

Diet

Diet is one of the most important factors affecting health, and the table shows what a balanced diet should contain.

Ingredient	Action
Carbohydrates (found in grains such as rice and wheat)	For oxidation and energy release; for storage as starch (plants) or glycogen (animals); cellulose strengthens plant cell walls and provides fibre roughage for animals
Fats (found in dairy products, red meat, fish and poultry)	For oxidation and energy release (twice the energy per gram of carbohydrates); energy storage; insulation
Proteins (found in meat and pulses)	For growth and repair (muscles, tendons, ligaments, skin, hair are made from proteins); enzymes control metabolic rate
Minerals (such as calcium found in dairy products)	For building bones and teeth; for nerve function; for haemoglobin (oxygen carrier) in red blood cells
Vitamins (found in dairy products, fresh fruit and vegetables)	To help control metabolic reactions
Water	For transport inside the body; as a medium for metabolic processes
Fibre (found in vegetables, fruit and whole grains)	Indigestible plant tissues – 'roughage' – help the passage of food through the gut

'Healthy' diets are those that derive the above 'ingredients' from a range of foods, contain plenty of fresh or unprocessed foods, including fruit and vegetables, which cut down on saturated (animal) fat products, and contain dietary fibre (Figure 2.26).

A useful idea is that, literally and metaphorically, *'we are what we eat'*. Awareness of the importance of a balanced diet has increased recently, but many nutritionists (and teachers) are concerned about the effect on the long-term health of children of convenience foods, monotonous diets and irregular mealtimes, all of which are potentially unhealthy. It has been suggested, for example, that a daily intake equivalent of five pieces of fruit or vegetables can significantly decrease the chance of heart disease, cataracts (which occur when the lenses of the eye become opaque) and some cancers. (See also Key Idea 2.2: Nutrition systems.)

Figure 2.26 Balanced food plate

WORKING SCIENTIFICALLY

Children can work with the school kitchen to produce posters to communicate healthy food and drink choices and portions. Finding out and displaying how much sugar is found in different drinks and healthy portion sizes will help develop a whole-school approach to healthy diets.

Researching and debating the UK's sugar tax is a good way of raising awareness of the effects too much sugar can have on our bodies.

Teeth

A related component of healthy living is the need for people to look after their teeth. The pattern of teeth (dentition) in humans reflects an omnivorous diet and comprises eight incisors (for cutting), four canines (for tearing – relics of the carnivores' fangs), eight pre-molars (for grinding and crushing) and twelve molars (adults only; also for grinding and crushing).

The basic structures of human teeth are shown in Figure 2.27. The outer coating of enamel is almost entirely made of calcium phosphate and is harder than the dentine it covers, which in turn is harder than the bone of the jaw. The pulp cavity at the centre of the tooth contains the blood supply and the nerve endings.

Tooth decay (dental caries) can begin when acids are formed in the mouth during the breakdown of sugars by bacteria. These bacteria form a layer on the teeth (known as plaque), and the acids they produce literally dissolve the tooth enamel and dentine. Toothache results when the nerves in the pulp cavity are affected.

It is important to maintain healthy teeth for as long as possible, both to ensure that food can be properly chewed and to prevent or limit the discomfort and pain of toothache. Methods of preventing or slowing down tooth decay include:

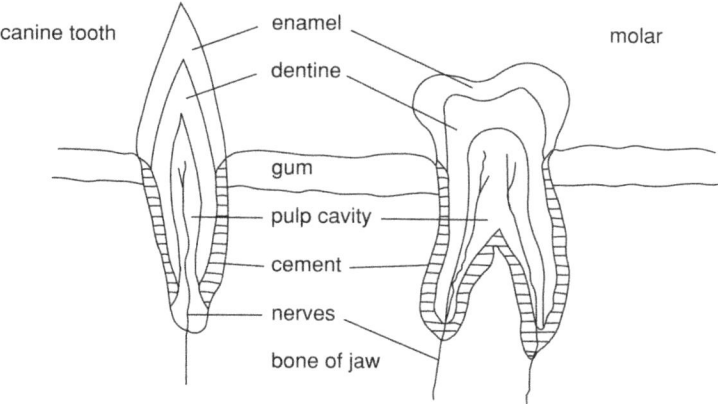

Figure 2.27 Sections of human teeth

- the regular brushing of teeth to remove plaque (toothpaste is slightly alkaline, and this also helps to neutralize mouth acid);
- cutting down on sugary foods and drinks (less acid is likely to form);
- regular dental check-ups (and filling of cavities if necessary);
- the use of a fluoride toothpaste or tablets (strengthens enamel);
- fluoridation of water supply.

FACT POINT

What is endocarditis?

Practising good oral and dental hygiene, including tongue brushing, can reduce the risk of developing endocarditis. This is a rare heart infection caused by bacteria entering the blood and travelling to the heart.

Personal hygiene

At the heart of personal hygiene is the attempt to prevent infection (and perhaps a wish not to offend the noses of companions!).

Leaving aside the persuasive advertising copy of the cosmetics industry, some important practices and functions of personal hygiene can be listed as follows:

- the washing of self and clothing will minimize the possibility of bacteria multiplying in sweat on the body or clothes;
- regular brushing of teeth will neutralize mouth acid and remove or slow down the build-up of bacteria in the mouth;
- the washing of hands after visiting the lavatory lowers the risk of infection, as does the regular disinfection of toilet areas;
- food hygiene may be practised by the prevention or slowing down of decay by refrigeration, the minimizing of risk of infection by use of clean utensils and the careful protection of food, appropriate cooking at the correct temperature (boiling kills most bacteria), the washing of hands before eating, and the proper disposal of unwanted food;
- the use of a handkerchief when suffering from a cold will remove infected mucus from the nasal cavity and will lessen the 'droplet cloud' effect of an unprotected sneeze.

Lifestyle

The effect of exercise

In order to maintain physical fitness, the body needs regular exercise. In recent years, concern has been expressed about the lack of fitness of the population, caused partly by lack of exercise, and health promotion programmes exhort people to increase their rates of exercise in order to stay healthy. However, promoting exercise during events such as the Olympics and the World Cup has helped to promote participation in a wide range of sports. Whether it is gymnastics or tennis, cycling or swimming, jogging or tight-rope-walking, exercise is an important aspect of improving fitness.

WORKING SCIENTIFICALLY

Investigating exercise

The best way to keep healthy is to lead an active lifestyle (using the stairs, walking more, watching less television), along with dedicated exercise. Children can record the activities they do in a week and consider how they could increase the number of physical activities they do. Not only will this help to reduce obesity and increase bone and muscle strength, but it is also beneficial to their mental health.

Whatever form the exercise takes, it should have the common effect of raising the heart rate through physical activity. This increases the circulation of blood round the body and allows the increased development of the blood capillary network, making for a more efficient transport system for the action of cellular respiration. Exercise allows all the 'moving parts' to develop, particularly the muscles, and the increased blood supply promotes the maintenance of healthy tissues. In addition, exercise frequently brings with it a sense or feeling of well-being, perhaps associated with the exercise-induced release into the bloodstream of substances known as endorphins. It has even been suggested that these self-generated substances are mildly addictive, hence the obsession of some people with fitness and exercise!

Just as it is unwise to do too little exercise, it is also unwise to over-exercise. It is not a good idea to overload the muscles, joints and bones of children who are still growing, as this can cause deformity, breakdown or burn-out. This can be seen by the numbers of prodigious young athletes who, as adults, fail to fulfil the promise shown in their younger years.

The need for rest

No organism can simply 'keep going' for ever. After any long period of sustained physical and/or mental activity, the body 'tires' – it becomes less efficient, and a recovery period becomes necessary. In physical terms, this need may be signalled by muscle fatigue (caused by the build-up of waste products such as lactic acid), the 'making of mistakes' when undertaking some mental activity such as counting or typing, or lack of coordination in some physical activity, such as driving a car or hitting a ball.

To restore the body to its full capacity again, a period of rest is needed. During the day, this can take the form of stopping the present activity and beginning a different one (what teacher has not introduced a completely different activity to rejuvenate a jaded class?), or rest and relaxation in a position of comfort, with little or no activity going on.

The daily pattern of activity and rest is an important consideration for people, particularly those with repetitive jobs, such as assembly workers, or those with jobs that demand long periods of high concentration, such as bus or train drivers. Variation in physical and mental activity is important in the establishment of a healthy lifestyle.

The body's main mechanism for rest is sleep, and most adults need about 8 hours of sleep (preferably unbroken) each night, in order to recover from the exertions of the previous day. Children, whose metabolic rates tend to be higher because of general growth and activity levels, need correspondingly more sleep in order to recover fully. The frequent lack of sleep caused by modern lifestyles (late-night TV watching, for example) has obvious effects on children in classrooms – inattentiveness, listlessness, irrational and sometimes antisocial behaviour. It may be appropriate for teachers to point out the effects of sleep deprivation, even if they are in no position to change things.

FACT POINT

Why is sleep important?

For about a third of our lives, we are asleep. While we are asleep, the heart rate goes down, muscles relax, the energy sources are replenished in brain cells, and activities that occurred in the day are committed to the memory. Sleep has been an area of research for neuroscientists for a long time More recently, it has been discovered that sleep improves learning and concentration.

The harmful effects of drugs, alcohol and tobacco

A number of substances can affect the central nervous system and cause physiological changes in people.

Drugs

Some drugs can be used for medical purposes, and some chemical solvents affect the nervous system (possibly by altering the way in which nerve impulses are transmitted), causing changes in perception. If a drug is used regularly, the body becomes tolerant to low doses of it, and increasingly high doses are needed to produce the same effects. Eventually, with continued use, an individual becomes drug-dependent (or addicted) and has a physiological need for the drug. Once a person is habituated to the use of a drug, its withdrawal can be accompanied by the symptoms of serious illness. A common behaviour pattern is that such a person may have no effective life outside the need to satisfy the drug dependency, often resorting to crime to finance the necessary supply.

Examples of drugs derived from medicines are those that depress the awareness of pain (analgesics) – for example, morphine and heroin – and those that slow down the nervous system (sedatives), such as barbiturates.

Drugs that distort perceptions (hallucinogens) include plant derivatives (cannabis or marijuana) and manufactured substances (LSD and solvents).

TEACHING IDEA

It is important to highlight to children that the word *drug* is sometimes used instead of medicine, but that drugs may also be substances that can be addictive or make people ill. Medicines are always beneficial, to help people get better or stay healthy. However, it must be emphasized to children that this is only the case when they are taken under clear instructions from a doctor or adult. Children could conduct a sorting activity to identify 'good' and 'bad' drugs.

Alcohol

Alcohol is a sedative drug. In small quantities, it is said to be beneficial, as it can relieve tension and bring about a feeling of well-being. Physiologically, it is vasodilatory – that is, it causes blood vessels to expand (hence, a 'flushed' appearance after alcohol intake). This property is said to be beneficial in the prevention of heart disease. Also, it is a diuretic – it promotes the passing of urine – which can cause dehydration of the body (said to be one of the causes of the 'hangover' headache).

An excess of alcohol turns the feeling of well-being into an abandonment of caution, causes serious impairment of judgement, coordination, speech and vision, and eventually leads to unconsciousness and, in severe cases, coma and death.

Long-term addiction to alcohol causes an impairment of liver function due to liver cell death, and the destruction of brain cells. The social effects can be similar to those of the pursuit of any drug dependency – lack of personal and social effectiveness, violent and irrational behaviour, and the allocation of all possible resources (to the point of indebtedness) to the purchase of alcoholic drinks.

Tobacco

Tobacco, like alcohol and the other drugs described, has two types of effect. First, it is a stimulant and is an example of the group of drugs that speed up nervous activity and increase alertness (cocaine and pep pills also fall into this category). The nicotine in tobacco makes it an addictive substance.

Second, inhaled tobacco smoke has a number of effects on the physiology of the body:

- Tar irritates the ciliated epithelium of the trachea, causing an increase in mucus secretion and paralysis of the cilia, which would otherwise remove unwanted particles. This results in mucus congestion of the bronchial tubes, a resultant 'smoker's cough' and a likely increase in infection (bronchitis).
- Tar also causes the break-up of the alveoli – the small air sacs at the end of the bronchioles (see Key Idea 2.2: The cardio-vascular system). This has the effect of decreasing the surface area for gaseous exchange. Clinically, this condition is known as emphysema and it causes chronic shortage of breath.
- Tar is carcinogenic (causes cancer). It can cause the cells in the lungs to divide rapidly, and eventually uncontrollably, forming a malignant tumour.
- Carbon monoxide in inhaled tobacco smoke combines with haemoglobin in the blood, making the oxygenation of the blood less efficient and reducing capacity for physical exercise.
- Carbon monoxide also increases sclerosis (deposition of fat) in the arteries, increasing the likelihood of a heart attack.

KEY IDEA 2.3 SUMMARY

Plants need a safe place for germination, water, carbon dioxide and oxygen, nutrients, sunlight, space, warmth and a system for pollination. They are able to make their own food through the process of photosynthesis. Animals require food, water, oxygen, warmth, safe shelter and exercise. Maintaining an active lifestyle, good hygiene habits and avoiding harmful drugs will also promote good health.

Working scientifically

- Mystery seeds: Present children with unnamed seeds (e.g. carrot and pumpkin seeds) and ask them to *predict* what kind of plant they may grow into and *investigate* the optimal conditions for growth and survival.

- How water travels through a plant can be *observed* by putting white carnations into some water with food colouring and seeing how the colour travels up through the stem to the flowers.
- Children could find out about the world of exercise, energy and movement by *researching* famous athletes.
- Children can *investigate* the impact of different liquids on their teeth by leaving eggshells in each liquid (such as water, milk, cola and orange juice) for 24 hours, then carefully replacing the liquid daily. *Observations* can be made as to which liquid corrodes the eggshells (representing teeth) most quickly.

Discussion points

- Why do animals eat plants, but plants do not eat animals?
- What is the difference between the ways plants and animals keep healthy?

Cross-curricular links

- *Literacy*: Children might demonstrate their understanding of the digestive system by describing the journey of a piece of food, either in the form of a story or stages in a cartoon. Children may also use books such as *James and the Giant Peach* (Roald Dahl) or the story of Jack and the Beanstalk as an introduction to learning about plant growth and survival.
- *Art*: Children can build their own plant model using craft materials, such as cardboard tubes, tinfoil, paper cake cases, pipe cleaners, drinking straws and tissue paper, labelling the main parts.
- *Maths*: Food labels provide great data for maths. Children can compare the amount of sugar in different snacks and drinks or even make top trump cards to compare the amount of each nutrition group in different foods. Children may calculate how many calories they eat each day, or the calories in their favourite breakfast cereal.

Real-life science

Biomechanics is the study of the mechanics and engineering of living things Scientists study athletes' movement, exploring how bones and muscles work together. Developing a better understanding helps to ensure exercises and sports are carried out safely, preventing injury and assisting recovery.

Nutrition scientists are continually developing specially formulated foods and drinks for athletes. For example, isotonic drinks, with specific quantities of salt and sugar, can aid rehydration and boost energy levels.

Health and safety

- When growing and working with plants, children should be warned not to eat anything or put things/fingers in their mouths. Hands should be washed after working with plants.
- During investigations with food and drinks, children's allergies should be taken into consideration to ensure that nothing is consumed unintentionally.

Assessment for learning

Homework learning log: Children may be invited to reflect on school learning by conducting thinking activities at home – for example, considering what they and their family could do to lead a healthier lifestyle. This will allow them to apply their learning to their own life and will identify their understanding of key aspects of keeping healthy.

KEY IDEA 2.4

The variety of life

There is a large variety of life forms on Earth.

CONCEPTS TO SUPPORT KEY STAGE 1

The classification of plants and animals

There are, supposedly, more than 8.7 million different kinds of species on Earth. For their study, or even identification, they have been classified into groups. The basis of classification is similarity and difference – how are the members of a group similar, and how do they differ from all other groups? These questions can be asked repeatedly until it is possible to identify individual types of plant or animal (these ideas are explored further in Concepts to support Key Stage 2, below).

It is now commonly accepted that present-day plants and animals have arisen by adaptation of previous forms (see section on natural selection below), and most classifications of plants and animals are evolutionary, with groupings based on common ancestry. People involved in the science of classification (taxonomy) take into account the outward appearance, the internal organization and biochemical and chromosomal evidence when assigning organisms to their appropriate groups.

The classification of plants and animals therefore involves the division of large groups of organisms into progressively smaller groups with similar features. The hierarchy is as follows:

> kingdom, phylum (from the Greek word for tribe), class, order, family, genus, species

To borrow an idea from mathematics, each succeeding refinement within the classification represents a 'subset' of the previous grouping. Two examples are shown in Figure 2.28.

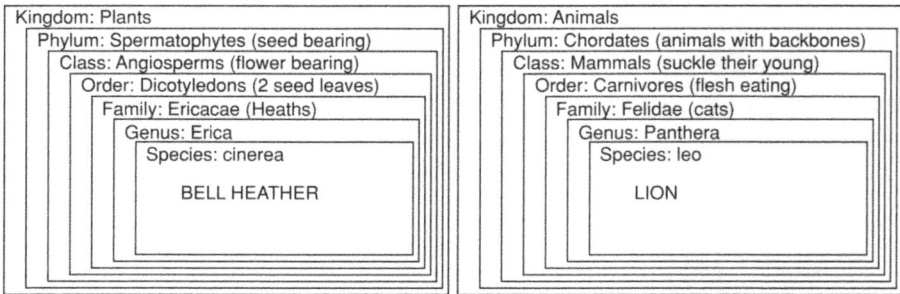

Figure 2.28 Examples of the classification of a plant and an animal

Conventionally, the generic name begins with a capital, and the specific name, with a small letter. Hence: *Erica cinerea* (bell heather) and *Panthera leo* (lion).

FACT POINT

Latin names for common plants and animals

Plants		Animals	
Apple	Pyrus malus	Cat	Felis Catus
Banana	Musa paradisicum	Crocodile	Crocodilia nicoticus
Carrot	Daucus carota	Dog	Carinis familiaris
Lemon	Citrus limonium	Frog	Anura ranidae
Potato	Solanum tuberosum	Horse	Equus caballus
Wheat	Triticum aestivum	Tiger	Panthera tigris

It is common to view all life forms as grouped into either the *plant* or *animal kingdom*. Some modern classifications include four other kingdoms, and these are *viruses*, *bacteria*, *protoctista* and *fungi*. From the point of view of children's understanding of classification, the awareness of animals and plants is probably sufficient for Key Stages 1 and 2, but brief details are given here of the other four groups, as each has some significance for, or potential effect on, people.

Kingdom: Viruses

Viruses are very small (about one-hundredth of the size of a bacterium) and so are beyond the resolution of a light microscope. They are subcellular structures that exist as chemicals outside living cells, but are able to reproduce once they have invaded their hosts. Viruses 'inject' their nucleic material (DNA) into host cells and 'take over' the host enzymes for their own metabolism. The virus DNA continues to replicate, until eventually the host cell ruptures, releasing the newly produced virus copies to invade further host cells. They have obvious significance for human health, as their replication destroys the tissues that they have invaded. Examples of diseases caused by viruses are:

- in plants: tobacco mosaic disease;
- in humans: measles, mumps, herpes (cold sores), influenza, smallpox, HIV.

Kingdom: Bacteria

Bacteria represent the smallest life forms that are organized on a cellular basis (although they have no distinct cell nucleus). They are about one-hundredth of the size of a human cheek or liver cell. They can be spherical, rod-like or spiral in shape, and can occur in chains or clumps.

Most bacteria obtain their energy from the breakdown of living or non-living organic matter. They play an important role in the decomposition of plant and animal remains and the eventual recycling of nutrients.

Some bacteria are valuable – they are involved in the production of yoghurt and cheese, and others are sources of antibiotics – for example, streptomycin.

Those that are parasitic on living organisms are potentially harmful, and examples of bacterial diseases are diphtheria, leprosy, tuberculosis and typhoid. These diseases are often transmitted through poor water supply, when personal hygiene is of a low standard or when bacteria are airborne in small water droplets (resulting from coughing or sneezing). Again, the implications for healthy living are obvious.

Kingdom: Protoctista

Protoctista are single-celled organisms. The plants are sometimes classified within the algae, as they contain chlorophyll, but all are single-celled, or colonial, and some are motile, that is, they are self-propelled. As a group, they have huge significance, as they make up much of the plankton in the oceans. It is thought that the plant component of plankton (phytoplankton) is responsible, through photosynthesis, for most of the Earth's oxygen supply (certainly for a significantly larger proportion than that produced by equatorial forest). Similarly, the phytoplankton provides the 'plant layer' that is at the base of all the marine food webs (see Key Idea 2.6, below). Some of the blue-green algae produce toxic waste products that can threaten water supplies if the summer-time algal 'bloom' is extensive enough.

The animals (protozoa) are almost all motile. Each individual cell contains organelles, specialized to perform certain functions – digestion, protein synthesis, transport and so on. Two groups of marine protozoa secrete hard shells that, on their death, form the marine sediments that can eventually become chalk or limestone. Some protozoa are harmful parasites, causing malaria (*Plasmodium*), dysentery (*Entamoeba*) or sleeping sickness (*Trypanosoma*).

Kingdom: Fungi

The fungi used to be classified as a group within the plant kingdom, but, as they contain no chlorophyll, they are now commonly excluded, so that the plant kingdom contains only *green* plants.

As fungi contain no chlorophyll, they gain their food from dead organic remains (saprophytic nutrition) or from living hosts (parasitic nutrition). They consist of multicellular filamentous threads called hyphae that grow over the substrate, secreting enzymes that digest the plant or animal remains before being reabsorbed. As with bacteria, fungi thus play an important role in the decomposition of dead remains and the recycling of nutrients in the soil. Fungi are useful, too, in the production of alcohol (a product of the anaerobic respiration of yeast cells) and antibiotics (*Penicillium* produces penicillin).

Their harmful effects include moulds spoiling food, plant diseases – for example, potato blight – dry rot in timber and parasitic attack of animals, including humans – for example, athlete's foot and ringworm.

The main division of classification, however, is into plants and animals, and Figures 2.30 and 2.31 summarize the main groups in each kingdom.

Here is a brief description of the major groups within the plant and animal kingdoms.

Kingdom: Plants

Phylum: Algae

The multicellular versions include *filamentous forms* (*Spirogyra*, *Cladophora*), and more complex forms are brown, red, green and blue-green *seaweeds*.

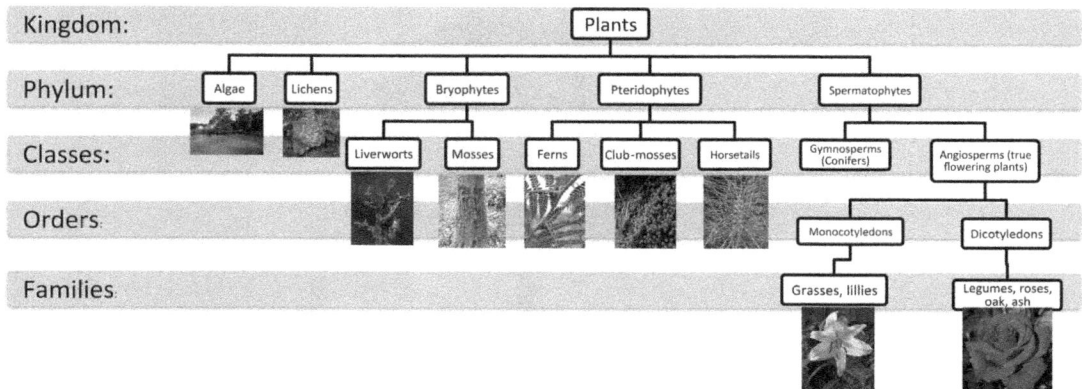

Figure 2.29 A classification of the plant kingdom

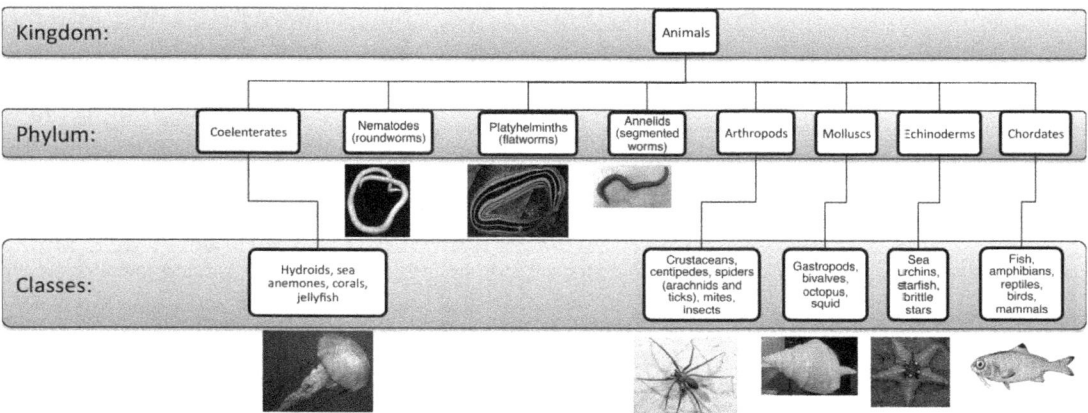

Figure 2.30 A classification of the animal kingdom

Phylum: Lichens

Lichens are a *symbiosis* (living together for mutual benefit) of specific *fungi*, which provide protection, and unicellular *algae*, which photosynthesize food. They are simple plants that are often the first colonizers of bare rock – the first soil formers. They grow very slowly and are sensitive indicators of atmospheric pollution.

Phylum: Bryophytes

Classes include *liverworts* and *mosses*. Each of these groups favours damp situations, and most can tolerate shady conditions.

Phylum: Pteridophytes

Classes include *ferns*, *club-mosses* and *horsetails*. These are the forerunners of the flowering plants. Many fossil forms were very large, and in some cases they grew in the forests from which coal deposits have developed.

Figure 2.31
Oak tree

Phylum: Spermatophytes

These are seed-bearing plants. Classes are as follows:

- gymnosperms: conifers: pines, spruces, firs, larches, yews
- angiosperms: monocotyledons, dicotyledons: iris, lily, bluebell, grasses, rose, dandelion, birch, oak

This classification is 'scientific' and is based on similarities between groups of like kind, arranged in ascending order of complexity. It also reflects an evolutionary series, evidence for which exists in the fossil record. However, it will be difficult for children to see the common sense behind a system that places grass plants from a meadow or playing field in the same group as oak trees, blackberry bushes or daffodils. They are, however, all examples of flowering plants!

Kingdom: Animals

Phylum: Coelenterates

Classes include *hydroids, sea anemones and corals, jellyfish*. They have two basic layers of cells with a single body cavity. Stinging cells help with food capture.

Phylum: Nematodes

These are *unsegmented, cylindrical worms*. Many are parasitic and cause diseases in plants, animals and humans.

Phylum: Platyhelminths

These are *flatworms*. Many are parasitic and alternate between two hosts, causing disease in humans and animals.

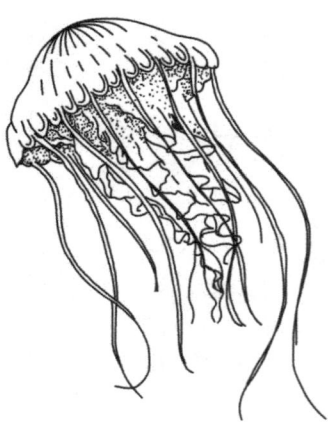

Figure 2.32 A jellyfish

Phylum: Annelids

These are *segmented worms – earthworms, lugworms, leeches*. Separation of the gut and body wall allows movement and digestion to take place independently. Earthworms are useful for improving soil aeration, drainage and nutrient availability.

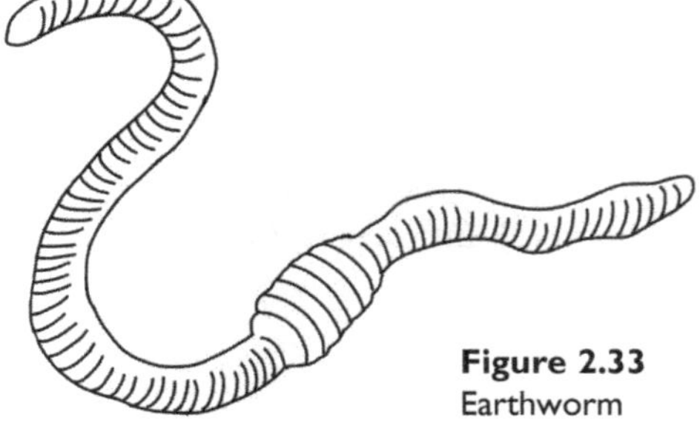

Figure 2.33
Earthworm

Phylum: Arthropods

This is the largest and most successful animal phylum.
Classes include:

- *crustaceans* – *woodlice, barnacles, crabs, shrimps*;
- *centipedes* (carnivores) and *millipedes* (herbivores);
- spiders and ticks – two body regions, four pairs of legs; some are parasitic and carry disease;
- *insects* – three body regions, three pairs of legs; the power of flight has allowed worldwide colonization (adaptive radiation); insects can be helpful – honey bees, pollination of crop plants, control of harmful organisms (ladybirds eat aphids) – or harmful – destruction of crops (locusts), carrying disease (malarial mosquito), domestic pests (clothes moth, housefly, death watch beetle).

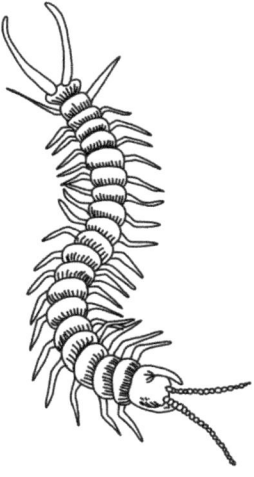

Figure 2.34
Centipede

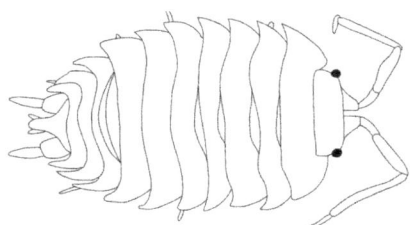

Figure 2.35 Woodlouse

Phylum: Molluscs

These are animals with shells (which may be absent or internal).
Classes include:

- *gastropods* – *snails, winkles*;
- *bivalves* – *cockles, mussels, oysters, octopus* and *squid*.

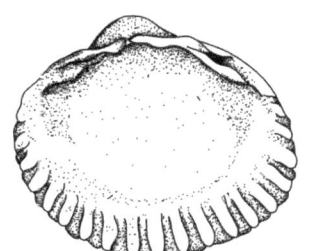

Figure 2.36
Cockle

Phylum: Echinoderms

Starfish and *sea urchins* have five-way symmetry.

Phylum: Chordates

Subphylum: *vertebrates* – animals with backbones.
Classes include:

- *fish*:
  – cartilaginous – sharks, rays and dogfish
  – bony – cod, herring, mackerel.

Fish live all their lives in water and breathe through gills (lungfish represent the evolutionary 'move on to land'). They are cold-blooded, use external fertilization, have a body covering of bony scales and their limbs are fins.

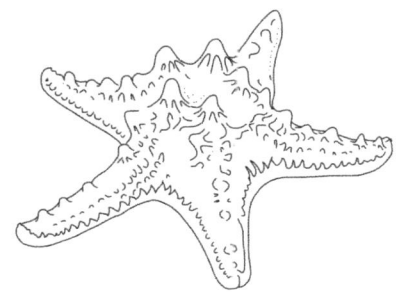

Figure 2.37
Starfish

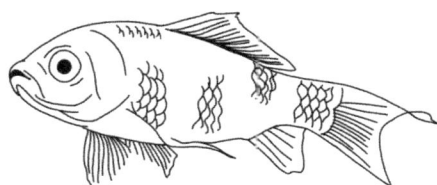

Figure 2.38 Fish

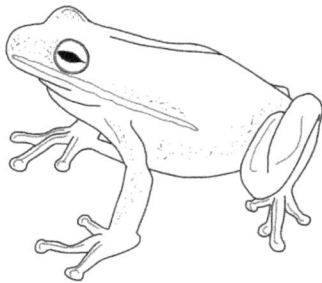

Figure 2.39 Frog

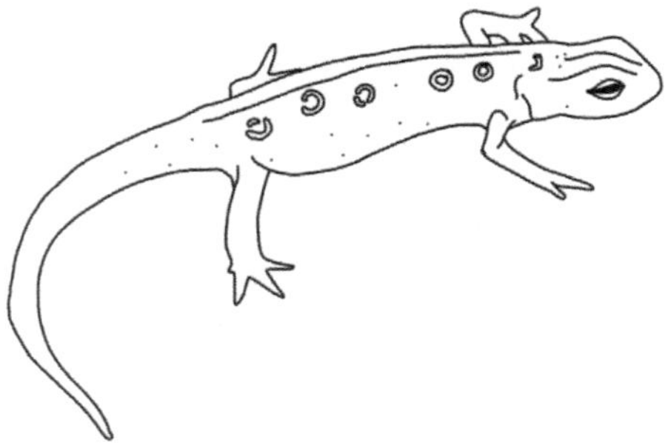

Figure 2.40 Lizard

- *Amphibians* – frogs, toads, newts.

Larval forms (tadpoles) breathe through gills; adults have 'legs'. They are cold-blooded, fertilization is external and aquatic, and they have a body covering of smooth skin.

- *Reptiles* – lizards, snakes, crocodiles, turtles.

Mainly terrestrial, adults have legs (vestigial in snakes). They are cold-blooded, use internal fertilization, with eggs laid in a soft shell, and have a body covering of leathery scales.

- *Birds* – sparrow, raven, ostrich.

Power of flight has allowed worldwide adaptive radiation. Forelimbs are wings. They are warm-blooded, use internal fertilization, with eggs laid in chalky shell, and they have a body covering of feathers.

- *Mammals* – shrew, cat, elephant, bat, dolphin, humans. They are warm-blooded, use internal fertilization, with young born live and fed milk from female mammary glands, and have body covering of hair (except marine mammals).

Figure 2.41 Sparrow

Figure 2.42 Mouse

Again, this classification represents a supposed evolutionary sequence of development. The ordering of the groups makes the assumption that the history of the animals has involved, first, an increase in the variety of life forms and, second, a 'migration' from the water to the land. Hence, successive groups in the classification represent more complex life forms. (Note that there is no such group as 'minibeasts'. In terms of scientific classification, that particular grouping is unhelpful.)

The story is not so simple, however. It is believed, for example, that the marine mammals – whales, dolphins and porpoises – have 'gone back' into the sea in evolutionary terms, and that their ancestors were probably land-dwelling animals.

It is generally accepted that the increasing variety of life forms, and their migration from the sea on to land, can be explained in terms of the theory of evolution, and this is dealt with in a later section (Key Idea 2.5).

WORKING SCIENTIFICALLY

Children in Key Stage 1 should be given the opportunity to identify living things in their local area. Using digital cameras or hand-held devices, they can take photos of different organisms and group them by their own criteria. This type of activity will help the children raise lots of questions about the similarities and differences of living things.

CONCEPTS TO SUPPORT KEY STAGE 2

The identification of plants and animals using keys

Similarities and differences: The basis of classification

How is it possible to identify an unknown plant or animal? As has been seen in the previous section, all plants and animals can be assigned to groups in a scientific classification. There are a number of these, each containing variations, but all agree on the main groupings of plants and animals, and the groupings in a classification allow for the construction of 'keys', the use of which will enable the naming of an unidentified organism.

Classifications and keys are based on grouping together organisms that are similar to each other, but different from all other groups. The grouping begins at a general level and proceeds through increasingly detailed levels of organization until it is possible to identify the individual species of organism. As a reminder, the various levels of classification (reflected in the construction of identification keys) are:

> kingdom, phylum (from the Greek word for tribe), class, order, family,
> genus, species

Identification keys have been produced with a variety of detail. Many field guides contain keys to the species described in them – for example, the wild flowers, or birds, of Britain and Europe. Other keys have been specifically produced for smaller groupings of organisms – for example, woodland mosses, seashore lichens, water animals or deciduous trees. Some are pictorial, or combine illustration with text-based questions, but all are based on similarity with, and difference from, smaller and smaller groupings of organisms.

The dichotomous or binary key

This is the most common type of identification key, so named because it is based on a 'splitting into two'. The basic feature of such a key is a progressive series of questions, each of which has only two possible answers, which relate to characteristics of the unidentified plant or animal. If these characteristics are directly observable features of the 'look' of the organism, the key is said to be a 'morphological' key. Plant keys that depend on descriptions of the flowers are of limited use out of the flowering season, and in these cases it is possible to use keys based on 'vegetative' characters alone. In working through the layers of questions, more and more specific details can be considered, until, eventually, the individual species can be identified.

Some keys expect the user to be familiar with morphological and structural details, and these are perhaps of limited use in classroom or field situations, but it is possible to find (or even produce) keys based on questions about general features, including information about life cycles. Many teachers produce their own identification keys for use in well-known local habitats, or to support a study of major groups of plants or animals.

Famous scientist factbox

Name	Carl Linnaeus (1707–78), Rashult, Sweden
	Swedish botanist, physician and zoologist
Link to NC	Living things and their habitats (specifically in the Year 6 programme of study)
Famous for	Carl Linnaeus is famous for his work in taxonomy, the science of identifying, naming and classifying organisms (plants, animals, bacteria, fungi)
	In his book *Systema Naturae*, he presented his new system of taxonomy and gave organisms two-part names, one for the genus and another for the species. Although some names have later been changed, we still use this system – for example, humans are *Homo sapiens*
Working scientifically	Linneaus used grouping and classifying to create a system to name and identify organisms
Impact on society	Classification is used to make sense of biodiversity. If living things are grouped into defined ladders and given individual names, it becomes easier to study the complex natural world. Carl Linnaeus' classification system is the same one we use today. The system helps scientists to identify and classify new species, adding to our knowledge about the world's diversity of organisms

A dichotomous key to the five vertebrate classes

Here is a simple example of a dichotomous key for the five groups (classes) of vertebrate animals. It is based on some of the diagnostic characteristics of each of the classes and is structured in such a way as to identify one class per question (Figure 2.43).

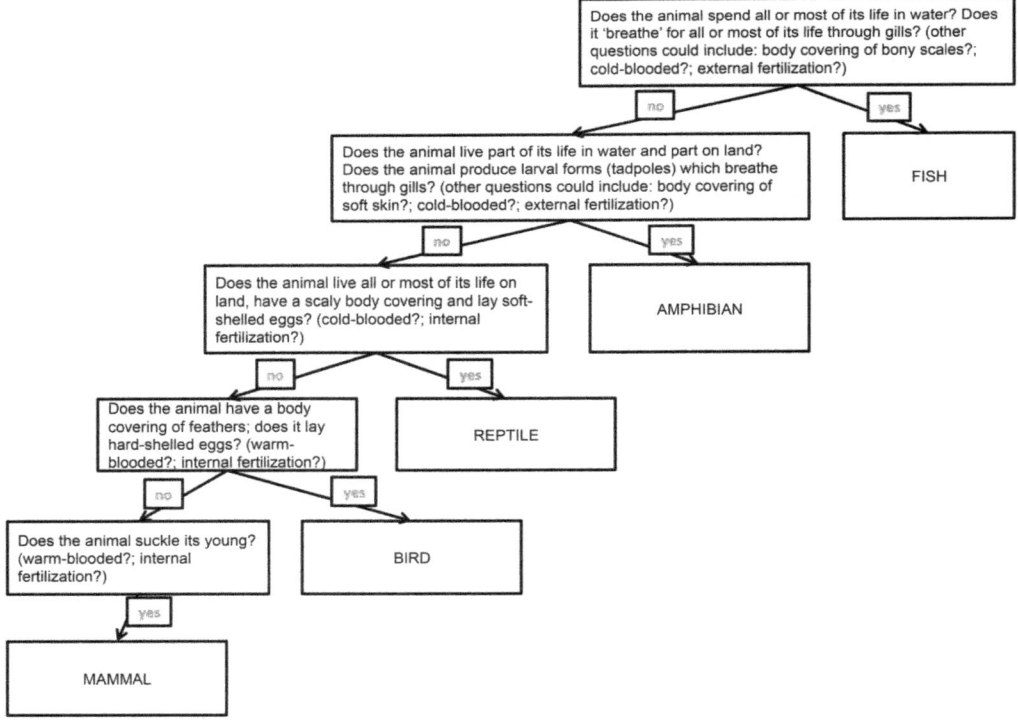

Figure 2.43 Dichotomous key to the five vertebrate classes

The questions in the key have been chosen to avoid pitfalls. Here are some that could cause problems for general identification:

> Q: 'Does it live in water? Yes? – The animal is a fish.'

Not necessarily true, as the marine mammals (whales, dolphins and porpoises) also live in water, and some fish spend most of their lives in mud.

> Q: 'Can it fly? – Yes? – The animal is a bird.'

Again, not necessarily true, as animals other than birds can fly (bats), and not all birds can fly.

So, some care is needed when selecting questions for the production of keys.

Lateral keys

Lateral keys are based on the principle of comparison. The features of the unidentified plant or animal are compared against a list of general characteristics. The exhibition of a particular set of these characteristics allows the organism to be placed in a group that shares the set.

Using the example of the five classes of vertebrate animal again, the list of characteristics could include: type of body covering, type of limb and type of mouth parts. To use the lateral key, each of the animals to be classified would be compared against the list of characteristics, and those belonging to the same group would be seen to have the same 'set' of features.

Figure 2.44 shows an example of a lateral key designed to classify vertebrate animals into groups.

	Body covering				Limbs			Mouth parts		
	Hair	Feathers	Scales	Other	Legs	Wings	Fins	Teeth obvious	Teeth small or absent	Beak
Goldfish			√				√		√	
Pigeon		√			√	√				√
Human	√				√			√		
Frog				√	√				√	
Mouse	√				√			√		
Sparrow		√			√	√				√
Lizard			√		√					
Herring										
Crocodile										
Newt										

Figure 2.44 An example of a lateral key

KEY IDEA 2.4 SUMMARY

Appreciating the diversity of life on planet Earth is essential for its conservation. There are approximately 8.7 million species of organism on Earth, but only around 1.9 million have been discovered and given scientific names. Classification is a way of grouping different living things together based on similar features.

Working scientifically

- *Classifying minibeasts*: By using soft brushes, pooters, hand lenses and clear containers, children can identify invertebrates from the local environment with the aid of simple identification charts.
- *Outdoor learning*: Exploration of organisms by going on plant and animal hunts will develop the children's understanding of biodiversity. Discussing the difference between fungi and plants and even learning that coral is made by animals rather than being a plant or rock will help challenge some potential misconceptions.
- *Classification*: Classification keys can be used to identify a range of different things. Children can practise by making keys for types of sweet or characters from storybooks. It is important to remind them that questions must have yes or no answers.

Discussion points

- *Why are fungi-like mushrooms not classified as plants?* Although they grow in the soil, they don't photosynthesize to get food. Instead, they have similarities to animals, as they obtain their food by absorbing dissolved molecules. They do this through their cell walls.
- *Why do scientists give Latin names to the living things we identify and discover?* Not only does this universal naming system prevent the same thing being named more than once, but the names are also important as they enable people around the world to communicate about animal species with less confusion.

Cross-curricular links

- *Computing*: Children can use PowerPoint programs or other computer software to make keys, using yes/no buttons with hyperlinks to different pages within a presentation.
- *Literacy*: Through the speaking and listening game of '20 questions', children can write the names of different organisms on paper, getting their partner or class to ask yes and no questions until the organism has been correctly identified. Children may also use their literacy skills to create spotter guides to identify organisms in their local area.

Future application

A deeper understanding of biodiversity can help scientists to make developments in different fields – for example, discovering new medicines. Learning about how animals and plants behave and depend on each other can help us to better protect them in the future. There are many career opportunities in the area of conservation and ensuring humans reduce their impact on animal and plant diversity.

Health and safety

- When going outside to observe and identify living things in the local environment, advise children on boundaries and dangers. Ensure adults keep visual contact with their groups and consider adult-to-pupil ratios.

- Be aware of children with allergies (e.g. nuts, insect stings, hay fever). Check that children with severe allergies have their asthma pump or emergency treatment for anaphylaxis.
- Ensure that a first aid kit is carried when conducting outdoor learning.
- Conduct a safety sweep of the area before outdoor habitat activity takes place.

Assessment for learning

KWL grids: When exploring and classifying the diversity of living things in the local area (or even further afield), children could write down what they already *know* about the organisms they may find and *what* they would like to find out. Once they have conducted their exploration and learning, they could return to their grid to consider what they have *learned*.

KEY IDEA 2.5

Adaptation to environment

Animals and plants tend to adapt to their environments (natural selection).

CONCEPTS TO SUPPORT KEY STAGES I AND 2

The explanation of the theory of evolution is generally credited to Charles Darwin, although another nineteenth-century naturalist, Alfred Wallace, had separately come to similar conclusions. In the end, they 'launched' the theory with joint papers to the Royal Society in 1858, and Darwin published his book *On the Origin of Species by Means of Natural Selection* in 1859.

Between 1831 and 1836, Darwin had been the naturalist on board the Admiralty ship HMS *Beagle*, which had made a round-the-world voyage of scientific discovery. During his travels Darwin had gained an appreciation of the huge variety of plants and animals on Earth, but he was particularly struck by one location. Having rounded Cape Horn, the *Beagle* visited the Galapagos Islands, 600 miles west of the coast of Ecuador, in South America. Darwin noticed that the animals of the Galapagos Islands bore a resemblance to those of the South American mainland. Two things struck him, however: first, the island populations were not identical to the mainland animals of a similar kind, and, second, each island appeared to have its own separate population of animals. Examples that Darwin recorded and collected included the so-called Darwin finches and the giant tortoises.

Darwin had noticed that, although all the islands were of volcanic origin, they were roughly the same height and experienced the same climate, each had its own population of finches, which appeared to be adapted to feed on the available vegetation of the island concerned. Similarly, the populations of tortoises had adapted to feed on the particular vegetation of each island. A striking example of this was the shape of the shells of the giant tortoises. Those that lived on grass-covered islands had normal-shaped shells, whereas those that lived on bouldery, scrub-covered islands had shells with high peaks that enabled the animals to raise their heads to browse on overhanging vegetation (see Figure 2.45).

All of these insights were eventually to lead Darwin to the realization that species of animal and plant were not created and immutable, but that, by small, slow steps, new species gradually evolved from previously existing forms. A distillation of Darwin's work can be presented in terms of four observations, from which three deductions are possible, as follows.

Figure 2.45 'Normal' and 'high-peaked' forms of Galapagos tortoise shell

Charles Darwin's observations and deductions

Observation 1: Organisms show the potential for 'geometric' increase

In modern terms, 'geometric' means 'exponential', that is, 2, 4, 8, 16, 32, 64 . . . and so on. This is true both for plant and animal populations. A single grass head could contain 1,500 seeds, and some fish produce millions of eggs each time they spawn.

Observation 2: Populations remain relatively stable

Although populations do rise and fall in numbers, the fluctuations bear no resemblance to the potential for 'geometric' increase cited by Darwin.

Deduction 1: There is a 'struggle for existence'

As in all plants and most animals there is a very high wastage of embryonic or juvenile forms, there must be a continuing struggle for survival. Birds such as the house sparrow or greenfinch commonly lay four to six eggs and may produce three broods in a season – a potential production of twelve to eighteen offspring per pair per year. Clearly, however, the population of either of these species does not increase six- or ninefold annually.

Observation 3: Individuals vary, and some variations confer advantage

Darwin had noticed, as had many naturalists before him, that all individuals vary – that is, they are all different from all other individuals of the same species (except, as we now know, in the case of identical twins). Some of the variations between individuals were advantageous to survival in specific environments. So, the tortoises with high-peaked shells on shrubby islands that were able to 'crane their necks' to browse on overhead vegetation were more likely to survive than normal-shelled individuals living on the same island. The 'high peak' gave them an advantage in the battle for survival.

Deduction 2: Organisms that survive are those best adapted to the environment – the 'survival of the fittest'

In the Darwinian sense, 'fitness' means 'best adapted to the particular environment' and is not necessarily a function of size, strength and so on. To continue the tortoise example, both normal- and high-peak-shelled forms would survive on a grassy island – neither would be disadvantaged by grazing the ground plants. On a shrubby island, however, the high-peak shells would have a distinct advantage over the normal forms and would be the 'fittest' for that particular environment. There is a 'cart before horse' danger here. The high-peaked tortoises do not *become* high peaked because of 'craning their necks' to browse on overhead vegetation; those tortoises that are *born* high peaked are more likely to survive because they are *able* to 'crane their necks' to graze the shrubs above them.

Observation 4: Characteristics that confer advantage tend to accumulate (and tend to be inherited)

As long as the environment remains stable and unchanged, the characteristics that confer advantage will tend to accumulate. This is because there is more chance of 'fitter' forms surviving to breed and, therefore, of the advantage being inherited by subsequent generations. Sadly, Darwin did not know of the work of Gregor Mendel, who first laid out the principles of 'inheritance' (modern-day genetics). Had he done so, it would have 'completed the story' for him.

Famous scientist factbox

Name	Mary Anning (1799–1847), Dorset, England Fossil collector and palaeontologist
Link to NC	Year 3 – Rocks Year 6 – Evolution and Inheritance
Famous for	Mary Anning was a *famous fossil hunter and collector*. She found and identified many prehistoric fossils from the time of the dinosaurs. Anning was the first person to uncover a full *Ichthyosaurus skeleton*
Working scientifically	Although Mary did not go to school, she could read and write. She used books and *scientific research* to find out about rocks and fossils
Impact on society	*Science communication*: Anning was one of the earliest fossil hunters to identify these *prehistoric* fossils, and she shared her specimens and impressive knowledge about them with scientists at the time. How evolution works was explained by Charles Darwin, not long after Mary Anning died. Her fossils had helped scientists understand how things began *Women in science*: Although recognized by the science community, Anning was not admitted to the Geological Society – women were not allowed to join it until 1904. However, the Geological Society did record her death in 1847, demonstrating her importance

Deduction 3: Natural selection gives rise to new species

This, in a sense, is the final explanation of Darwin's observations of the animals of the Galapagos Islands. It is possible that all of them descended from ancestors from the mainland populations. Over very long periods of time, however, each island population, responding to the natural selection of each separate island environment, would slowly adapt to become the 'fittest' form for that particular island and would, of necessity, look different from similar species of island neighbours. Natural selection, driven by the different environments on each of the islands, had given rise to different species on each island.

It is worth remembering that the ideas implicit in natural selection represent a theory – not established fact. Although much of the evidence points to the theory being a reasonable one, it cannot be verified on a short timescale. It has taken much of geological time to produce the variation in life forms that we see today!

A further point is that it is possible to offend religious sensibilities by proclaiming the theory of evolution as fact – with these, as with many ideas in science, we tread the boundary between knowledge and belief – it is unwise to declare as fact something that cannot be verified.

FURTHER CONCEPTS TO SUPPORT KEY STAGE 2

The sources of variation in plants and animals

At the heart of the theory of evolution is the idea that natural selection acts on the great variability within individual species of plants and animals in an area to bring about the survival of the fittest – those best adapted to the particular environment of the area concerned.

Remembering Darwin's third observation – individuals vary, and some variations confer advantage – it is appropriate now to ask what causes the variation between individuals of the same species. A useful idea can be expressed in the form of a simple formula:

Phenotype = genotype × environment

FACT POINT

An example of evolution: Polar Bears

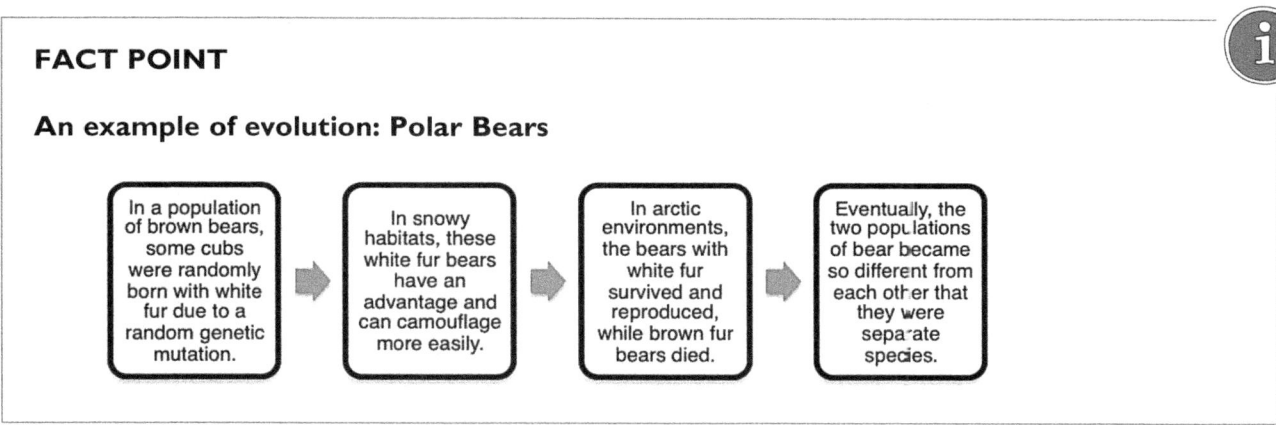

The phenotype of any organism is the totality of its expression as a living thing – the way it looks and functions. All individual phenotypes (with the exception of those of identical twins) are unique. An individual's phenotype will result from the interaction of its genotype – the total genetic capacity inherited from its parents – with the environment in which it finds itself. All individual plants and animals look as they do because of the way in which their environment has acted on their own genetic coding.

This concept is particularly helpful with consideration of the 'nature versus nurture' debate. Much heat has been generated in the past over the extent to which characteristics such as intelligence or musicality are governed by heredity or environment. Will intelligent parents produce intelligent offspring? Can a child become musical if surrounded by the wherewithal of music? Phenotype = genotype × environment shows us that these are not the correct questions to ask. A child's intelligence will be a function of the way in which its capacity for intellectual activity (genotype) is acted on by the environment in which it finds itself (or which is provided for it). A child surrounded by music will achieve little unless it has inherited some capacity for musical activity.

Environment can have a significant effect on phenotypes. Hydrangea flower colour can be controlled by soil additives, resulting in flowers ranging from blue to purple, depending on the calcium content of the soil.

Genetic variation

So, the variation shown by all individuals (phenotypes) can be related to the genetic coding inherited from their parents. The code is made up of sequences of bases, strung together in long molecules of the chemical DNA, which is the main constituent of the cell nucleus. The bases are arranged in pairs that are linked in a 'double helix'. The particular sequence of the bases in the DNA strand allows for the assembly of particular amino acids, and these are the building blocks of the proteins used in each cell in the organism.

The base sequences are grouped together in *genes* and are linked together on the DNA molecules to form *chromosomes* (a useful model is of carriages – the genes – making up a train – the chromosome). At fertilization, the two parental gametes, each containing half the required number of chromosomes, fuse to form the embryo, restoring the full chromosomal complement to the new individual. Each individual is thus a unique 'mixture' of its parents' genetic coding. The variation achieved by this continual mixing of genetic material as a result of sexual reproduction is the 'raw material' that is tested by natural selection for the ability of the species to adapt to changing environmental circumstances.

A further source of genetic variation can arise when 'copying errors' occur in the replication of DNA base sequences during cell division or gamete formation. Such errors usually result in what are known as *mutations*. If part of a base sequence is missing, or repeated, or inverted, the subsequent assembly of amino acids (and, hence, proteins) maybe faulty. Mutations are frequently deleterious to the organisms concerned (Down's syndrome occurs as a result of the occurrence of an *extra* chromosome, for example), but this may not always be the case. The Darwinian view would be that the variation provided by such genetic mutations may confer unforeseen advantage in the event of environmental change.

FACT POINT

Cystic fibrosis – a genetic disease

Cystic fibrosis is a disease affecting the whole body and it shortens life expectancy by blocking the lungs with thick mucus, causing chest infections. Cystic fibrosis is a result of a mutation in a single gene. Although the cause of cystic fibrosis was discovered in 1989, important research in gene therapy still continues to find a cure for this genetic disease.

Environmental variation

Individual plants and animals also vary within species, depending on the nature of their environments. A well-fed animal will tend to be bigger and stronger than a malnourished one, with a correspondingly greater chance of survival to reproduction. The important feature of environmental variations – characteristics 'acquired' during the lifetime of the individual – is that they cannot be inherited. A tree that grows tall simply because it germinates in a favoured position will not produce tall offspring as a result. A person who has put on weight because of a programme of body-building will not produce large, well-muscled offspring as a result.

The mechanism of natural selection

Given the variability within species of plants and animals, how does natural selection operate? The answer comes from Darwin's second deduction: organisms that survive are those best adapted to the environment – the survival of the fittest.

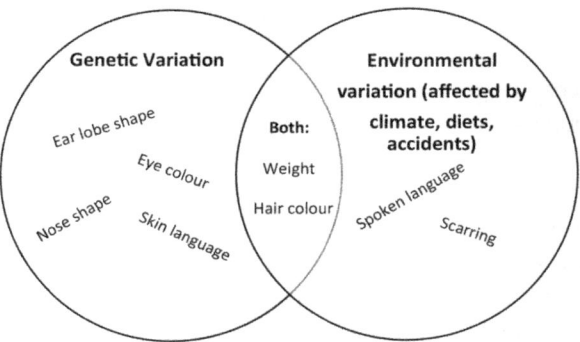

Figure 2.46 A Venn diagram showing genetic and environmental variation

FACT POINT

Artificial selection

Intentional breeding of different animals and plants is called *artificial selection*. Some farmers select their strongest animals for breeding (e.g. to produce more meat or milk). Dog breeders hand-pick dogs with desirable traits, such as hair colour or a better coat. Children might discuss or debate the pros and cons of artificial selection.

It is clear from any study of plants and animals and their habitats that particular (and generally predictable) groups of plants and animals are associated with particular habitats. It is important to remember that plants and animals are able to survive in specific locations because they are able to *tolerate* the conditions found there, not because they 'like' them. Salt-marsh plants survive in salt marshes because they can tolerate high levels of sodium in their systems, not because they 'like' salt. Conversely, meadow grasses do not grow on salt marshes because they cannot tolerate sodium in their systems. Similarly, rhododendron bushes will not survive on calcium-rich (chalky) soils (they are said to be calcifuges – 'fleeing from calcium'), but they can tolerate acid soil conditions and will thrive in the absence of calcium.

In Darwinian terms, the survivors in any habitat will be those plants and animals best adapted to that environment – the 'fittest' – and it is the environmental conditions that 'select' the survivors. While the environmental conditions remain relatively stable, the characteristic plant and animal species in the area will tend to be unchanged. However, any changes in conditions will immediately favour those plants and animals best suited to coping with the changes, and natural selection will operate to 'filter out' those organisms unable to survive.

The environmental conditions are governed by physical factors such as rock type, soil type and depth, slope gradient, aspect (the direction a slope faces), climate and seasonality (temperature, water availability, length of growing season, day length), and biotic factors such as availability of food, shading, presence of predators and so on.

Using the micro-to-macro theme again, it is possible to imagine that the basic unit within an environment is the individual of a species. A species is sometimes defined as being all those individual organisms capable of interbreeding to produce fertile offspring. What happens in natural environments is that *individual plants and animals* in a particular habitat form *breeding pairs*. The total grouping of individuals (or breeding pairs) of a species in the habitat concerned would constitute a *population* of that species. Populations of individual species in a habitat interact with populations of other species to form a *community* or

CONCEPT CONFUSION

It is important that teachers elicit the misconceptions children may hold about how organisms evolve through discussion. The misconceptions may include:

*   *evolution on demand*: individuals may think that some species (or individuals within a species) will evolve traits/features necessary to survive under new conditions or environmental changes;

*   *anthropomorphism*: individuals may liken other organisms to humans and believe they survive because they prefer ('they like') particular conditions.

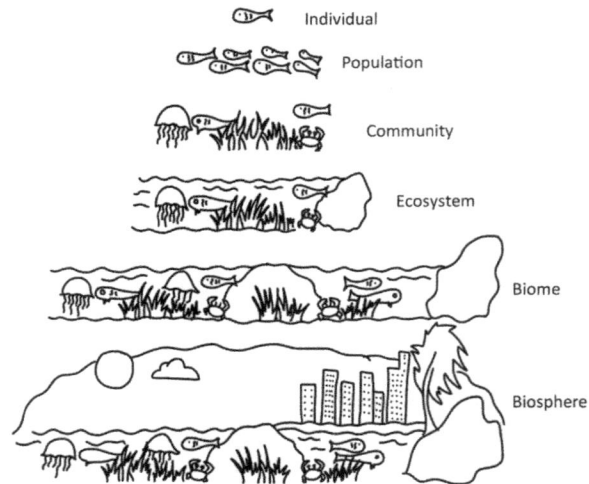

Figure 2.47 A diagram of biosphere organization

assemblage, and the community of species in a habitat interact with the environmental conditions to form a self-sustaining *ecosystem*. Examples of ecosystems are woodlands, grasslands, rocky shores, ponds and so on. The sum total of all the Earth's ecosystems is called the *biosphere*.

Some care is needed when interpreting such ideas, as the terms used are not very precise. A population could mean a species grouping at a number of different levels: for example, the population of caterpillars on an oak tree, of mistle thrushes in a wood, of red kites in Wales, of elephants in Africa, or the world population of blue whales.

Similarly, the general idea of 'community' is usually a positive one based on mutual tolerance, respect and well-being. This is emphatically not the case in 'communities' of plants and animals (hence, the alternative, but not as descriptive, term: assemblage). If Darwinian theory is correct, all plants and animals are competing fiercely with each other all the time for the essentials of survival – food, water, shelter, space, light and so on.

All ecosystems are dynamic and evolving. Even though it may appear that a particular habitat is stable and unchanging, slow change is always taking place. As young trees in a woodland grow to maturity over many years, the woodland floor becomes more shaded, particularly during the summer months, and the ground flora of the wood gradually changes from 'open-clearing' to shade-tolerant plants. Similarly, the colonization of bare ground by plants and animals can show a succession in time, as in the 'reclamation' of abandoned farmland by woodland, or in space, as in the succession of vegetation commonly visible when one moves inland from a belt of seashore sand dunes. Most natural environmental change takes place slowly, allowing organisms time to respond and adapt over many generations. A disturbing modern trend is the rapid environmental change brought about by human activity – for example, mining or quarrying – and the subsequent despoliation as plants and animals are unable to respond at a suitable evolutionary speed.

Adaptation to environment

As a result of natural selection, the plants and animals in a particular habitat are those best adapted to survive the environmental conditions found there. The adaptation may be seen in terms of:

- *changes in appearance*: for example, 'dwarf' forms of plants growing on exposed upland surfaces;
- *modifications to life cycle*: for example, seeds that fall in autumn 'overwintering' in the soil before germination the following spring, with increased chances of survival;
- *specialized physiology*: for example, tolerance to toxic levels of heavy metals in the soil, and so on.

Some of these adaptations are best examined by looking at the plants and animals found in a variety of differing habitats.

Examples from local habitats

Woodland environments

Very few of the woodlands in Britain are completely natural. Since Neolithic times, and particularly since the Middle Ages, the native woodlands of the UK, which are broadleaved deciduous woodlands, have been managed to a certain extent – even if this has meant the slow depletion of trees by felling through the centuries.

A typical surviving woodland would show four 'layers' of vegetation, conforming to the 'skyscraper' model: the *ground layer* of low-lying mosses, liverworts and fungi; the *field* or *herb layer* of ferns and flowering plants (grasses and wild flowers); the *shrub layer* of woody shrubs (holly, hawthorn, elder); and the *canopy layer* of large trees (oak, ash, elm, beech, birch; see Figure 2.48).

Examples of adaptation to the woodland environment include the following:

- Some of the plants of the woodland floor have little or no strengthening tissue – they are 'floppy' – a response to the sheltered conditions in woodland (example: wild garlic).
- Many woodland plants have large flat leaves, presenting the maximum surface area to the light – woodlands are dark places, particularly in summer, when limited sunlight penetrates the canopy (examples: dog's mercury, wild garlic).
- Many of the plants of the field layer flower early in the year – flowering and seed set are complete before the canopy trees are in full leaf and the woodland floor darkens for the summer (examples: wood sorrel, wood anemone).
- Later-flowering plants are shade tolerant (example: bluebell).

Famous scientist factbox

Name	David Attenborough (born 1926)
Link to NC	Year 5 – Living things and their habitats
Famous for	Attenborough studied natural sciences at Cambridge University. He is famous for his wildlife television documentaries, in which he has surveyed and presented his observations of almost every aspect of life on Earth
Working scientifically	Through observation, grouping and classifying and recording, David Attenborough has had the distinction of having a number of newly discovered species and fossils being named in his honour
Impact on society	Attenborough has made biodiversity accessible to people, explaining animal and plant behaviour and fascinating characteristics

Raising awareness of environmental issues, David Attenborough has contributed to ensuring that humans support the conservation of life on Earth |

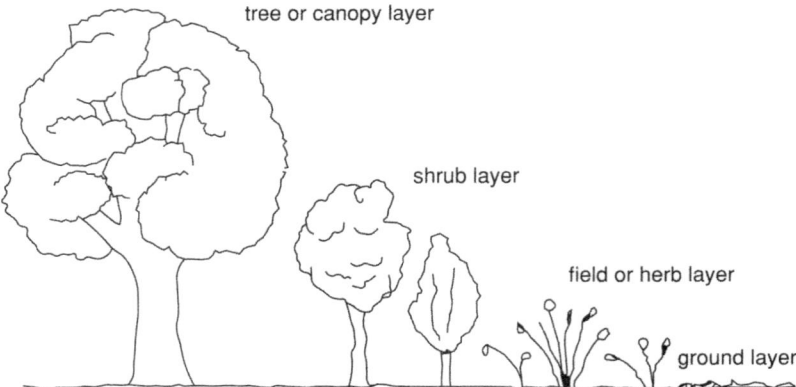

Figure 2.48 The layers in a deciduous woodland

- Animals are specialized for feeding in woodlands – on tree trunks (examples: wood-peckers, tree creepers, nuthatches, squirrels) or in the canopy (examples: pied flycatchers, wood warblers).
- Woodland birds have short, rounded wings for rapid manoeuvring between trees (examples: sparrowhawk for hunting, warblers and flycatchers for hunting insects and escaping predators).

Many of these adaptations to the woodland environment can be easily seen, particularly if it is possible to visit a local wood at different times of the year, so building up a seasonal picture of the changing nature of the woodland. In some deciduous woodlands, the shrub layer appears to be missing. This may be because animals have been allowed to graze the wood during winter seasons in the historic past, or the shrub-layer plants have been cut, for firewood or for cottage industries, such as hurdle- or furniture-making.

Coniferous woodlands in the UK are formed almost entirely from introduced species (with the notable exception of the Scots pines of Rothiemurchus Forest). They tend to have a much simpler structure. Although the thinned, open plantations may have ground and field layers present, the canopy of mature coniferous plantations is so dense that the shrub and field layers are usually absent, and the ground layer is formed from shade-tolerant mosses and liverworts.

The intertidal zone: Rocky shores

The intertidal zone is one of the most hostile environments on Earth. It is exposed to drying winds, rainwater, large temperature fluctuations and inundation by sea water. In simple terms, because of the pattern of tides on the coast, a large part of the zone is covered at least twice a day by sea water (along most of the British coast, the time interval between successive high tides is about 12 hours 50 minutes). In addition to the daily pattern, there is also a 28-day pattern to the range of the tides, linked to the phases of the Moon. Following the appearance of the full and new moons, when the gravitational pull of the Moon or the Sun is at its greatest, the spring tides will produce the greatest range of movement, with the highest and lowest water levels in the cycle. One week after each spring tide, when the Moon is at 'first and last quarter' phase and the combined 'pull' of the Sun and Moon is at its least, the smallest range of movement results, the neap tides. The sequence during a complete lunar cycle would be:

- Day 1 – new moon – spring tides – maximum range of high and low water;
- Day 8 – first quarter – neap tides – minimum range;

- Day 15 – full moon – spring tides – maximum range;
- Day 22 – last quarter – neap tides – minimum range.

It is interesting to check this range in tide tables or almanacs (available online or in the reference section of most public libraries) and to see how the pattern repeats itself throughout the year. The very highest (and lowest) tides of the year coincide with the equinoxes, in March and September.

The plants and animals of the intertidal (or littoral) zone are basically marine organisms that have adapted to the changing conditions imposed by the pattern of the tides. Some examples of adaptation to life on a rocky shore include the following:

- Plants (seaweeds) are tough and flexible, to resist the destructive action of waves.
- They have strong fixing points (holdfasts, not roots) attaching them to rock surfaces or boulders, to prevent them from being torn loose and carried out of their 'zone'.
- They secrete a slimy mucilage that prevents them from drying out when exposed to the air and lubricates the movement of the fronds to minimize physical damage.
- Some seaweeds have air bladders that help to buoy up the fronds in the waves.
- Some animals are able to 'shut down' on exposure to the air: periwinkles close the 'trap door' (the operculum) to their shells; limpets attach themselves firmly to the rock; anemones withdraw their tentacles and become 'blobs of jelly'.
- Other animals, mainly worms, burrow into sand to avoid drying out.

Because of the tidal patterns described above, the time spent exposed to the air varies according to position on the shore. The plants and animals of the upper shore are covered least often, and for the shortest time – perhaps for a few hours on 2 or 3 days in every 14. Those of the middle shore will be covered for half their lives (12 hours in 24). Finally, those of the lower shore will spend almost all their lives covered with sea water, drying out only for a few hours during the 'low spring tide' phase of the tidal cycles – a 'mirror image' of the upper-shore conditions.

Consequently, seashore organisms are to be found in broad 'zones', according to the extent to which they are able to tolerate drying out (desiccation) during periods of low water. Two good examples of this zonation are provided by the seaweeds known as 'wracks' and by the periwinkles. Figure 2.49 shows the positions of these organisms relative to tidal levels on a rocky shore. As well as linear zonation across the intertidal zone, it is also possible to see vertical zonation on rock 'islands' on the shore.

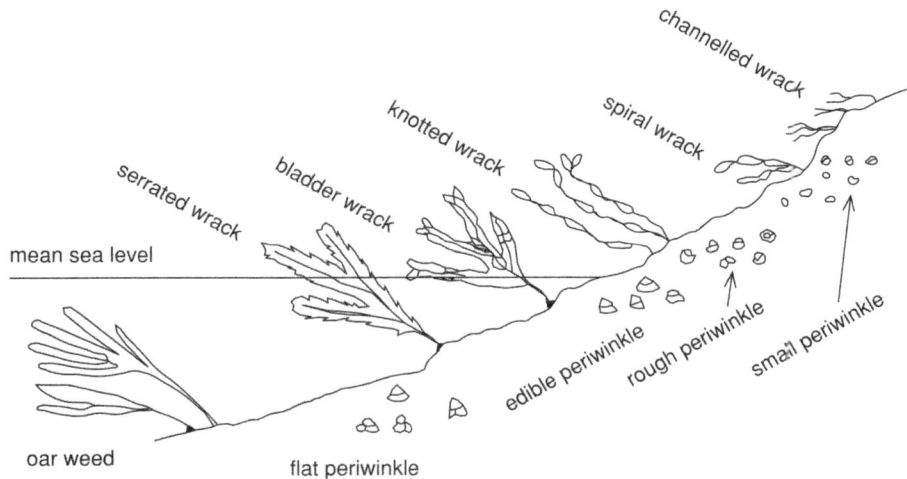

Figure 2.49 The zonation of some seaweeds and periwinkles on a rocky shore

An important consideration when studying seashore life is that any plants or animals collected should be returned, not simply to the shore, but to the approximate position of collection, in the appropriate zone. Many organisms would not survive for long if replaced in a position other than the zone to which they are adapted.

KEY IDEA 2.5 SUMMARY

Within an individual species of plants and animals, there is great variation (some of which is genetic, some of which is environmental). There is always a struggle for survival. Organisms that persist are those best adapted to the environment. Natural selection leads to new species. It is important to highlight that this evolutionary process is slow, taking thousands or millions of years.

Working scientifically

- *Data collection and pattern-seeking*: Collecting class data on characteristics such as hair colour, eye colour and foot size can help children learn about variation. Children may look for *patterns* between different characteristics: for example, do taller people have larger head circumferences?
- *Observation*: Children can *observe* fossils and *predict* what the preserved organisms may have been like in real life. Children may also observe and investigate different features of animals – for example, teeth shape or body colour and pattern – to identify how they survive in a particular habitat.
- *Bird beaks*: Children can observe how some animal variations confer advantages by playing the bird beak game. Using a spoon, straw and tweezers, children can race to see how much food they can collect from a bowl of chocolate honeycomb balls, rice and strawberry laces. It should reveal that only certain beaks can pick up certain items, in the same way that different beaks can grab different foods.

Discussion points

- What would the Earth be like today if dinosaurs were still around?
- *Why are there still apes, if humans evolved from apes?* This is a common area of confusion, and it is important to highlight that chimpanzees and other modern apes are our distant relatives, and we share common ancestors that lived millions of years ago.
- What are the advantages and disadvantages of artificial selection? Is it ok to breed crops that are resistant to disease or deliberately breed animals to be different shapes, sizes and colours?

Cross-curricular links

- *Maths*: Measuring out 100 m on the school playground and working with children to create a timeline of life on Earth will support the awareness of how long it takes for species to evolve.
- *Literacy*: Learning about the work of Darwin and Wallace could allow children to create cartoons, animations and short stories to explain the processes of natural selection and evolution.
- *Geography*: Children could map out the voyage of Darwin on HMS *Beagle*, learning about the countries he visited and the diversity of species within them.
- *Art*: Pupils may design plants or animals that could live in a particular habitat. They could be given images of animals and create new creatures using body parts from several different animals. They could be encouraged to explain how the animal is adapted.

Application

An understanding of environments helps children understand how they might change over time and how they can be conserved, perhaps inspiring the next generation of environmentalists and conservationists. Palaeontologists continually work to use fossils to develop records of what lived on Earth millions of years ago. They demonstrate the gradual change in living things from simple to more complex forms and provide evidence for evolutionary change.

Health and safety

As with Key Idea 2.4, care should be taken when conducting outdoor learning activities to observe living things and their habitats.

Assessment for learning

Peer assessment: Children may create cartoon strips to demonstrate how different animals, such as the giraffe, have evolved. Partners could evaluate learning against a known criterion, identifying any evolution misconceptions and providing next steps for learning. Each individual should get an opportunity to respond to the peer marking in order to improve their understanding of evolution.

KEY IDEA 2.6

The transfer of energy

Life is sustained through the transfer of energy (from the sun to the tissues of living organisms).

CONCEPTS TO SUPPORT KEY STAGES 1 AND 2

As shown above (Key Idea 2.2), all living things need energy in order to sustain the processes of life. The initial source of this energy is light from the sun. The basic process of energy transfer starts in green plants, which differ from all other life forms in that they are able to make their own food. They do this by combining simple molecules – water (H_2O) and carbon dioxide (CO_2) – into energy-rich sugars (carbohydrates), using the light energy from the sun.

The process is known as photosynthesis (from Greek words meaning 'light' and 'putting together'), and the energy from the sunlight is transferred to the plant through the molecules of a green pigment called chlorophyll. This tends to be concentrated in the leaves of the plant.

Photosynthesis

The process of photosynthesis has already been described in Key Idea 2.2, (Plant nutrition – photosynthesis), but a summary would be as follows:

$$\underset{\substack{\text{carbon} \\ \text{dioxide}}}{6CO_2} + \underset{\text{water}}{6H_2O} \xrightarrow{\text{sun's energy, through chlorophyll}} \underset{\text{glucose}}{C_6H_{12}O_6} + \underset{\text{oxygen}}{6O_2}$$

Carbon dioxide (from the atmosphere) and hydrogen (from water in the plant) are converted into glucose, and oxygen (also from the water) is released to the air through the pores (or stomata) in the leaves of the plant.

The *energy* from the sunlight has been *transferred* into the chemical bonds of the glucose molecules, which can be:

- converted to sucrose, for transport elsewhere in the plant;
- converted to starch, for storage;
- converted to cellulose, for cell walls (growth and support);
- used in respiration;
- used in amino acid or fat synthesis.

The factors that can affect the rate at which photosynthesis takes place include: the amount of light, water, carbon dioxide and minerals available, and the temperature of the environment.

WORKING SCIENTIFICALLY

Investigating phototropism

To photosynthesize, green plants move and grow towards the light (phototropism). Using a shoebox and a fast-growing plant (for example, a bean plant), children can observe how the plants will grow towards the light. Creating a mini maze inside the shoebox and cutting a big hole in one size will encourage the plant to grow around the maze towards the light.

Energy transfer

The green plants, then, are the *producers* – they are able to synthesize their own food. They represent the first trophic (nourishment) level in any ecosystem, and they support, directly or indirectly, all animal life on Earth.

Much of the light energy 'trapped' by plants is used to sustain the plants themselves, for respiration, growth, reproduction and so on. It has been estimated that up to 90 per cent of the energy 'fixed' by the plant may be used in the operation of these life processes or be converted through decay, by bacteria or fungi for example.

This means that only about 10 per cent of the energy fixed by plants is available for transfer to animals, which cannot produce their own food and which, therefore, rely on plants to provide it for them. These animals, the *primary consumers*, are known as *herbivores* and they have developed digestive systems that will deal with plant tissues in such a way as to make the products of photosynthesis available to them in a useful form. The herbivores represent the second trophic level in an ecosystem, and, because of the small transfer of energy from producer to primary consumer, the herbivores in an ecosystem will be less numerous than the plants and will produce less total living matter, or biomass.

Similarly, the animals that themselves live on the herbivores – the *carnivores* – represent the less numerous third trophic level, and those animals that live on carnivores, the top carnivores, will represent the smallest numbers and lowest biomass in the ecosystem.

In its simplest form, this concept can be seen in terms of an 'ecological pyramid', and at each step up the pyramid there will be a large drop in both numbers of organisms and biomass (see Figure 2.50).

As only about 10 per cent of the total energy within a particular trophic level is available for transfer to the organisms of the next level, it is easy to see how small a proportion of 'original' energy from green plants is available to top carnivores. If the original energy available at the first level (plants) was 100 units, then there would be 10 units available to the herbivores, 1 unit available to the carnivores, and 0.1 units available to the top carnivores.

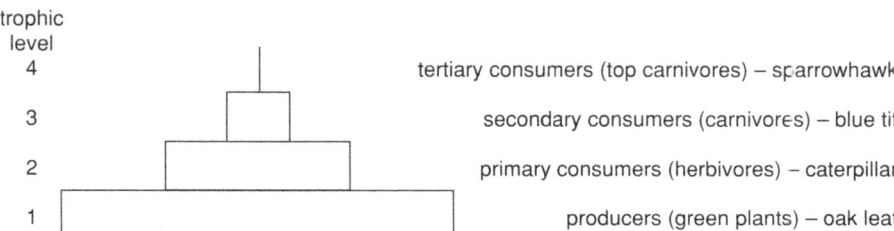

Figure 2.50 A pyramid of biomass in a simple food chain

Food chains and webs

This transfer of energy through the trophic levels of an ecosystem is often described in terms of food chains.

Environment	Producer	Consumers		
		Primary (herbivore)	Secondary (carnivore)	Tertiary (carnivore)
Urban garden	Cabbage	Caterpillar	Blackbird	Sparrowhawk
Pond	Pondweed	Tadpole	Stickleback	Perch
Ocean	Algae	Herring	Shark	
Woodland	Oak leaves	Caterpillar	Flycatcher	Owl
Grassland	Grass	Rabbit	Weasel	

In natural environments, however, such food chains rarely exist. It is unusual for a plant to be the only food species of a particular herbivore, or for that herbivore to be the only food for one particular predator. Most edible plants act as food for a number of herbivores (or omnivores), and similarly, most predators feed on a variety of prey species. If, for any reason, the preferred food of any consumer begins to decline or disappear, possibly owing to environmental change or population reduction, there are a number of options open:

*   the consumer can seek other food (different species);
*   the consumer can move to an area where the preferred food is in greater supply;
*   the consumer may die.

Given these kinds of interaction, a more useful idea is that of a food web (see Figure 2.51), with a variety of possible interrelationships between the trophic levels.

The food cycle

An often neglected component of food webs is the role played by the 'decomposers' in an ecosystem. These include the small animals that live in the soil, such as woodlice and

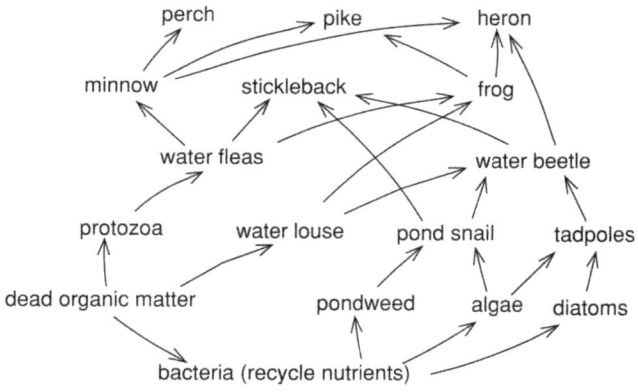

Figure 2.51 A food web: Some feeding relationships in a pond ecosystem

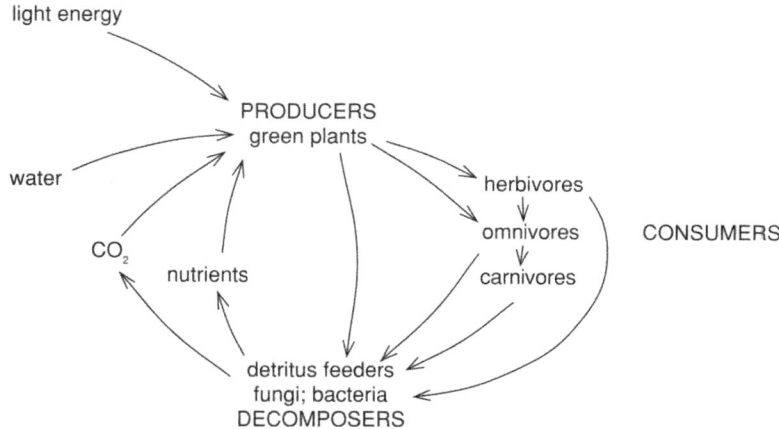

Figure 2.52 The food cycle

earthworms, and feed on dead and decaying organic matter, and the fungi and bacteria that decay plant and animal remains by 'digesting' them with enzymes.

The activities of the decomposers cause the breakdown of once living material into mineral salts and inorganic molecules (such as CO_2), thereby making them available once again to producers (plants). This results, in effect, in the recycling of nutrients and other mineral salts back into the food webs (see Figure 2.52).

FURTHER CONCEPTS TO SUPPORT KEY STAGE 2

Cycles of matter

The biosphere, the totality of life on Earth, exists in a narrow band at or near the Earth's surface. It is now thought that the earliest life forms appeared on Earth about 3 billion years ago, and the sustaining, evolution and expansion of life forms since then have required a series of mechanisms for recycling the 'raw materials' of life.

Some of the key raw materials of life are water, carbon, oxygen and nitrogen. The ways in which these elements and compounds are cycled through the biosphere are now described.

The water cycle (see also Key Idea 3.5)

Water is removed from the biosphere by:

- drainage: the 'run-off' of surface and groundwater into rivers and lakes, and their drainage into the oceans;
- evaporation from water surfaces – lakes, rivers, the ocean – from rocks and soil, and from plant surfaces – leaves, stems and so on;
- transpiration: the diffusion of water as vapour from the aerial parts of a plant;
- perspiration: the excretion of water, as sweat, by animals.

Water is returned to the biosphere from the atmosphere when water vapour condenses to form droplets that fall as rain or snow. Most rainfall occurs over the oceans, but that which does occur over the land masses replenishes the groundwater on which most plants depend for their supplies of water for photosynthesis (see Figure 2.53).

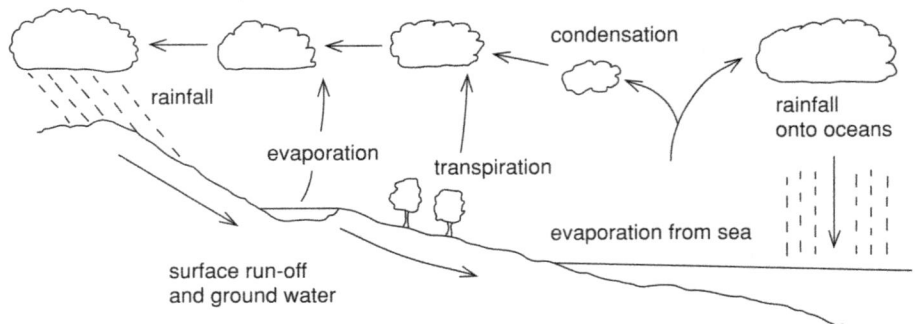

Figure 2.53 The water cycle

FACT POINT

The Earth's water

Today, around 71 per cent of the Earth's surface is covered with water, but, 4.6 billion years ago, there was no water on Earth at all. There are many theories of the origin of water on Earth. Scientists have been uncertain as to whether water was present when the planet formed, or if it was carried by comets and asteroids later on.

WORKING SCIENTIFICALLY

A model water cycle

A model water cycle can be created by filling a large jar a third full of hot water and putting a plate over it, with ice cubes on top. Children can observe the water evaporating, rising as water vapour and then condensing back into the jar.

The carbon cycle

Carbon, an essential ingredient of carbohydrates, is available in the atmosphere as a component of carbon dioxide gas. This is used by plants in the process of photosynthesis and is then transferred through the trophic levels of the ecosystem, being combined with other elements and compounds in the tissues of living organisms. Most of the carbon is returned directly to the atmosphere as a waste product of the organisms' respiration processes, but some is 'fixed' in the form of undecayed plant and animal remains, or in the shells of animals, as carbonate (see Figure 2.54). It is thought that the formation of limestone in the geological past removed large amounts of carbon from the atmosphere, as did the formation of coal and oil – the 'fossil' fuels. The rapid rate at which fossil fuels are now being used is the cause of an increase in atmospheric carbon dioxide (the present level may have doubled by the mid-twenty-first century). There are at least two opposing theories as to the possible effects of this increase.

Theory 1 expects that the increase in carbon dioxide in the atmosphere will prevent heat loss by radiation from the Earth, so causing 'global warming', with the possible implication

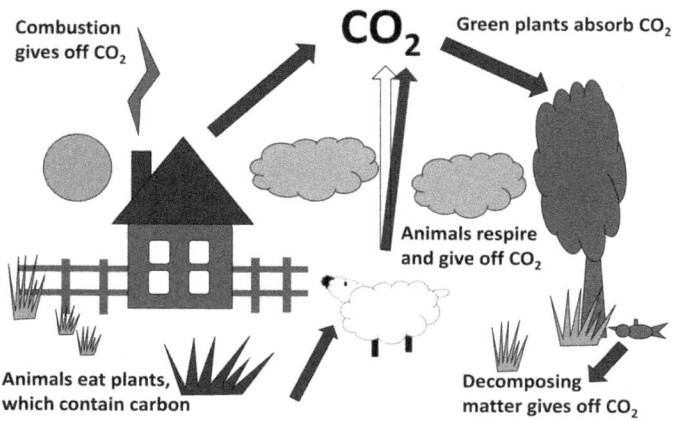

Figure 2.54 The carbon cycle

of the melting of the polar ice caps, the subsequent rise in sea level (up to 70 m is predicted) and the 'drowning' of many of the world's largest cities.

Theory 2 states that the increase in the burning of fossil fuels will cause an increase in the layer of dust particles in the upper atmosphere. This in turn will cause a reflection of the sun's rays back into space, with a consequent cooling of the Earth's surface and atmosphere (a lowering of average temperatures by 3°C is predicted, sufficient to cause the onset of an ice age).

Time will tell!

FACT POINT

Could biofuels be the answer?

Plants such as sugar cane and corn are being used to produce biofuels that are being used as alternatives to petrol and diesel. The carbon dioxide emissions are less than those from fossil fuels. However, the extra land needed to grow crops for biofuels would mean cutting down forests and clearing land that stores carbon dioxide, which may result in the levels of carbon dioxide in the atmosphere being increased.

The oxygen cycle

Most of the oxygen present in the atmosphere is produced by green plants as a by-product of photosynthesis. It is used by plants and animals for respiration and becomes combined with carbon to form carbon dioxide, and with hydrogen to form water, as waste products of this process. It is thus a component of both the water and the carbon cycles.

The nitrogen cycle

Nitrogen, a gas that comprises 80 per cent of the atmosphere, is 'fixed' by bacteria and algae in the soil as nitrate, in which form it can be absorbed in solution by plants. It is then incorporated into amino acids and proteins in the tissues of plants and then animals, and returned to the soil in faeces and urine, or in decaying plant and animal remains. Decomposers

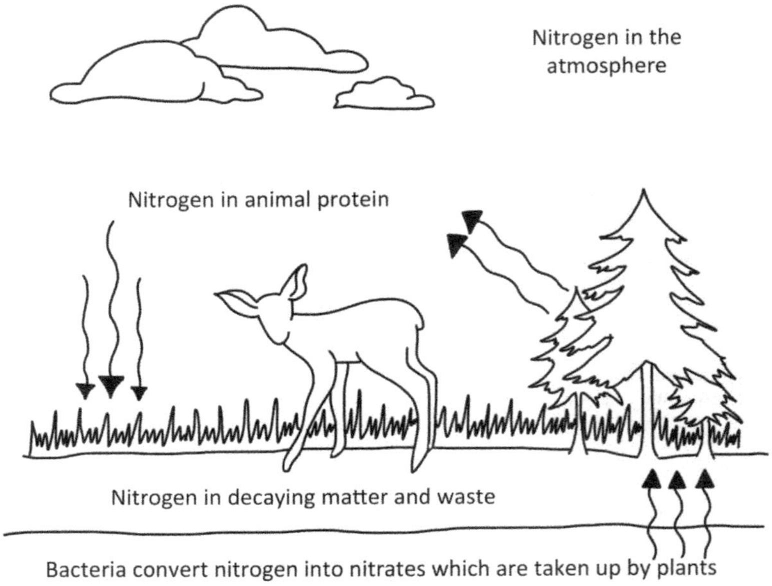

Figure 2.55 The nitrogen cycle

FACT POINT

Uses of nitrogen

If nitrogen is cooled below $-196°C$, it condenses into a liquid. Liquid nitrogen has many uses. It is used in medicine to remove warts and skin lesions. It is also used in laboratories to store living cells, such as blood, sperm and eggs, at a very low temperature. Liquid nitrogen can also be used in engineering to make metal alloys stronger.

---

in the food cycle convert nitrogenous wastes to ammonia, which is in turn converted to nitrates again. These either re-enter the food cycle at this point, being absorbed by plants, or are denitrified and returned to the atmosphere as nitrogen gas (see Figure 2.55).

Energy transfer: Micro to macro

During photosynthesis, *photons* of light energy enable *hydrogen ions* from the *water molecules* in green plants to combine with *carbon dioxide* absorbed from the atmosphere, forming *carbohydrate molecules*. These carbohydrates help to form complex molecules within the *cells* of the plant and help to supply energy for the metabolism of the *individual organism*. The individual plant forms part of the *producers' trophic level*, and energy is transferred through the trophic levels of the *ecological pyramid* of the particular habitat (Figure 2.56).

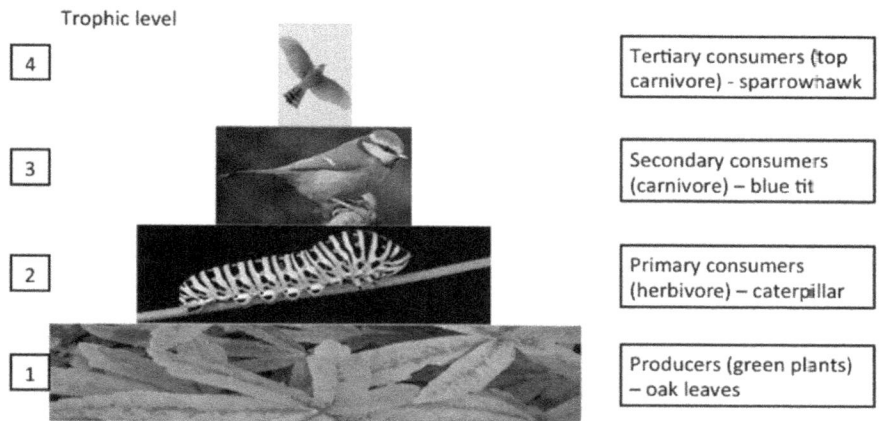

Figure 2.56 Ecological pyramid

KEY IDEA 2.6 SUMMARY

Life on planet Earth is a balance of living organisms and their relationships with each other and with their physical environment. Most of the planet's energy comes from the sun. Plants use sunlight to create food and oxygen. Animals obtain their food by eating plants or other animals. Decomposers break down dead organisms so that the chemicals trapped inside them can be reused. A food chain describes the flow of energy from one organism to another. The food chains of interdependent organisms can be represented as food webs. Energy is a fundamental part of the universe and is necessary for everything. The amount of energy in the universe remains constant, but is transferred from one form to another.

Working scientifically

- *Compost heaps and wormeries*: Children can *'observe over time'* how dead plants are broken down to release their nutrients back into the soil using compostable materials such as scraps of food, vegetable peelings, grass cuttings and tea-bags. Putting these, with soil, into a sealed transparent container such as a 2-litre pop bottle will allow children to observe the process of decay. Using hand-held lenses, the children can observe the invertebrates breaking down waste plant material.
- *Food chain models*: Children can *research* different food chains within a particular habitat. They can present these as a food chain mobile or label the organisms on polystyrene cups and stack them in the correct order of energy transfer.
- *Endangered species*: Children can *research* endangered species, creating presentations, displays and leaflets explaining why they are endangered and how they could be saved.

Discussion points

- What did you eat for lunch? Where do you think it came from?
- What do you think happens to all the leaves that fall off the trees every autumn?
- Why do Venus flytraps and other carnivorous plants eat insects, even when they make their own food?

Cross-curricular links

- *Geography*: Looking at global environmental issues such as pollution, climate change and human impacts on the environment can encourage whole-school initiatives to conserve energy, reduce carbon footprints and use less water.
- *Maths*: Children can carry out surveys and produce graphs to show the amounts of different materials that households are recycling.
- *Art*: Children can create models (perhaps of plants and animals) using recycled materials that they have collected, highlighting how materials can be reused for different purposes.

Global dimension

Our global energy demand increases as the world's population continues to grow. It is important that we help children to understand the importance of finding more efficient and cleaner ways of supplying energy to people. Scientists are working to develop different ways of capturing the sun's energy to make electricity. Solar panels are already being used successfully around the world. Scientists are now working to develop the use of solar fuel by using the sun's energy to split water into hydrogen and oxygen and then using the hydrogen as a fuel.

Application

If we teach children about the environment and our impacts upon it, they can gain a deeper understanding of how the environment may change over time, and how they can contribute to its conservation and management.

Health and safety

- When creating a mini water cycle in a jar, conduct it as a teacher demonstration if using boiling water.
- When making compost, children should be advised to wash hands thoroughly if they have touched the soil. Certain items should not be composted (meat, dairy and cooked food), as they can attract vermin.

Assessment for learning

Food web/ecosystem challenges: At the end of a topic looking at food webs or interdependence, children could be tasked with a range of increasingly more challenging activities – for example: Can you create a food chain with three organisms? Can you create a food web with six organisms? Can you predict what would happen if the number one species in your food web became extinct?

Biology: Schools National Curriculum coverage and progression

Below is listed each of the component parts of the relevant programme of study of science in the NC (DfE, 2013). The table demonstrates how each Key Idea is developed through progression of knowledge in the Key Stage 1 and 2 programmes of study.

Year group	Programme of study	Statutory requirements
Key Idea 2.1: The characteristics of living things		
Year 1	Animals, including humans	Identify, name, draw and label the basic parts of the human body and say which part of the body is associated with each sense (*The characteristics of living things*)
Year 3	Plants	Identify and describe the functions of different parts of flowering plants: roots, stem/trunk, leaves and flowers Investigate the way in which water is transported within plants (*The characteristics of living things*)
Key Idea 2.2: Life processes		
Year 2	Living things and their habitats	Explore and compare the differences between things that are living, things that are dead, and things that have never been alive (*Life processes*) Identify and name a variety of plants and animals in their habitats, including micro-habitats (*Life processes*)
Year 2	Plants	Observe and describe how seeds and bulbs grow into mature plants (*Growth*)
Year 2	Animals, including humans	Notice that animals, including humans, have offspring that grow into adults (*Reproduction*)
Year 3	Plants	Explore the part that flowers play in the life cycle of flowering plants, including pollination, seed formation and seed dispersal (*Reproduction*)
Year 3	Animals, including humans	Identify that humans and some other animals have skeletons and muscles for support, protection and movement (*Movement*)
Year 4	Animals, including humans	Describe the simple functions of the basic parts of the digestive system in humans (*Nutrition systems*)

Year group	Programme of study	Statutory requirements
Year 5	Living things and their habitats	Describe the differences in the life cycles of a mammal, an amphibian, an insect and a bird (*Reproduction*) Describe the life process of reproduction in some plants and animals (*Reproduction*)
Year 5	Animals, including humans	Describe the changes as humans develop to old age (*Growth*)
Year 6	Animals, including humans	Identify and name the main parts of the human circulatory system, and describe the functions of the heart, blood vessels and blood (*The cardio-vascular system*) Describe the ways in which nutrients and water are transported within animals, including humans (*Nutrition systems*)

Key Idea 2.3: Optimum conditions for survival

Year group	Programme of study	Statutory requirements
Year 2	Plants	Find out and describe how plants need water, light and a suitable temperature to grow and stay healthy (*Healthy plants*)
Year 2	Animals, including humans	Find out about and describe the basic needs of animals, including humans, for survival (water, food and air; *Healthy animals*) Describe the importance for humans of exercise, eating the right amounts of different types of food, and hygiene (*Healthy animals*)
Year 3	Plants	Explore the requirements of plants for life and growth (air, light, water, nutrients from soil, and room to grow) and how they vary from plant to plant (*Healthy plants*)
Year 3	Animals, including humans	Identify that animals, including humans, need the right types and amount of nutrition, and that they cannot make their own food; they get nutrition from what they eat (*Diet*)
Year 4	Animals, including humans	Identify the different types of tooth in humans and their simple functions (*Teeth*)
Year 6	Animals, including humans	Recognize the impact of diet, exercise, drugs and lifestyle on the way bodies function (*Lifestyle*)

Key Idea 2.4: The variety of life

Year group	Programme of study	Statutory requirements
Year 1	Plants	Identify and name a variety of common wild and garden plants, including deciduous and evergreen trees (*The classification of plants and animals*) Identify and describe the basic structure of a variety of common flowering plants, including trees (*The classification of plants and animals*)
Year 1	Animals, including humans	Identify and name a variety of common animals, including fish, amphibians, reptiles, birds and mammals (*The classification of plants and animals*) Describe and compare the structure of a variety of common animals (fish, amphibians, reptiles, birds and mammals, including pets; *The classification of plants and animals*)

Year group	Programme of study	Statutory requirements
Year 4	Living things and their habitats	Recognize that living things can be grouped in a variety of ways (The identification of plants and animals using keys) Explore and use classification keys to help group, identify and name a variety of living things in their local and wider environment (The identification of plants and animals using keys)
Year 6	Living things and their habitats	Describe how living things are classified into broad groups according to common observable characteristics and based on similarities and differences, including micro-organisms, plants and animals (The basis of classification) Give reasons for classifying plants and animals based on specific characteristics (The basis of classification)
Key Idea 2.5: Adaptation to the environment		
Year 2	Animals, including humans	Identify that most living things live in habitats to which they are suited and describe how different habitats provide for the basic needs of different kinds of animal and plant, and how they depend on each other (Adaptation to environment)
Year 4	Living things and their habitats	Recognize that environments can change, and that this can sometimes pose dangers to living things (The mechanisms of natural selection)
Year 6	Evolution and inheritance	Recognize that living things have changed over time, and that fossils provide information about living things that inhabited the Earth millions of years ago (The mechanisms of natural selection) Recognize that living things produce offspring of the same kind, but normally offspring vary and are not identical to their parents (The sources of variation in plants and animals) Identify how animals and plants are adapted to suit their environment in different ways and that adaptation may lead to evolution (Adaptation to environment)
Key Idea 2.6: The transfer of energy		
Year 1	Animals, including humans	Identify and name a variety of common animals that are carnivores, herbivores and omnivores (Food chains and food webs)
Year 2	Living things and their habitats	Describe how animals obtain their food from plants and other animals, using the idea of a simple food chain, and identify and name different sources of food (Food chains and food webs)
Year 4	Animals, including humans	Construct and interpret a variety of food chains, identifying producers, predators and prey (Food chains and food webs)

REFERENCE

DfE. (2013) National curriculum in England: Primary curriculum. Department for Education. Available at: www.gov.uk/government/publications/national-curriculum-in-england-primary-curriculum (accessed 9 April 2017).

SECTION THREE

Chemistry

SOME KEY IDEAS IN CHEMISTRY

3.1 *The particulate nature of matter*
3.2 *The classification of materials: Materials or substances can be classified according to their origin, properties or uses[1]*
3.3 *Changing materials: Materials can be changed, and these changes can be permanent or reversible*
3.4 *The rock cycle*
3.5 *The water cycle*

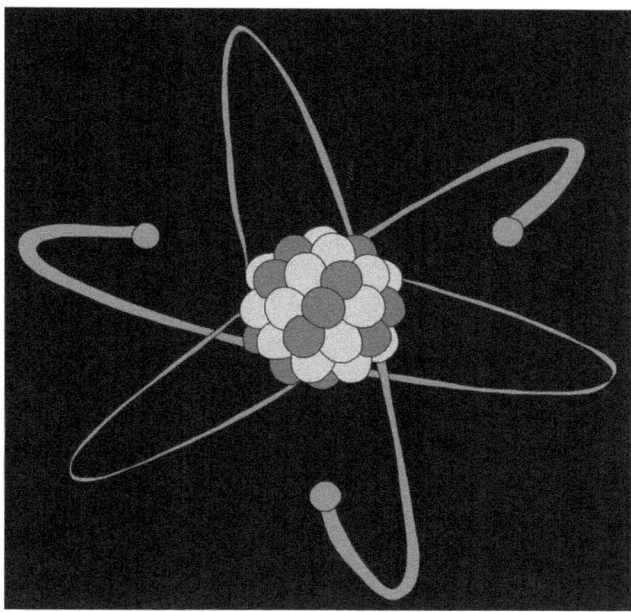

Figure 3.0 Everything in our universe is made of matter

NOTE

1   Please note that Key Idea 3.2 has been subdivided into three sections for easy reference: The origin of materials, The physical properties of materials and The uses of materials.

KEY IDEA 3.1

The particulate nature of matter

Although this concept is not part of the curriculum for primary schools, and some of the ideas involved are difficult (though by no means impossible) for children to grasp, an understanding of the nature of matter is helpful for teachers, particularly in terms of an explanation of the way in which materials behave.

CONCEPT CONFUSION

It is important that children have the opportunity to explore a wide range of solids, liquids and gases. Including soft solids such as cotton and powdery/granular solids such as sugar can ensure that the stereotype of solids being strong and hard is challenged. The weight of gas can be demonstrated by hooking two balloons on opposite ends of a coat hanger. Inflating one balloon should unbalance the suspended coat hanger, demonstrating that the air inside has weight.

THE KINETIC THEORY

At the heart of the explanation of the nature of matter is the kinetic theory. This assumes that all the materials that surround us in our everyday lives (and, indeed, all the materials in the observable universe) are made up of a variety of substances. These substances themselves are made up of collections of particles, and the kinetic theory holds that the particles are in constant motion. The particles concerned are very small and may be atoms of an element or molecules of a compound (see below). It has been estimated that molecules of a light oil are 2 millionths of a millimetre (2×10^{-6} mm) in diameter and are, therefore, well below the resolution of ordinary light microscopes.

THE STATES OF MATTER: SOLID, LIQUID AND GAS

The concepts of solid, liquid and gas *are* part of the Key Stage 2 curriculum, and, although children may well recognize and differentiate them in operational terms, the kinetic theory of matter also allows teachers to understand their properties in particle terms.

However, the Schools NC implicitly categorizes materials as solids, liquids and gases (emphasis added), and it is important to remember that these are not *types* of material, but *states* in which substances can exist. Theoretically, any substance can exist in any of these three states, and whether a substance exists in solid, liquid or gas state is governed by the grip or attraction that the particles of the substance have for each other.

In a sample of a *substance in solid state*, strong forces of attraction hold the particles close together in a tightly packed, rigid, lattice-like formation. Particle movement is confined to vibration in a fixed position. This accounts for the density of substances in solid state and

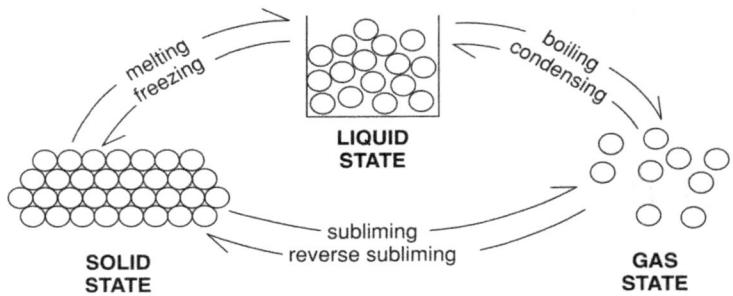

Figure 3.1 The states of matter and changes of state

the fact that they have a *fixed shape and volume*. A useful mental model might be to imagine apples packed in layers in a box representing the particles in a solid material.

In *substances in liquid state*, the forces of attraction between the particles are weaker than in a solid state. The particles are therefore released from the rigid lattice and are able to move more freely around each other. A liquid substance will therefore be less dense than a solid substance and will have a *fixed volume, but not a fixed shape* (although it will take up the shape of the bottom of a container into which it is poured). A mental model for the particles in a liquid substance might be the movement of marbles in a bag, or of balls in a 'ball pool'.

In *substances in gas state*, the particles are widely spaced and are moving independently of each other, at high speed (500 m/s^2) and at random. A substance in gas state will therefore have a very low density – about 1,000 times less dense than a liquid substance – and will have *no fixed volume or shape*. A mental model for the particles in a gas might be the 'flying balls' inside the National Lottery number dispenser!

FACT POINT

What about plasma?

Plasma is the fourth state of matter and is also the most plentiful in the universe. Plasma has luminescent characteristics and is responsible for lightning and the Northern/Southern Lights. Man-made plasma can be found in fluorescent light bulbs, neon lights and some television screens.

 Ensure children don't confuse the state of matter plasma with blood plasma (which is actually a straw-coloured liquid component of blood!).

CHANGES OF STATE

When a substance in solid state is heated, the heat energy transferred causes the particles to vibrate more rapidly. In doing so, they move apart, causing the substance to expand. If enough heat energy is transferred, the particles vibrate rapidly enough to break free from their fixed positions in the lattice and they are able to move around each other. At this point (the melting point), *the substance melts. It changes from solid to liquid state.*

Note: water is unique in that it is *less dense* in solid state at 0°C than it is in liquid state (it is at its densest at 4°C), and that is why ice floats on water.

Similarly, if heat energy is transferred to a substance in liquid state, the particles will move more and more rapidly until, eventually, the particles are moving so fast that they are able to escape from liquid state into gas state. The escape of particles from the surface of a

FACT POINT

The boiling point of water

At sea level, water boils at 100°C. However, as altitude increases, the air becomes less dense, decreasing the air pressure and causing water to boil at a lower temperature. As a result, cooking an egg at a higher altitude will take longer, as the boiling water will be less hot.

liquid substance is known as *evaporation*, and the temperature at which bubbles escape from the body (rather than the surface) of the liquid is known as the *boiling point*.

Conversely, if heat energy is transferred out of a substance in gas state, the particles begin to slow down until they no longer move independently of each other, but become loosely bonded together, so that they move around each other. At this stage, the substance has *condensed* from gas to liquid state. The process is a reversal of evaporation, and the temperature at which condensation occurs will be the same as the boiling point of the liquid state of the same substance.

To continue the process, if heat energy is transferred out of a substance in liquid state, the particles will slow down until they are unable to move around each other and can only vibrate in a fixed position. The sample contracts in size and changes from liquid to solid state at a temperature known as the *freezing point*. As with the above case, the freezing point (liquid to solid state) for a material will be the same as the melting point (solid to liquid state).

A small number of substances change state directly from solid to gas and vice versa. This process is known as *sublimation* (and reverse sublimation). Carbon dioxide, a substance in solid state at −70°C, sublimates to form carbon dioxide gas at normal atmospheric temperatures and pressures. Under some circumstances, and owing to a process known as ablation, ice sublimates directly to water vapour.

To use the commonest example, on heating, ice (water in solid state) melts at 0°C to become water in liquid state. On further heating, water boils and evaporates at 100°C to become water vapour. Conversely, on cooling, water vapour condenses at 100°C to become liquid water. On further cooling, liquid water freezes at 0°C to form ice.

Another useful classroom demonstration of the states of matter is that paraffin wax can be seen in solid state (in an unlit candle, for example) and in liquid state (at the base of the wick of a lit candle). The liquid wax in turn boils and vaporizes to form wax in gas state. Although it is transparent and effectively invisible, it is the paraffin wax vapour that is reacting with oxygen gas from the air to produce the candle flame.

THE COMPRESSION OF GAS

Because the particles in a substance in gas state are moving independently of each other and are relatively widely spaced, it is possible to force them together into a smaller space, a process known as compression. When the particles of a gas are compressed, they collide with each other, and with the sides of any container, more frequently. The increased frequency of collisions in the container results in an increase in pressure. This pressure can be felt if a finger or thumb is held over the end of a bicycle pump while the plunger is being pushed in.

Similarly, a blown-up balloon has had 'extra' air forced into it under pressure. The increased number of air particles, and hence collisions, causes pressure to be exerted on the inside surface of the balloon, and, as the inside pressure is greater than the outside (atmospheric) pressure, the balloon is kept in shape by the pressure of the air inside it pushing against the elasticity of the rubber.

ELEMENTS, COMPOUNDS AND MIXTURES

A substance made up of particles that are all of the same kind, and that cannot be broken down into any other substances, is known as an *element*. There are 118 elements, most of which occur naturally in the crust of the Earth or the atmosphere. Most of the elements are solid metals such as iron (chemical symbol, Fe), zinc (Zn), copper (Cu) and lead (Pb) – mercury (Hg) is a liquid metal, and carbon (C) is a non-metallic solid. Some elements are gases, such as hydrogen (H), oxygen (O), nitrogen (N) and chlorine (Cl).

When two or more elements combine together chemically, a new substance known as a *compound* is formed. A compound is characterized by the specific proportions of each constituent element that it contains and is a different material, with different properties from any of them. In order to retrieve the original elements in a compound (in some cases, a difficult process), a chemical reaction is necessary. Simple examples of compounds would include common salt – sodium chloride (NaCl) – water (H_2O) and carbon dioxide (CO_2). An example of a compound made from three elements is chalk – calcium carbonate – C_aCO_3 (calcium, carbon and oxygen).

When two or more substances are combined together without a chemical reaction taking place, a *mixture* is formed. In contrast to compounds, mixtures do not form new substances, they can contain any proportion of constituents, they have similar properties to those of the original constituents, and they can usually be separated into their component ingredients. Mixtures can be made of elements – alloys are solid mixtures of metallic elements; air is a mixture of gaseous elements – or of compounds – emulsion paint is a mixture of water, pigments and compounds that speed up the curing and drying process; sea water is a mixture of water and dissolved salts; petrol is a mixture of compounds of hydrogen and carbon (hydrocarbons).

THE STRUCTURE OF ATOMS

The behaviour of substances in solid, liquid and gas states can be explained in terms of kinetic theory and the particulate nature of matter. But what are these particles like?

The basic units of matter are known as *atoms*. Under normal conditions of temperature and pressure, atoms cannot be broken down into simpler or smaller particles (this is possible, of course, but lies in the realms of nuclear physics).

Famous scientist factbox

Name	Dorothy Hodgkin (1910–94), Cairo, Egypt Biochemist
Link to NC	Year 5 – Properties and changes of the material
Famous for	She used X-ray crystallography to study interesting biological molecules. She was awarded a Nobel Prize in 1964 for mastering her technique and determining the structures of penicillin, vitamin B12 and insulin
Working scientifically	Through observation and identification, she was able to discover biomolecular structures. Her meticulous perseverance allowed her to develop skill and mastery in X-ray crystallography
Impact on society	Hodgkin decoded the structure of insulin and was a pioneer scientist in X-ray crystallography studies of biochemistry. X-ray crystallography is now a widely used tool and enabled the understanding of structures and functioning of many biological molecules

An atom is thought to contain:

- a *nucleus* composed of *protons* (positively charged) and *neutrons* (no charge);
- *electrons* (negatively charged) orbiting the nucleus at high speed.

The atom is electrically neutral, and this state is achieved because there are always the same number of (positive) protons in the nucleus as there are (negative) electrons surrounding it (see Figure 3.2). Almost all the mass (the amount of matter) in an atom is contained in the protons and neutrons of the nucleus. It is thought that electrons have a mass nearly 2,000 times less than protons and neutrons, so that their contribution to the total mass of an atom is negligible.

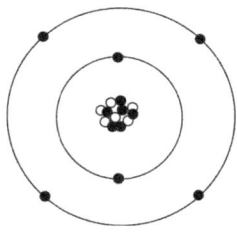

Figure 3.2
The structure of a carbon atom

TEACHING IDEA

The building blocks of all matter: The atom

Although children in Key Stage 2 do not need to understand the structure of atoms, some may be curious about what the building blocks of all matter look like. They can be compared to solar systems, with the central nucleus of an atom being like the sun, around which electrons orbit, like planets. However, unlike planets, electrons do not orbit in circles or ellipses, but in all kinds of random shapes.

Although conventional diagrams show the electron shells as being relatively close to the nucleus, it has been suggested that this is not the case. Using a greatly enlarged scale for the size of an atom (the diameter of an atom is estimated at one five-millionth of a millimetre), if the nucleus at the centre of the atom was 1 cm in diameter, the closest electron shell would be 1 km away! In other words, almost all the 'content' of an atom is empty space.

THE PERIODIC TABLE

Each of the elements has a characteristic number of protons (and therefore electrons) and neutrons, and the conventional way of describing these details is by listing them in the periodic table. Each entry in the table consists of the name and chemical symbol of the element concerned, together with two numbers, one corresponding to the total number of protons and neutrons in the nucleus (the mass number) and the other to the number of protons (the atomic number). This is illustrated in Figure 3.3 for carbon and copper.

Although beyond the scope of this book, reference to a copy of the periodic table will allow the reader to admire the beautiful simplicity of the arrangement. Basically, the elements are differentiated by the numbers of electrons that surround their nuclei, and these can be found by reference to the atomic number, as there is always the same number of electrons as protons in an atom. Each successive element in the table can be seen to have one more electron (and, hence, one more proton) than the preceding element. So, phosphorus, with fifteen electrons surrounding the nucleus of each atom, is placed before sulphur, with sixteen electrons.

A feature of the periodic table is that elements are arranged in such a way as to place those with similar properties in the same vertical column or *group*. The position of an element in the group is an indication of its reactivity. For example, those elements in group I, the alkali metals, react on contact with water. The least reactive is lithium, followed by sodium, potassium, rubidium and caesium, which generates enormous explosive force immediately on contact with water.

| 12 |
| C |
| Carbon |
| 6 |

| 64 |
| Cu |
| Copper |
| 29 |

Figure 3.3
Periodic table entries for carbon and copper

All the elements to the left of the stepped line are metals, and the transition elements are also known as the heavy metals. Those to the right of the line are metalloids (elements such as silicon, with some properties similar to those of metals), non-metals or gases. The lines (or *periods*) in which the elements are arranged also correspond to the number of electrons in each shell surrounding the nucleus, and the significance of this is explained in the next section.

Some elements have more than one kind of atom, and the explanation for this lies with the number of neutrons in the nucleus. Carbon atoms, for example, usually have six protons and six neutrons in their nuclei, and the atomic mass of 'normal' carbon is 12. Some carbon atoms, however, have six protons (this is invariable – if the proton number changed, the element would not be carbon) and eight neutrons. These alternative atoms are known as *isotopes*, and C-14 is the radioactive isotope of carbon. Because the decay rate of the isotope is predictable and measurable, C-14 is very useful in dating any remains that contain carbon.

Carbon also demonstrates another feature of some elements, namely that they can exist in a number of different physical forms, known as *allotropes*. Two well-known allotropes of carbon are graphite and diamond, and a newly discovered allotrope of the same element (with a spherical molecular structure) has been given the name of Buckminsterfullerene.

FACT POINT

Making sense of elements

In 1869, a Russian chemist called Dmitri Mendeleev published the periodic table. He was a passionate chemist who wanted to make sense of elements by arranging them by their atomic mass and by grouping those with similar properties into vertical columns.

TEACHING IDEA

An interactive periodic table

Even in primary school, children love learning about the periodic table. Why not have an interactive display sharing fun and interesting facts about different elements. Children could be challenged to find out about different elements to add to the display.

ATOMIC BONDING

The behaviour of all materials, substances and matter (including living matter) can be explained in terms of the nature of the bonding between atoms, and between groups of atoms known as molecules, and the transfer of energy between them by the movement of electrons.

The negatively charged electrons spinning round atomic nuclei are held in layers or 'shells', depending on their energy levels and the degree of attraction to the positively charged protons in the nucleus. Each shell can hold a fixed maximum number of electrons – the four shells closest to the nucleus can hold a maximum of two, eight, eight and eighteen electrons, respectively. Each electron shell corresponds to a line (or period) of the periodic table, and the shells of successive elements in the table 'fill up' with electrons in sequence. So, an atom of carbon (atomic number 6) will have six electrons orbiting the nucleus, two in the inner shell and four in the next shell. An atom of silicon (atomic number 14) will have

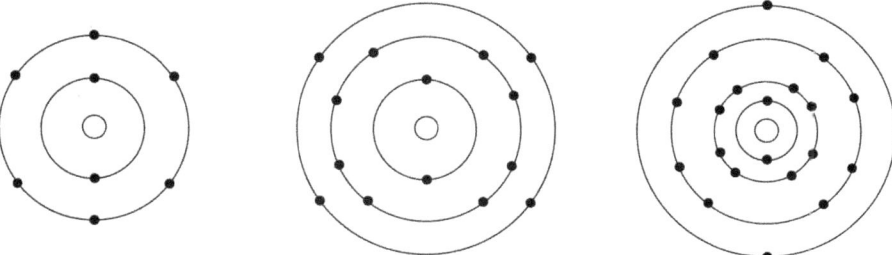

Figure 3.4 Electron diagrams of some common elements

fourteen electrons orbiting its nucleus, two in the inner shell, eight in the next shell and four in its outer shell (see Figure 3.4).

During chemical reactions, the tendency is for the electrons in the outer shells of atoms to form stable bonds with those of other atoms. The most common types of bonding are ionic, covalent and metallic.

Ionic bonding occurs when electrons from the outer shell of atoms of a metallic element are transferred to the outer shell of atoms of a non-metallic element. A common example of this transfer is in the formation of sodium chloride. Sodium atoms have eleven electrons, arranged two, eight, one in the first three shells. Chlorine atoms have seventeen electrons, arranged two, eight, seven. The transfer of the single electron from the outer shell of the sodium atom (resulting in a positively charged sodium ion, Na^+) to the outer shell of the chlorine atom (resulting in a negatively charged chlorine ion, Cl^-) bonds the ions together with a strong electrostatic charge. The result is a cubic lattice of alternating sodium and chlorine ions, visible as crystalline salt.

FACT POINT

Salt

Salt contains two basic elements: sodium and chlorine. Sodium (Na) is a reactive metal that reacts with water to oxidize in air. Chlorine (Cl) is a toxic gas at room temperature. However, together, they are integral to life. Not only does salt help control fluid balance, but it also controls the way muscles and nerves work.

Covalent bonding occurs when electrons are shared between atoms. In the previous example, the chlorine atoms, two, eight, seven, will tend to combine with other atoms to form a stable outer shell. If each of two chlorine atoms shares one outer-shell electron, the effect is to stabilize the outer shell, and a chlorine molecule results.

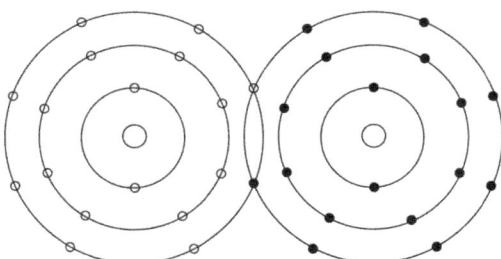

Figure 3.5 Covalent bonding: A chlorine molecule

In Figure 3.5, the electrons of one atom have been depicted as 'solid' to distinguish them from those of the other atom. The outer shell of each of the chlorine atoms has seven electrons in it. When two chlorine atoms combine to form a molecule, one electron from each of the outer shells is 'shared' in a covalent bond between the atoms, creating a stable arrangement that holds the atoms together.

Similarly, compounds can be formed with covalent bonds. In water, the molecules are formed with strong covalent bonds between the hydrogen and oxygen atoms, but weak bonds between the molecules allow them to move around each other, thus demonstrating the properties of a liquid. Similarly, the giant covalent structures of the loosely linked long-chain polymer molecules of plastics and rubber are able, up to a point, to stretch and then return to their original shape – clearly the basis of elasticity.

Materials with covalent structures tend to be poor conductors of heat and electricity, as there are few 'free' electrons to effect the energy transfers necessary.

Finally, *metallic bonding* consists of a densely packed lattice of positively charged metal ions (atoms that have lost or 'given up' one or more electrons from their outer shells) surrounded, and held tightly in place, by a 'sea' of those electrons. The very strong forces of attraction between the ions and the 'free' electrons result in the properties of metals – strength, hardness and toughness, and the 'sea' of electrons accounts for the high thermal and electrical conductivity of metals. Also, the atoms in the tightly packed lattice of a metal are able to 'slip' in layers across each other, and it is this feature that gives metals their malleability.

FACT POINT

Shape-memory alloys

A shape-memory alloy is an alloy that remembers its original shape and that, when distorted, returns to its original shape when heated. The innovative material has already been used for spectacle frames, dental braces and stents.

KEY IDEA 3.1 SUMMARY

Everything is made of particles called atoms. These are arranged in different ways to make different states of matter: solids, liquids and gases. Understanding how particles behave can help children understand how matter can change from one state to another.

Working scientifically

- *Fair testing*: Children can investigate how to slow down the process of ice-lollies melting by wrapping them in different materials or different layers and identifying the most effective way to insulate them.
- *Observing over time*: Children can explore the factors affecting the rate at which clothes or puddles dry – helping them understand the process of evaporation.
- *Making slime*: Borax and PVA can be mixed to make slime; or cornflour and water can be mixed to make oobleck – both interesting substances to explore.

Points for discussion

- *Why does water expand when it freezes, but other substances, such as metal, expand when they get hot?* When most materials get hotter, they get bigger and they shrink when they cool. Uniquely, water expands as it freezes. When water cools, the molecules move closer and lock together. However, with cooling down below 0°C, the molecules rearrange themselves into a more open structure. As a result, ice is less dense, and so it can float on water.
- *How do snowflakes form?* Water molecules forming weak hydrogen bonds with one another when they freeze cause snowflakes to form symmetrical, hexagon shapes. More intricate patterns are formed at lower temperatures.

Cross-curricular links

- *Numeracy*: Children can draw bar graphs comparing melting and boiling points of different materials.
- *Literacy*: Children can be encouraged to research different elements of the periodic table, presenting information to their class about their uses. They can be encouraged to choose elements that are often found in our food, such as magnesium, potassium, zinc and iron.
- *Drama*: Children can explore particle models by acting out solid, liquid and gas states. This may support their ability to explain the different properties of solids, liquids and gases.

Future application

New materials are continually being developed to have special properties perhaps to be stronger, more flexible or able to absorb energy in a certain way. Children can be challenged to research different *smart materials*. Smart materials are able to react to changes in their environment. From colour-changing materials to shape-memory materials, they provide great potential for future design. Exploring new materials with children may inspire them to become engineers or chemists.

Health and safety

- When exploring changing state, avoid using thin plastic cups to hold hot water because of the risk that they may easily be knocked over, spilling the hot water.
- Hot water should be no hotter than 70°C unless it is used in an adult-demonstrated activity.
- When exploring a range of solids, liquids and gases, children's allergies should be considered to ensure substances are not consumed accidently.

Assessment for learning

Pre- and post-thought showers: Children come with a wide range of experiences related to materials and states of matter. They could work independently or in groups to record a thought shower on everything they know about materials at the start of a topic, and then add to this at the end to show their acquisition of increased understanding about solids, liquids and gases.

KEY IDEA 3.2

The classification of materials

Materials or substances can be classified according to their origin, type, properties or uses.

INTRODUCTION

Since the beginning of human history, people have been using a variety of materials to help them in their daily lives. As technology progressed, the materials became more sophisticated, from the stone tools of the Neolithic people to the metal weapons of the Bronze and Iron Age people. In general, materials were used to make objects with specific purposes – sharp bone needles for sewing, wooden rollers and wheels for transport, golden ornaments for decoration – all designed to improve the quality of life in the period concerned.

Today, we are surrounded by a bewildering variety of materials, capable of being put to many uses. Some are related to the necessities of life – the need for food, clothing and shelter. Others are more related to wants than needs – 'domestic consumer goods' such as washing machines, digital cameras, cars and so on. There are many ways in which to classify or group these materials, and the first part of this section will deal with some of them.

No matter how they are classified, it is important to remember that all of the materials that are available to people are derived from the resources of the Earth. In some cases, the materials are 'natural' and can be used with little or no modification, whereas, in other cases, the natural (or raw) material needs to be processed in some way before being used to make something else. An issue of increasing concern is the awareness that the Earth's resources are not limitless, and that it will not be possible to go on depleting those resources at the present rates of consumption. Attention is now turning to the importance of 'renewable' resources when new supplies of materials are being sought for people to use.

CONCEPT CONFUSION

Ensure children are aware that the word 'material' refers to all solids, liquids and gases, and not just fabrics. Anything made up of matter, occupying space and having a mass is a material.

THE ORIGIN OF MATERIALS

CONCEPTS TO SUPPORT KEY STAGE 1

Natural and manufactured materials

A simple first classification is to divide materials into natural and manufactured (or processed or synthetic) types. The main groups of materials can be listed as:

- natural: rocks, soil, air, water, wood;
- manufactured: metals, glass, ceramics, polymers (including rubber), paper, fabrics.

CONCEPTS TO SUPPORT KEY STAGE 2

Natural materials from the physical environment

In terms of human survival, one of the most important natural materials is the soil.

Soil is composed of weathered remains of bedrock, which contains the mineral nutrients needed for plant growth, mixed with humus – the decaying remains of dead organisms. In addition, soil contains water from rainfall and air from the atmosphere (see Figure 3.6). It is the combination of these components that makes it a suitable growing medium for the plants that form the base of the ecological pyramid (see Key Idea 2.6).

Most other natural materials derived from the physical environment of the Earth are the products of geological processes that have been operating in and on the crust of the Earth for millions of years (see Key Idea 3.4: The rock cycle). These 'geological' raw materials are the products of extractive industry – mining, quarrying, dredging, drilling and so on. They are rarely usable in their completely natural state, and some minor processing, usually physical, takes place before they can be used for their intended purposes. Quarried stone is broken into movable pieces, dredged sand is washed, and gravel is sorted for size, for example.

'Geological' raw materials include:

- granite, dolerite and other 'hard' *rocks*, which are quarried for roadstone;
- limestone, which is quarried for cement production and metal smelting;
- sand and gravel, which are dredged or dug for use in the building and glass-making industries;
- clays, which are dug for the production of earthenware and ceramics;
- coal, which is deep-mined or open-cast for fuel;
- oil, which is drilled from deep wells for fuel.

(It could be argued that the last two examples are of 'biological' materials, as they are 'fossil' fuels.)

Figure 3.6 A soil profile

Two other important natural materials from the physical world are air and water.

Air is the mixture of gases that make up the Earth's atmosphere, and the relative abundance of the components, together with their uses, can be seen in the table.

Gas	% present in air	Uses
Nitrogen	78.0	Nitrates in soil (plant nutrients) used in ammonia production
Oxygen	21.0	Respiration, oxidation, smelting, medical applications
Argon	0.9	Domestic light bulbs
Carbon dioxide	0.03	Photosynthesis, 'dry ice'
Neon	Trace	Lighting
Helium	Trace	Airships (non-flammable)
Krypton	Trace	High-temp. light bulbs
Xenon	Trace	High-temp. light bulbs

Water is a colourless, odourless liquid that originally derived from the Earth's atmosphere. It is 'recycled' from the atmosphere to the crust of the Earth and the oceans (see Key Idea 3.5: The water cycle). It is important because it supports life on the planet, as almost all the significant reactions at cellular level depend on aqueous solutions. It is also a key component in many industrial processes – as an ingredient in the brewing industry, as a coolant in the steel-making process or as a power source in the generation of hydroelectricity, for example.

Natural materials from the biological environment

From the biological environment comes:

- *wood* (timber);
- vegetable fibres (wood pulp, cotton, flax, hemp, sisal, coir);
- vegetable waxes, oils and sap (carnauba wax, linseed and sunflower oil, latex);
- animal fibres (wool, alpaca);
- animal products (leather from skins and hides, tallow for candles, lard).

Again, although each of these materials is natural, some processing is required before they can be used to their best advantage – timber is sawn to size, fibres are spun into yarn, latex is cured to make rubber, leather is tanned, and so on.

FACT POINT

Recycling copper

Copper, like many other metals, is extracted from naturally occurring ore in large quantities, using advanced technology. Copper has many useful properties, including its good conductivity, making it suitable for electric cables. Unfortunately, the world is running out of ores rich in copper. The recycling of the metal is, therefore, cheaper and uses less energy and fewer resources and is thus much more sustainable than extracting copper from its ores.

Manufactured materials

Manufactured materials are made from raw materials that have been processed in a variety of ways. Basic manufacturing frequently uses relatively simple processes, often involving irreversible chemical reactions (see below, Key Idea 3.3), in order to provide further raw materials for more complicated secondary processes.

The manufacturing of materials derived from 'physical' raw materials would include the following processes:

- the refining of *metals* from ores;
- the firing of *ceramics* (bricks, tiles and porcelain) from clays;
- the making of *glass* from sand and other minerals;
- the fractional distillation of paraffin and petrol from crude oil;
- the production of coke (for smelting) from coal.

The basic manufacturing processes involving 'biological' raw materials would include:

- the sawing of timber;
- the production of *paper*, card and board from wood pulp;
- the production of *fabrics* from plant and animal fibres;
- the production of *rubber* from latex.

Secondary industries would include the production of:

- *polymers* (*plastics*; including synthetic fibres such as nylon and terylene) from crude-oil derivatives;
- detergents, paint and perfume from coal.

Types of manufactured materials

The basic processes used in the production of the main groups of manufactured materials are now described.

Metals rarely occur in their pure form. Those that do tend to be unreactive and valuable – for example, gold. Most other metals occur as ores, which are compounds of the metal and unwanted impurities, and, in order to produce the metal, a process of smelting is necessary.

Famous scientist factbox

Name	Charles Macintosh (1766–1843), Glasgow, Scotland
Link to NC	Year 2 – Everyday materials
Famous for	– Inventing bleaching powder with Charles Tennant – Developing a conversion process using carbon gases to convert iron into steel – Inventing a solution that made cloth waterproof. While analysing the by-products of a works making coal gas, he discovered dissolved indiarubber. This solution was sandwiched between two sheets of cloth, making it waterproof
Working scientifically	Macintosh's interest in chemistry and his ability to *compare and test* new solutions, considering their applicability, is what makes him a model scientist
Impact on society	Macintosh's waterproof cloth was first used in the clothing for an Arctic expedition led by Sir John Franklin (1819)

Metals commonly used in the manufacturing industry include *iron, copper, lead, tin, zinc* and *aluminium.*

The commonest method of producing metals is by removing the oxygen from the ore by a process known as reduction. In the production of iron, this involves the following sequence:

- *Iron ore* (haematite – iron oxide) is loaded into a blast furnace along with *coke* and *limestone.*
- *Hot air* is blasted into the base of the furnace, and *carbon* from the coke reacts with *oxygen* from the air to form *carbon monoxide.*
- The *carbon monoxide* reacts with *oxygen* from the *haematite* (*iron oxide*) to form *carbon dioxide* and *iron.*
- The *limestone* combines with *impurities* in the ore (mainly silicates) to form *slag.*
- The *molten iron* is tapped from the base of the furnace and solidifies into billets known as '*pigs*' – hence '*pig iron*'.

At this point, the iron is impure. To form steel, which is an alloy of iron and carbon, it is necessary to reheat the iron to drive off the impurities and then to add up to 1.5 per cent of carbon. Other metals can give the steel particular properties – the addition of chromium will produce stainless steel, for example.

Other alloys (mixtures of metals) include:

- *brass* (copper and zinc), which is used for electrical contacts and corrosion-resistant fixings (screws, bolts, etc.);
- *bronze* (copper and tin), used for decorative or artistic purposes;
- *solder* (lead and tin), which is used for electrical connections;
- *duralumin* (aluminium, magnesium, copper and manganese), which is used in aircraft production.

Ceramics include those products that are made by baking or firing mixtures of clay, sand and other minerals – *bricks, tiles, earthenware, pottery, china.* There is a sense in which the kiln firing process is creating 'artificial metamorphic rocks' by using heat to fuse together the individual ingredients of the product into a matrix. The main constituent of all these products is silicon – clay is aluminium silicate; sand is silica dioxide.

This category would also include those products made by 'curing' mixtures of sand, gravel, water and a setting agent (usually cement) to form *concrete*, and *mortar*, a sand, water and cement mixture.

Glass is also produced by the melting together of minerals. The basic ingredients are sand (silica dioxide), calcium carbonate and sodium carbonate. The resulting mixture of calcium and sodium silicates cools to form glass. Again, additives can change the character of the product. The addition of boron will produce heat-resistant 'Pyrex'-type glass, and added lead will produce hard, 'crystal' glass.

Polymers (*plastics*) are products of the oil industry. When crude oil (petroleum) is refined by fractional distillation, petroleum vapour is fed into a fractionating column, and different products condense out at different temperatures. Bitumen collects at the base of the column, followed (at increasing height) by heavy fuel oil, lubricating oil, diesel oil, paraffin, petrol and petroleum gas. The chemical differences between the fractions result from the number of carbon atoms present in the molecules. The general arrangement of hydrogen and carbon atoms in a hydrocarbon molecule is shown in Figure 3.7.

Heavy fuel oils have twenty to thirty carbon atoms per molecule, whereas petrol has five to ten carbon atoms.

In a separate process, those molecules with eight to twelve carbon atoms per molecule (i.e. between paraffin and petrol) are chemically 'cracked', or split, into smaller units, one of

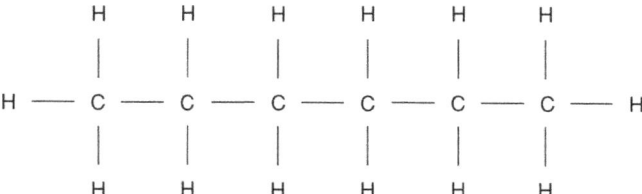

Figure 3.7 A hexane molecule

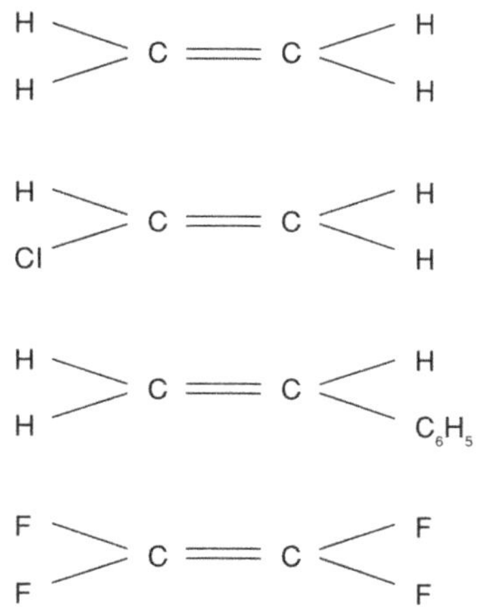

Figure 3.8 Plastics from ethene

which is ethene. *Ethene* is the basis of much of the plastics industry. Under conditions of high temperature and pressure, and in the presence of a catalyst, molecules of ethene (*monomers*) can link together in long chains (*polymers*) – hence, *polythene*. If the ethene monomer is modified by the replacement of one of the hydrogen atoms by another atom or molecule, further monomers result, which leads to the production of other plastics or polymerization (see Figure 3.8).

Rubber is an example of a natural polymerized material, produced by the curing of latex, the sap of the rubber tree. The natural rubber is heated with a small amount of sulphur (about 3 per cent) in a process known as vulcanization, which hardens and strengthens the rubber. (The white sap that exudes from the broken stem of a dandelion plant is a type of latex. Its rubbery and sticky nature can be felt if it is rubbed between the fingers.) Synthetic rubbers include neoprene, widely used for wetsuit material, and butyl, which is used for pond linings.

Paper is basically a product derived from wood. Wooden billets, usually of softwood (the coniferous Sitka spruce is most frequently used), are shredded to a pulp, both by mechanical and chemical means. Chemical binders and bleaches are added, and the water is removed from the pulp, either by it being sieved in thin layers or by it being fed from vats in a continuous strip. The resulting sheets or strips of paper are dried and pressed and finished according to the required properties (see next section).

A sheet of paper is, therefore, a mat of wood fibres (which can easily be seen with a hand lens held to the torn edge of a sheet of paper). Some paper is made up of more than one layer, with the fibres 'laid' in a particular direction. Kitchen roll and table napkins are good examples of 'two-ply' laid papers. The individual layers can usually be separated, and the sheets can be torn into narrow strips very easily in one direction (usually 'along the roll'), but not at all easily 'across the roll'.

Paper is a material that is relatively easy to recycle, and 'paper bank' containers are increasingly common in public places. It is also possible to produce paper from rags, in particular those made from 'natural' fabrics.

Fabrics are usually made from woven fibres, which may be natural or synthetic. Natural fibres derived from plants such as cotton, flax and hemp, or from the fleeces of animals such as sheep, alpaca or angora rabbits, can be spun together to form a thread or yarn. These yarns can then be woven into cloth, braid, rope and so on.

In a similar fashion, yarns can be spun from synthetic fibres made from long-chain polymer molecules, as described above. The properties of such fibres differ significantly from those of natural fibres, and some of these will be detailed in the next section.

THE PHYSICAL PROPERTIES OF MATERIALS

CONCEPTS TO SUPPORT KEY STAGE I

For young children, the classification of materials will tend to be based on direct sensory experience of a range of objects. The 'properties' that they investigate may not, therefore, be those that engineers or materials scientists would use. In describing any object or material, a young child is unlikely to differentiate between descriptions of 'scientific' properties such as strength, stiffness and so on, general characteristics such as flexibility and buoyancy, or specific attributes such as colour and shape.

An understanding of the distinction between properties, characteristics and attributes of materials may not be important for the Early Years child (although it may be helpful for the teacher). What *is* important is that children should have the opportunity to examine and explore a wide range of common materials with which they may come into contact.

As with the identification of animals and plants, the initial investigation of the properties of materials can be based on *similarities* – those features that group materials together – and *differences* – those features that separate the groups. Some of the 'properties' questions that may be asked about objects made of different materials are listed below. Some will relate to similarities and differences. Others may lead to a description of the characteristics of particular objects or materials. All of them, however, help to build an experiential awareness of the materials under investigation. Where appropriate, the property or characteristic implicit in the question is added in brackets (it is not suggested, of course, that these properties would be identified and named in scientific terms for Key Stage 1 children).

Questions about objects and materials

With reference to a particular object or material, is it:

- heavy or light? (density);
- rough or smooth? (texture);
- shiny or dull? (reflectivity, thermal (heat) conductivity, insulation);

- bendy or stiff? (flexibility);
- hard or soft? (hardness);
- large or small? (size is not a property, but, coupled with 'heavy or light'?, this can help to build an awareness of density).

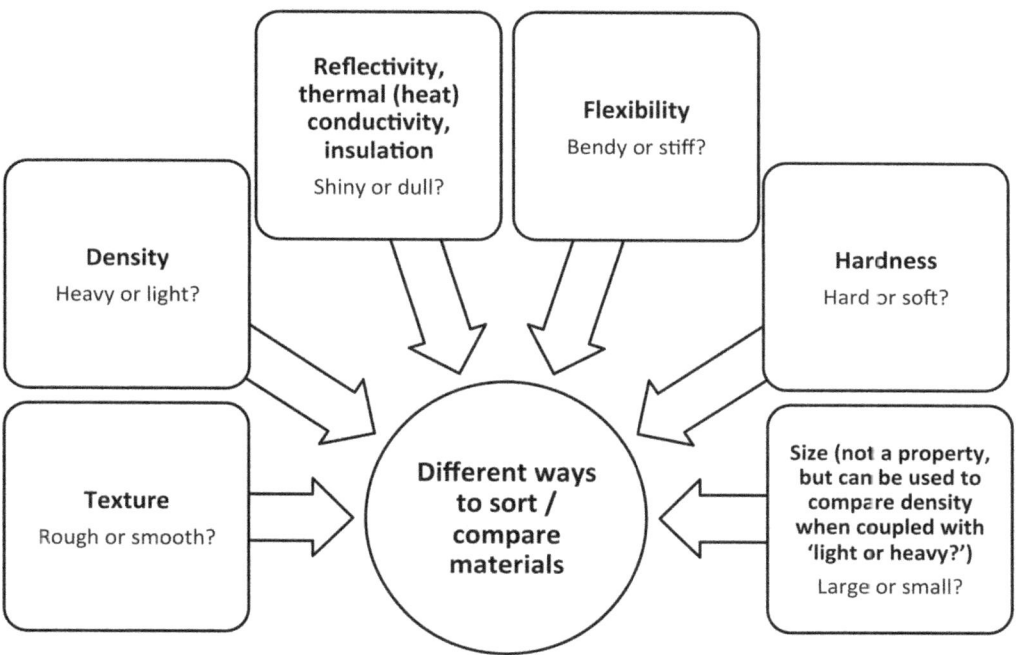

In addition:

Shape	• What shape is it?
Heat absorption / insulation	• Does it feel cold or warm?
Buoyancy	• Does it float or sink?
Hardness	• Can we scratch a mark on it? • Does it make a mark on paper?
Malleability	• Is it squashy, can we mould or press it into shapes?
Opaque, translucent, transparent	• Can we see through it?
Viscosity	• How quickly does it pour? • Can we pour it?
Compressibility	• Can we press it into a smaller shape?
Elasticity	• Is it bouncy, stretchy?
Magnetic	• Does it attract metals?
Taste / Smell	• Can we smell or taste it? (when comparing foods or perfumes)
Material	• What is it made of?

The sorting and grouping of unknown materials and objects using these simple questions will allow for discussion and increasing awareness of the major properties of materials and of the way in which these properties are exploited in the design and manufacture of everyday objects – rubber bands, paper clips, polythene bags and so on.

It is sometimes important to distinguish the *properties* of the *material* or substance from the *characteristics* or attributes of the *objects* made from that substance. For example, iron (the substance from which iron (wire) wool is made) has metallic properties related to hardness, strength, flexibility and so on, whereas a ball of iron wool (the object) is relatively soft, springy, bendy, can be squashed into a smaller shape and so on.

TEACHING IDEA

Grand designs

Children can be challenged to design their dream house, identifying which materials they would use and justifying their choices by identifying the useful properties for different parts of their house.

CONCEPTS TO SUPPORT KEY STAGE 2

Properties and characteristics of materials

Materials can be investigated and classified according to a variety of properties and characteristics. The properties can be measured as the materials react to a variety of influences and they include:

- *mechanical* properties, such as *hardness, strength, elasticity, toughness, stiffness;*
- *thermal* properties, such as *conductivity* (how well or poorly a material will conduct heat);
- *electrical* properties, such as *conductivity* (how well or poorly a material will conduct electricity);
- *chemical* properties, such as *reactivity* and *solubility;*
- *optical* properties, such as *transparency, reflectivity, refractivity;* and
- *magnetic* properties.

Some of the most important properties of materials for consideration here include *density, hardness, strength, elasticity, stiffness* (and *flexibility*), *toughness, compressibility, thermal and electrical conductivity,* and *magnetic properties.* Some of the chemical properties of materials will be explored in Key Idea 3.3, below.

Density

It is usually easy to characterize materials as 'heavy' or 'light', and these descriptions are an intuitive measure of the density of the materials concerned.

$$\textbf{density} = \frac{\text{mass}}{\text{volume}} \text{ (expressed as kg/m}^3\text{, or g/cm}^3\text{)}$$

In practical terms, the density of an object, or of a sample of material, is a measure of the mass of the object (the amount of matter in it), expressed in grams, compared with its volume (the amount of space it takes up), expressed in cubic centimetres.

A useful idea is to imagine a fixed volume (1 litre, for example) of a number of different materials and to consider how different their masses would be. One litre of pure water has a mass of 1 kg – the density of water is, therefore, 1 g/cm³ (1,000 grams/1,000 cubic centimetres). One litre of lead, however, has a mass of about 11,340 grams, and the density of lead would therefore be 11.3 g/cm³. Lead is 11.3 times denser than water. Similarly, 1 litre of aluminium has a mass of 2,700 grams, and, therefore, aluminium has a density of 2.7 g/cm³.

In addition to a feeling for relative heaviness or lightness, the density of a material also gives an indication of whether or not a sample of the material would float or sink. Materials with a density lower than that of water – that is, less than 1.0 g/cm³ – will float on water. Those with a density greater than 1.0 g/cm³ will sink. Interesting investigations can be performed with materials that are 'just floaters' or 'just sinkers'. If an uncooked egg is placed in a container of fresh water it will sink. The density of the egg will be about 1.1 g/cm³. If enough salt is dissolved into the water, the density of the solution will increase until, eventually, it is higher than that of the egg, and the egg will float to the surface of the solution. This increased density of salt water is also part of the explanation for people feeling that they 'float better' in the sea than in fresh water.

A similar experiment can also be performed with 'centicubes', which are commonly available as a mathematics resource and are made of a plastic material that has a density just greater than 1 g/cm³. Centicubes are, therefore, 'just sinkers' in fresh water, but will float to the surface once the density of the water has been increased by the addition of a sufficient quantity of salt.

Hardness

The *hardness* of a material is a measure of its resistance to permanent or plastic deformation by scratching or indentation. It is an important factor in materials that have to resist wear or abrasion – moving parts in machinery, for example – and frequently needs to be considered along with the strength of materials. Hardness is measured on a scale (Moh's scale) of 1 (talc) to 10 (diamond). Relative hardness can be demonstrated by investigating which materials can be scratched by a fingernail (hardness 2.5), an iron nail (hardness 4), a steel nail (hardness 6) and (if possible) a piece of quartz (hardness 7).

Strength

The *strength* of a material is the extent to which it can withstand an applied force or load (*stress*) without breaking. The load is expressed in terms of force per unit area (newtons per square metre, N/m²), and can be in the form of:

- *compression force*, as applied to the piers of a bridge, or a roof support;
- *tensile or stretching force*, as applied to a guitar string, tow rope or crane cable;
- *shear force*, as applied by scissors, or when materials are torn (see Figure 3.9).

Materials are, therefore, described as having compressive, tensile or shear strength.

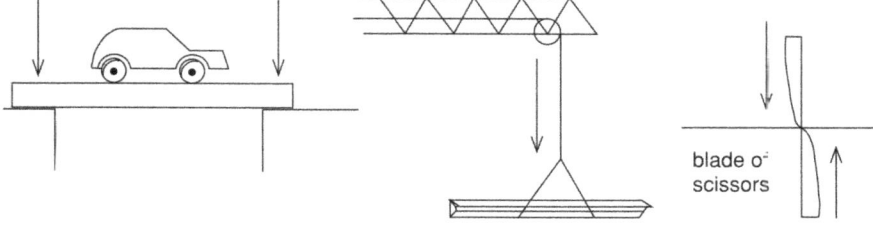

Figure 3.9 Examples of compressive, tensile and shear forces

Materials that can withstand high compression loading include cast iron, stone and brick, hence the common use of brick for building purposes. Cast iron, stone and brick, however, are brittle and break if subjected to high tension. If a building is to be designed that will resist tensile strain – in an earthquake-prone area, for example – steel, which has high tensile strength, would be a more suitable building material.

CONCEPT CONFUSION

Highlight the difference between the terms strength and hardness by demonstrating how these properties are tested in different ways. Strength indicates a material's ability to support a heavy load without breaking – testing the strength of shopping bags by adding weight until they break is a good example. Hardness is defined by a material's ability to withstand scratches – scratching different rocks to see if a nail or penny leaves a mark will compare how hard they are.

Elasticity

Almost all materials will stretch to some extent when a tensile force is applied to them, and the increase in length on loading, compared with the original length of the material, is known as *strain*.

The *elasticity* of a material is the extent to which it can regain its original shape or size following deformation (stretching or compression) by the application of a force. Robert Hooke (1635–1703) was the English scientist who first realized that increasing force, applied as a series of increasing loads, will result in a material extending proportionally. In simple terms, the change in length (extension) of a material is proportional to the applied load – *strain* is proportional to *stress*.

This can easily be seen in the classroom by hanging masses (weights) on to a rubber band and measuring the 'stretch' as each mass is added. In general, the 'stretch' or extension of the rubber band is directly proportional to the load added. A graph of the results should be a straight line passing through the origin. Up to a certain point, the removal of the applied load results in the rubber band regaining its original shape and size, and this tendency of materials to return to their original shape and size, when stress is removed, is known as elasticity.

As increased loading continues, a point is reached when the rubber band will no longer return to its original shape and size on removal of the load, and permanent deformation has occurred. The rubber band is said to have exceeded its *elastic limit* or *yield stress*, beyond which the rubber is suffering plastic deformation – it is being stretched irreversibly.

Eventually, at maximum stress, the material reaches its breaking point – *its ultimate tensile strength* – and failure or fracture rapidly follows. This sequence is illustrated for a variety of materials in Figure 3.10.

What can we learn about the materials from their stress–strain diagrams?

- *Mild steel* has little elasticity but has the highest yield stress of all the samples; it is fairly ductile, that is, it has a large range over which it can sustain plastic deformation; and it has the highest ultimate tensile strength.
- *Cast iron* is brittle – it has the lowest elasticity of the four samples and has no ability to sustain plastic deformation, although its tensile strength is higher than that of concrete.
- *Copper* has little elasticity but is the most ductile of the four samples. It has an ultimate tensile strength less than half that of mild steel.
- *Concrete* has little elasticity and the lowest tensile strength of the four samples.

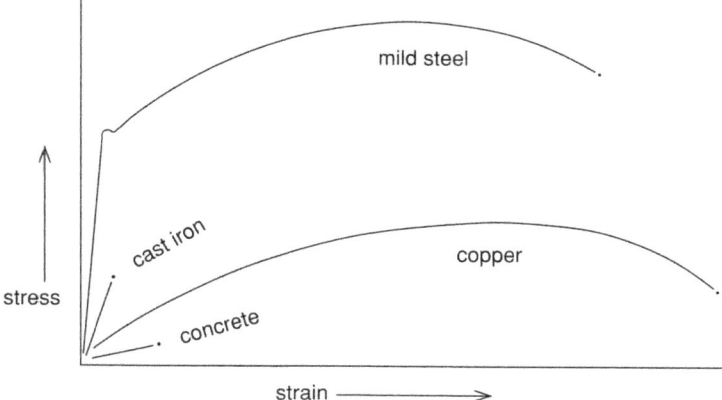

Figure 3.10 Stress–strain curves for a variety of materials in tension

Although rubber is the obvious 'elastic' material, metals too are elastic (a spring can be substituted for the rubber band in the above simple investigation), as, to a lesser extent, are plastics and wood. The elasticity or springiness in a metal can be shown in the classroom by investigating a bulldog clip or a paper clip.

Stiffness (and flexibility)

The part of the stress–strain curve (see Figure 3.10) that relates to elastic (reversible) deformation gives an indication of the *stiffness*, and therefore the flexibility, of the material. Stiffness is the resistance of the material to elastic deformation, and this resistance, or lack of it, results in the characteristic flexibility or rigidity of different materials.

A material with high stiffness will be brittle, will tend to be rigid and will shatter suddenly under the effect of a load beyond its elastic limit. Glass and ceramics are examples of brittle materials that are rigid and have little or no flexibility – they are more likely to fracture than stretch. Conversely, rubber and some plastics can easily be extended under tension and are said to have low stiffness, and hence, high flexibility.

Toughness

The part of the stress–strain curve that relates to plastic deformation gives a good indication of the ability of a material to change shape under load without breaking, and this is a reflection of its *toughness*. Materials that can absorb high tensile forces exhibit two further properties. They are said to be *ductile* if they can be elongated – metals can be drawn out into wires, for example – or *malleable* if they can be pressed, bent or beaten into shape – play dough, plasticine, copper pipe or wrought iron, for example. Again, the unbending of paper clips in the classroom will enable children to experience malleable metal at first hand.

This area gives us a good example of the difficulties of misunderstanding that can occur when a commonly used word with a generally understood, everyday meaning also has a specific scientific meaning that is different. In the examples given above, play dough, plasticine, copper pipe and wrought iron exhibit plastic properties in the sense that a force applied to them can change their shape permanently. They are not made of plastic, however, nor do they exhibit all of the properties of plastics. Some plastics, such as the nylon used in climbing ropes, demonstrate elastic properties, whereas others, such as perspex, are brittle and prone to shatter. Clear understanding of the terms involved, helped by a clear explanation of which of the meanings is being used in any particular context – do we mean plastic the *material*, or plastic the *property*? – and a careful use of language, will help to avoid confusion.

Compressibility

All materials have some ability to be compressed into a smaller space, although the compression of substances in solid and liquid states is usually too small to be obvious. Substances in gas state, however, can easily be compressed, and this characteristic can readily be experienced by attempting to work a bicycle pump when the outlet hole is held closed with a thumb or finger. The 'springiness' felt in the plunger is a result of the air in the barrel of the pump being compressed by the washer. Practical applications of this characteristic are considered in the next section (The uses of materials).

Thermal and electrical conductivity

Thermal conductivity is a measure of the extent to which heat energy can be transferred through a material. Metals are good thermal conductors, whereas plastics and natural materials conduct heat poorly. It is important to remember that conduction of heat can result in a rise or fall in temperature. This property of materials can be illustrated by comparison of the temperature of the handles of metal and plastic teaspoons after a short period of immersion in a hot liquid. The higher temperature of the metal spoon is a measure of the high thermal conductivity of the metal. Conversely, outdoors in winter, metal objects 'feel' colder than objects made of wood or other natural materials.

As with heat, *electrical conductivity* is a measure of the ease with which an electrical current can move in a material. Again, metals are good *conductors* of electricity – for commercial purposes, copper and silver have the highest conductivities. Plastics and natural materials are poor conductors, and those materials that oppose or resist the passage of an electrical current are known as *insulators* and are said to have high resistivity.

The table summarizes some properties of a variety of common materials. What does the table tell us about the materials listed? As has already been described, those materials that have a *density* greater than 1.0 g/cm^3 will sink in water, whereas those with densities lower than 1.0 g/cm^3 will float.

Material	Density (g/cm³)	Tensile strength (MN/m-)	Thermal conductivity (W/m/°C)	Electrical resistivity (10–8 ohms m)
Copper	8.96	215	385	1.67
Gold	19.30	125	296	2.3
Iron	7.87	210	80	9.71
Aluminium	2.70	80	201	2.65
Tin	7.30	25	65	12.8
Steel	7.86	690	63	12.0
Brick	2.30	5	0.6	10^{10} ohms m
Concrete	2.40	5	0.1	–
Glass	2.50	100	1.0	10^5 ohms m
Nylon	1.15	70	0.25	10^{16} ohms m
Water	1.00			
Polythene	0.92	13	0.2	10^{16} ohms m
Rubber	0.91	17	0.15	–
Softwood	0.60	100 (with grain)	0.15	–

The *tensile strength* of the materials is expressed in terms of the maximum force that a sample of the material can sustain under tension (the units are meganewtons per square metre). Perhaps not surprisingly, the harder metals (steel, copper and iron) demonstrate the highest tensile strengths, with glass and softwood performing better under tension than aluminium, tin, the ceramics and the plastics.

Thermal conductivity is expressed in terms of the efficiency with which heat can be transferred along a sample of the material (the units are watts per metre per Celsius degree). In this case, copper, gold and aluminium are the best conductors of heat, and the ceramics, plastics and softwood are the poorest.

The *electrical conductivity* of the materials may be inferred by looking at their *resistivity*. Resistivity is a measure of the extent to which the materials impede or resist the passage of an electric current (the units are ohm metres), so that a material with a high resistivity will be a poor conductor of electricity, and vice versa. It is easy to see from the table that metals in general, and copper in particular, are good conductors of electricity (because they have low resistivity) in comparison with the various non-metallic materials, with their high resistivity and correspondingly low conductivity.

Magnetic properties

Some materials have the property to attract iron, a property known as magnetism. Lodestone, an iron oxide, has natural magnetic properties (and reputedly was first discovered near Magnesia in ancient Greece), and other magnetic materials include iron, cobalt and nickel, and alloys of these metals such as steel, alnico (an *alloy* of *ni*ckel and *co*balt) and nichrome. In addition to pure metal magnets, some modern materials have incorporated magnetic metals into ceramics and plastics.

CONCEPT CONFUSION

It is important to help children discover that not all metals are magnetic, only objects made from iron, cobalt and nickel. Children often say that objects 'stick' to a magnet, and so it is important to introduce the vocabulary of attraction and repulsion.

FUTURE APPLICATION

Understanding magnetism can help children sort and recycle metals. Having recycling points at school where children can test cans to see if they are attracted to a magnet will help to identify aluminium cans for recycling (which saves 90 per cent of the energy needed to make new aluminium from raw materials).

The property of magnetism is a function of the atomic structure of the metals concerned. It is believed that the atoms of ferromagnetic materials are aligned in the same direction in very small areas (0.01–1.0 mm in diameter), known as domains. When brought into close contact with a magnet, the domains also align themselves in the same direction in such a way as to reinforce the overall effect, and magnetism is produced. In non-magnetic materials, the domains remain randomly oriented, cancelling out any overall magnetic effect.

It is difficult to provide a definition of magnetism, other than on an operational level – in other words it is easier to explain what magnets do than explain what they are.

Some operational characteristics of magnets and magnetism include the following:

- magnets attract other magnetic materials;
- this attraction may occur from a distance;
- it may occur through other, non-magnetic materials;
- every magnet has two areas (poles) that produce a stronger force of attraction than other areas;
- a magnet has a north-seeking (north) and a south-seeking (south) pole;
- a freely suspended magnet will come to rest with the north pole pointing northwards;
- unlike poles, that is, N–S, attract; like poles, that is, N–N or S–S, repel;
- the region around a magnet in which its magnetic force acts is known as a magnetic field;
- temporary magnets can be made by bringing iron into close contact with a magnet, by stroking a piece of iron with another magnet, or by inducing magnetism with an electric current (see Section 4);
- permanent magnets can be made by repeating the above processes with steel;
- heating or hammering a magnet will reduce its magnetism.

TEACHING IDEA

Making a magnet

Children can turn a paper clip into a magnet by stroking it repeatedly in one direction with one end of a bar magnet. This results in the negative and positive particles in the paper clip lining up, allowing it to become polarized. The paper clip will then point towards north when floating on water, like a compass.

FACT POINT

How does a compass work?

The Earth behaves like a magnet, with strong magnetic poles. These poles attract other magnets towards them. As a result, a compass needle (which is magnetic) always points north, allowing us to work out which direction we are travelling or facing.

Composite materials

These are materials that are formed to realize or exploit the properties of two or more other materials. Examples include:

- bone, which combines the flexibility of protein with the strength of calcium phosphate;
- reinforced concrete, which combines the compressive strength of concrete with the tensile strength of steel;
- glass-reinforced plastic (fibreglass), which combines the bonding property of polymer resins (the plastics) with the flexibility of woven glass cloth or fibrous mat.

Other combinations include electric cable, which uses the conductivity of the copper-wire core and the insulation of the plastic outer covering, and the technique of lamination, which increases the strength of materials by bonding together a number of layers. Plywood is an example of a laminate made from natural materials, and sailboards are composite laminates of a number of plastic products, including polystyrene, woven polyester cloth and polyester resin.

The characteristics of the main groups of materials

Although there are always exceptions to any large-scale groupings, it is possible to characterize the main groups of materials in terms of their general properties.

Metals are dense materials that are strong, hard, tough, ductile and malleable. They are excellent conductors of heat and electricity and have high melting points. Some metals have magnetic properties. Some are easily corroded.

Ceramics and *glass* are materials of low to medium density. They are resistant to abrasion and have compressive strength and good insulating properties. They have high melting or softening points and are resistant to corrosion. They are brittle and weak in tension.

Polymers are low-density materials that have low strength and hardness and high flexibility. They are easily moulded and are good insulators. They are highly resistant to corrosion, but have low melting points.

FACT POINT

Plastic fantastic?

Plastic is a man-made polymer, usually made from the carbon of oil or natural gas using high pressure and high heat. Although plastics are more lightweight and less expensive than things made from glass or wood, they do not break down easily. Plastic is not biodegradable (micro-organisms cannot break it down). It is, however, photodegradable (sunlight breaks it down into smaller pieces). A large amount of waste plastic ends up in oceans and as small pieces, killing many marine animals and seabirds as they accidently eat it. Reduction in the use of such plastics should, therefore, be encouraged, as should safe disposal.

Wood is a low-density natural material that, because of the arrangement of the lignin-strengthened fibres, has fairly good strength in tension and stiffness 'along the grain', coupled with shear strength 'across the grain'. It has high flexibility and is a good insulator. Wood is susceptible to decay and to destruction by fire.

Fabrics are highly flexible and have fairly good strength in tension. They are good insulators, but have poor resistance to abrasion. Natural-fibre fabrics are susceptible to decay and destruction by fire. Synthetic fibres may melt and give off toxic fumes if 'overheated' – this sometimes occurs when synthetic fabrics are ironed at too high a temperature setting.

FUTURE APPLICATION

Up-cycling

It once seemed logical to recycle materials. However, we should highlight to children that our first priority should be to reduce our use of newly manufactured materials such as fabric, plastic and paper. We should then consider reusing materials, or 'up-cycling'. Up-cycling is a creative process to convert old and discarded materials into something useful. This way, not only are we conserving valuable resources, but we are also reducing the amount of energy used to make them.

THE USES OF MATERIALS

CONCEPTS TO SUPPORT KEY STAGE 1

Fitness for purpose

The objects, structures and articles that are made for human use or consumption usually have a particular purpose or function. It is rare for an object to be 'completely useless', and, as a result of the demands that will be made on the object or structure, the materials of which it is made will have been chosen for their ability to 'do the job'.

The uses to which materials are put will reflect the exploitation of their properties. A simple, familiar example might be to consider the materials commonly found in houses and the ways in which these materials are used.

Material	Property	Household example
Metals	Strength	Structural components, for example, rolled steel joists
	Malleability, thermal conductivity, electrical conductivity, hardness	Water pipes, radiators, saucepans, ovens, core of electrical cables, drill bits, hammer heads
Ceramics	Strength (compression), heat resistance, abrasion resistance	Brickwork, concrete, paving slabs, ovenware, china, crockery
Glass	Thermal insulation, transparency	Loft and cavity-wall insulation, windows
Plastics	Flexibility	Moulded items, e.g. mixing and washing-up bowls
	Electrical insulation, thermal insulation, lightness and strength	Sheathing of electrical cables, saucepan handles Construction: window frames
Wood	Lightness and strength	Construction: doors, window frames, furniture
Fabrics	Flexibility, insulation	Curtains, furnishings, clothing

Sometimes, of course, a particular 'job' can be done by more than one type of material. A plate can be made of china, glass, plastic or paper, but the way in which it can be used will be limited by the properties of the material concerned. 'Ovenware' china and hardened 'Pyrex' glass plates can be used in an oven, but are more likely than plastic plates to break if dropped. Conversely, plastic plates, although lighter and almost unbreakable, will scratch more easily than glass or china and cannot be used in the oven. Paper plates, despite having very few of the properties of those made from china, glass or plastic, have been designed as disposable items and with the 'convenience' of users in mind.

Similarly, clothes made from synthetic fibres will tend to be longer lasting because they are more resistant to abrasion than those made from natural fibres. They are also stronger, because of the length of the fibres from which they are made. This is because the strength of natural fibres is limited by the length of the fibres available from the plant or animal concerned. Synthetic fibres can be spun to any length, and this results in an increased strength for a given diameter of yarn. In spite of the greater strength and durability of clothes made

Famous scientist factbox

Name	John McAdam (1756–1836), engineer, Glasgow, Scotland
Link to NC	Year 2 – Everyday materials
Famous for	He moved to New York City and, as a merchant during the American Revolution, he made his fortune working at his uncle's counting house. On his return to Scotland, he purchased an estate in Ayrshire and noted the poor condition of local highways. At his own expense, he undertook a series of experiments in road-making Under government appointment, he continued experimenting and made the recommendation that roads should be raised above the adjacent ground for good drainage. He proposed that they should be covered first with larger rocks, then smaller stones, and bonded with a fine gravel or slag. This process was called macadamization
Working scientifically	John McAdam used his engineering skills, his time and his fortune to benefit others apart from himself. He saw a *problem* and *investigated* possible solutions
Impact on society	The process of macadamization was instrumental in the facilitation of travel and communication and was adopted by many countries, including the US

from synthetic fibres, there are still many people who prefer the softer 'feel' (and the absorbency) of clothes made from natural fibres.

CONCEPTS TO SUPPORT KEY STAGE 2

Continuing the 'fitness for purpose' concept from the previous section, a further development is the idea that some materials demonstrate more than one property in their production and use for particular situations. An example of this is provided by the metal strings used on musical instruments such as guitars. First, these strings are produced as a result of the ductile nature of the metals used (often nickel steel, sometimes wound with copper wire). The *toughness* of the steel (see 'properties' above) allows the metal to be drawn out into fine wire. The *tensile strength* of the steel is then employed to allow the string to be tensioned enough to bring it to the required musical pitch. Finally, when the string is plucked, the *elasticity* of the metal allows it to vibrate consistently at the frequency that produces the musical note for which it has been tuned.

Considerations for the choice of materials

The materials that are used in the production of objects and structures are chosen because they exhibit particular properties. There are, however, other factors that are taken into account when any articles are produced, particularly on a large scale. Inevitably, the final choice of materials for a product represents a compromise between some or all of these factors. They may include the *cost* of raw materials (and, hence, the price of the finished product), the possibility of using *alternative materials*, the *availability* of the required materials, the degree of *maintenance* necessary and the *aesthetic qualities* of the materials concerned.

Cost/price: Today, the cost of materials is one of the most significant factors in manufacturing industry. 'Cost no object' products are rare and are usually products that involve national security, as in defence procurement, or prestige, as in the exploration of space. Most commercial and industrial operators want to produce at the lowest cost and sell at the highest price, and this mission is what drives the continuing search for alternative materials.

Alternative materials: These are the materials that can replace original materials, usually at lower cost, and still exhibit most of the required properties. Everyday examples of this tendency include the large-scale substitution of plastic objects for metal ones. In most kitchens, for example, metal colanders, sieves, cheese graters and tea strainers have been replaced by plastic versions (although tea strainers are themselves becoming obsolete, as leaf tea is superseded by tea bags).

Similarly, the baths in most houses are now made from glass-reinforced or high-density plastic. In the earlier years of this century, they would probably have been made from cast iron (if plumbed in) or galvanized iron ('tin' baths).

As a final example, motorists now sit on fabric (usually synthetic) seat covers rather than the leather seats that characterized cars during the early and middle decades of the last century.

Availability: Some materials are becoming scarce, and this has increased the need to develop substitutes. The scarcity of large-size hardwood timber for construction purposes has led to the development of laminated beams, or the substitution of metal alternatives.

Maintenance: Some of the newer materials are less demanding of maintenance than more traditional ones. A good example of the 'maintenance-free' tendency has been the large-scale substitution of glass-reinforced plastic for wood as a construction material for the leisure boating industry.

Aesthetic qualities: In some cases, materials are chosen for their aesthetic qualities, as well as for their properties, cost, availability and so on. Examples include decorative articles – jewellery, fabrics – and materials used in sympathy with a particular environment or location – the use of stone rather than brick - for buildings in national parks. Appeal is also made to shoppers on the grounds of 'quality' in the marketing of furniture made from solid wood rather than from veneered chipboard.

A materials case study: Drinks containers

Many of the issues raised above can be addressed simply in the classroom by a study of the wide variety of drinks containers available today. Containers can be found that are made from metal, ceramic, glass, plastic and paper. The properties of the materials from which the containers are made can be investigated, and the limitations of each can be discussed and tested. Some of the characteristics, design features and limitations are listed in the table.

Famous scientist factbox

Name	John Boyd Dunlop (1840–1921), Ayrshire, Scotland
Link to NC	Year 2 – Everyday materials
Famous for	Development of the pneumatic (air-filled) rubber tyre for his son's tricycle. His design was patented in 1888
Working scientifically	When his son's tricycle didn't appear fast or comfortable, he used *problem-solving* and *comparative testing* to develop tyres that allowed the ride to be smoother and faster
Impact on society	His design improved the bicycle and contributed to the success of the automobile
Controversies	It was later discovered that the pneumatic tyre had already been patented by Robert William Thomas in 1845. As a result, Dunlop's patent was removed; however, he is still credited for the development of the pneumatic tyre because of the timing of his invention (rubber was getting cheaper and road transport was being developed)

Drinks container	Properties	Disadvantages
Alloy drink can	Light – aluminium alloy has a density of 2.7 g/cm³ Strong in compression – with care it is possible to stand on the top of an empty drink can Designed to stack easily and be recyclable	Not reusable Malleable – it is easy to buckle an aluminium can by hand
China mug or cup (traditional hot drink container)	Keeps drinks hot Resists abrasion during washing-up Strong	Breakable
Glass (traditional cold drink container)	Transparent – can see the contents of the glass	Breakable, possibility of injury
High-density plastic (melamine) mug or cup	Light Strong Keeps drinks hot Virtually unbreakable	Liable to abrasion damage (possible health hazard, as bacteria can collect in surface scratches)

Drinks container	Properties	Disadvantages
Enamel mug	Light Unbreakable	Hot drinks lose heat quickly Now almost replaced by plastic versions
Thermoplastic cup	Very light Thin Disposable	Sometimes unstable Rapid, and sometimes uncomfortable heat transfer to user's hand Hot drinks lose heat quickly Non-biodegradable so sometimes the cause of litter problems Splits easily Not designed for reuse
Expanded polystyrene cup	Light Good insulation (hot drinks and no burnt fingers) Disposable	Non-biodegradable Not designed for reuse
Paper cup	Very light Cheap, disposable, but biodegradable	Not designed for reuse

KEY IDEA 3.2 SUMMARY

Everything around us is made of different materials. They are essential for all aspects of life. Understanding the behaviour and properties of different materials allows us to ensure they are suitable for different uses.

Working scientifically

- *Grouping and classifying*: Take a walk around the school and challenge the children to identify objects made from different materials, discussing the properties that make them suitable.
- *Fair testing*: Testing different materials to see which would make the strongest carrier bag can be done by cutting equal-sized squares of each material, hanging them with bulldog clips and suspending weights on them to see how much each material stretches.
- *Comparative testing*: Children could conduct a range of tests to identify the suitability of materials for different purposes. Identifying the best materials for a dolls house could involve a carousel of waterproof testing for the roof, transparency testing for the windows, and strength testing for the building structure.

Discussion point

- *Which material do you think you could not live without?* This could stimulate lots of discussion about the importance of different materials. Plastics, for example, can be used for anything from toothbrushes, to space shuttles, to drinks bottles. Nylon was also a revolutionary man-made material that is cheap and durable and can be used for anything from tights to bulletproof vests.

Cross-curricular activities

- *Maths*: A record of how much an elastic band stretches when weights are added can then be converted into a graph. Look at shapes in different buildings and investigate which shapes make the strongest structure. Make and test model bridges with different materials and measure how much weight they can hold before they collapse.
- *Geography*: Explore different materials used for houses around the world, such as mud huts, ice igloos and eco-friendly homes made of recycled materials, such as tyres and glass bottles.
- *Literacy*: Reading stories such as *The Iron Man* by Ted Hughes or 'The three little pigs' can introduce children to materials and their properties.

Application

'The three little pigs' can be a creative way to introduce the suitability of different materials. Alternatively, designing dream houses and researching grand designs or famous architecture can encourage children to identify the properties of different materials and their suitability. Materials scientists continue to develop new and interesting materials to improve our lives. Challenge children to consider what new material they would like to invent, and what properties it would have.

Global dimension

Becoming aware of our diminishing supply of natural resources is important for children to learn to be resourceful with the materials that they have. Learning about alternative uses for materials and learning how to reduce and reuse the things we already have are important aspects of appreciating the diversity of materials on our planet.

Health and safety

When testing the strength of carrier-bag materials, ensure that they are tested in a suitable place, in case the weights drop to the ground. Alternatively, measure how much they stretch rather than testing them to destruction, so that weights do not drop.

Assessment for learning

Talk partners: When learning about properties and uses of materials, children could be provided with photos of unusual objects or materials, or they may be led on a material/object hunt around the school. Questions could be posed to the children, such as 'What is it?', 'What do you think it is made from?', 'Why do you think that?'. The focus is on discussion, raising questions and explanations, and this will allow the children to share what they have learned.

KEY IDEA 3.3

Changing materials

Materials can be changed, and these changes can be permanent or reversible.

CONCEPTS TO SUPPORT KEY STAGE 1

Change in shape

Simple changes in the shape of objects are brought about by the application of forces, and the nature of the change in shape will be a function of the properties of the materials of which the objects are made (see above, Key Idea 3.2: The physical properties of materials).

Squashing

Objects that can be squashed will usually behave in one of two ways:

- they will return to their original shape once the applied squashing force is removed; example: a rubber ball, a football, a balloon – the materials are exhibiting the property of stiffness and have not been loaded beyond their elastic limits; or
- they will remain in their 'new' shape once the applied squashing force is removed; example: moulded or shaped play dough or plasticine – the materials have been loaded beyond their elastic limits, but are now exhibiting the property of toughness (malleability, the ability to sustain plastic deformation).

Bending

Similarly, objects that are bent will either:

- return to their original shape once the applied bending force is removed; example: bending a plastic or wooden ruler – again, the materials are demonstrating the property of stiffness (hence elasticity);
- remain in their 'new' shape once the applied bending force is removed; example: bent pipe cleaners or thin metal tube, folded paper – the materials are demonstrating the property of toughness (malleability, the ability to sustain plastic deformation); or
- fracture, if the elastic limit is exceeded with brittle materials, or the maximum tensile strength is exceeded with malleable materials.

Twisting

This process is usually achieved by applying a turning action (torque) to an object – for example, a ruler, a block of plasticine or play dough or a 'twist' of paper. An object held in this state is said to be under torsion. Again, the objects will either:

- return to their original shape (exhibiting stiffness);
- remain twisted (exhibiting toughness); or
- fracture (either at the elastic limit, or at the maximum tensile strength of the materials concerned).

Stretching

Objects that are stretched – for example rubber bands, metal springs and wire, 'rolls' of plasticine, cotton and wool fibres, fishing line – will usually lengthen, then either:

- return to their original length (exhibiting stiffness);
- remain 'stretched' (exhibiting toughness – ductility); or
- fracture (as above).

It is interesting for children to be able to investigate the nature of materials whose shape is changed, as they do not all behave in the neatly predictable ways described above. If a crisp packet is 'screwed up' – squashed and bent – it will begin to regain its original shape, but will never 'uncurl' completely. This shows that, even when materials are taken beyond their elastic limits, some residual elasticity remains.

It is relatively easy to discover that the physical processes that cause changes in shape do not result in any change in mass. 'Before and after' weighing will readily show that the mass of the material has remained constant, even though its shape may have changed owing to the application of force.

TEACHING IDEA

Modelling

Challenge children to shape a piece of play dough or modelling clay in as many different ways as possible. They can be encouraged to record different words to describe their actions – for example, twisting, stretching, flattening, squashing, rolling, squeezing, folding and bending.

Heating and cooling everyday materials

The effects of changes in temperature on materials can be explained in terms of the states of matter and changes of state (see Key Idea 3.1: The states of matter).

It is important for young children to realize that sometimes the effects of heating or cooling materials can be easily reversed, and sometimes changes occur that are difficult to reverse – in practical terms, they are permanent. Examples from the everyday life of children would include the heating and cooling of water, milk, chocolate, candle wax, cake mixture, clay and matchwood.

Water

Water boils (eventually) when heated. Steam is a cloud of minute water droplets at or near 100°C. The gas that evaporates from boiling water is water vapour and is invisible. When cooled, water vapour condenses to form water droplets. All of these processes can be easily demonstrated in a classroom (with care) by boiling water in a kettle and then holding a suitable surface (a pyrex plate is ideal) in the plume of steam. Condensation occurs almost immediately, and the water droplets that run down the plate can be collected in a suitable container.

When cooled below 0°C, water freezes to form ice (make 'lollies' in the school fridge). Uniquely, ice (the solid) is less dense than water and floats. When heated, the ice melts to form water. The heating and cooling processes are reversible.

WORKING SCIENTIFICALLY

Children can investigate factors that affect the boiling point of water. Pure water boils at 100°C. The addition of salt increases the boiling point of water, so that it takes longer to boil. If water contains impurities, such as tap water, which has lots of dissolved minerals, it also boils at a higher temperature. Altitude and pressure also affect the boiling point of water, but this may be not be a practical investigation in a classroom setting! Ensure safety procedures are followed when using hot water.

Milk

Milk also boils on heating (sometimes 'boiling over'). When frozen, milk separates out into water- and fat-based components, and these can clearly be seen as two different layers in the frozen milk.

Chocolate

Chocolate, a solid, melts when heated (either in a warm hand or a pan!). It is interesting to see what happens when a chocolate bar is broken up into small pieces before being heated, in comparison with one that is heated as a single large piece (the small pieces melt more quickly because of a larger surface area exposed to heat transfer). If allowed to cool, the chocolate will reconstitute, but will not resume its former shape. So, the process is reversible, but sometimes young children tend to think that the cooled-down chocolate is 'not the same' as the original, because of its different appearance and shape.

WORKING SCIENTIFICALLY

Melting chocolate

The fat content of chocolate affects its melting point. Children could compare the temperature at which different types of chocolate melt, perhaps using dark, milk and white chocolate. Hotter countries change ingredients in chocolate so that it is more resistant to melting!

Candle wax

A candle (made of paraffin wax) melts when heated or lit. The liquid wax vaporizes to form a gas, which burns as a flame (the brightness of the flame is as a result of white-hot particles of carbon). When the candle is blown out, and cooling begins, the vapour disperses, and liquid wax solidifies. In one sense, then, the process is reversible (the vapour is condensed to form liquid, then solid wax). In another sense, however, a permanent change has occurred, because the wax (a fuel) has been used up in the burning process – the candle 'burns down'.

CONCEPT CONFUSION AND CROSS-CURRICULAR LINK

Maths

Children can investigate how long a candle burns for. Using a sand tray, candles or tea-lights and different-sized glass jars, children can compare the length of time it takes for a candle flame to go out. They can then present their results in a graph. It is important to note that candles in closed containers do not go out because they use up all the oxygen. Instead, the hot carbon dioxide given off in burning builds up at the top, pushing down oxygen and eventually suffocating the flame. As a result, the children should discover that the smaller the jar, the quicker the carbon dioxide stifles the candle flame.

Cake mixture

To begin with, it is interesting to notice the changes that take place to the consistency and colour of the ingredients of a cake during the mixing process. When the mixture is heated (baked) in an oven, irreversible chemical changes take place. The liquid mixture solidifies and increases in volume, as carbon dioxide gas, produced during the baking process, is trapped in bubbles in the mix. The resulting cake, when cooled, is a fused matrix of the original ingredients, which cannot be reconstituted in their previous form. It has usually increased in size.

Clay

When clay is heated to very high temperatures in a kiln, the constituent minerals fuse to form a ceramic material. An irreversible chemical reaction has taken place, and a new compound has formed from a mixture of other compounds. Some modelling clays are plastics-based polymers and will harden at much lower (oven) temperatures.

Matchwood splint

If a splint, or paper twist, is heated by a match or other flame, the wood or paper will burn (carbon from the organic material combines with oxygen in the air to form carbon dioxide gas). As with the candle, the flame is composed partly of incandescent particles of carbon and partly of unburnt gas. The change in the wood is permanent, as it cannot be reconstituted in its original form.

One of the less obvious outcomes of heating everyday materials is the extent to which they expand. This can be seen outdoors where, on hot days, concrete road surfaces expand and squeeze out the tarmac filler placed between road sections. Many steel bridges have carriageways that are mounted on rollers at one end in order to allow for expansion of the metal during hot weather. The metal will regain its original length when temperatures return to normal. Railway lines are laid with gaps between adjacent rails to allow for expansion during hot weather. In exceptional circumstances, even this precaution is not enough to prevent the rails from buckling in the heat.

CONCEPTS TO SUPPORT KEY STAGE 2

Separating mixtures

Mixtures, as explained in Key Idea 3.1 (Elements, compounds and mixtures), are derived when two or more substances are combined together without a chemical reaction taking place.

In many cases, the original substances can be separated out by simple physical procedures that, in effect, reverse the mixing process.

Allowing for the three states in which substances can exist, there are nine different types of mixture. They are described here, with examples and, where appropriate, an explanation of a simple separating system. In each case, the use of the term *solid*, *liquid* or *gas* implies 'substance in solid state', 'substance in liquid state' or 'substance in gas state'.

Solid-in-solid (particles)

Solid-in-solid (particles) – for example, dried soil, sand and gravel – can be separated by *sieving*. Stones can be removed from topsoil with a sieve, before a garden is planted or a lawn is laid. The basic principle of a sieve is that large particles are trapped by a mesh, while small particles pass through the gaps – even a garden rake is a form of sieve.

Although solid particles of different sizes can be separated by sieving, it may not always be appropriate to do so. The traditional (but perhaps contrived) 'salt and sand' and 'sand and iron filings' mixtures are best separated by other means (although it is arguable as to why anyone might want to mix them in the first place!).

Solid-in-liquid

Some solid-state substances can be *dissolved* in liquid-state substances – salt or sugar in water, for example – to form a *solution*. What happens is that the crystalline salt or sugar pieces are bombarded by water molecules until they break down into particles so small that they cannot be seen, and these then become dispersed evenly in the water, weakly bonded to the water molecules.

It is important to realize that the process of dissolving is *not* a change of state. The solid substance is not melting. It is simply being broken into pieces too small to be seen. The pieces may have 'disappeared' from view, but the particles of the original solid-state substance are still there – mixed in with particles of the liquid-state substance.

A solid in solution (*solute*) can be recovered from a liquid (*solvent*) by causing the solvent to evaporate. This can be achieved by heating the solution until the solvent has been removed by *evaporation*. What has happened is that the additional heat energy has caused the loosening of the bonds between the salt or sugar crystals and the water molecules, which 'escape' from the solution as gaseous water vapour (this process can take place without heat, but takes much longer to complete). The original solute is recovered, once again in crystalline form.

There is a limit to the mass of substance that can dissolve in a given amount of solvent, and this limit is different for different substances. At the point at which no more of a particular substance will dissolve into a given amount of a solvent, a saturated solution has been produced. A key factor in this process is the temperature of the solvent. The amount

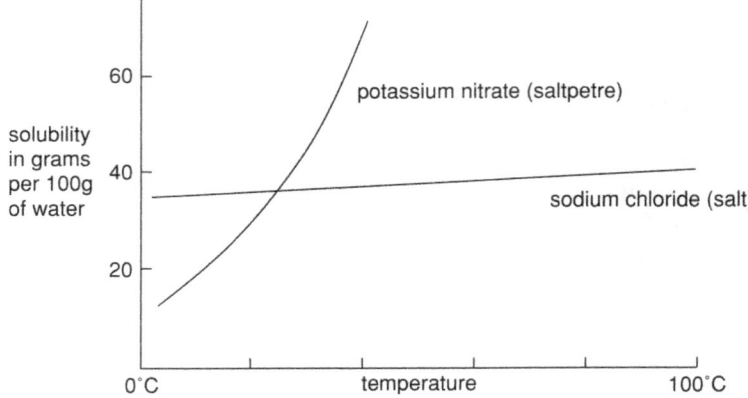

Figure 3.11 The solubility curves of two different compounds

of a substance that will dissolve in a given amount of solvent will increase with increasing temperature, and the solubility curves for different solids are characteristic for a range of temperatures (see Figure 3.19). Gases show the opposite tendency, and, as temperature rises, less gas will dissolve in a given mass of solvent.

The *mass* of a solute that will dissolve in a solvent is affected by the temperature of the solvent. The *speed* at which a soluble substance will dissolve is also affected by the size of the grains or pieces of the substance. The smaller the pieces, the faster the substance will dissolve. This is because, as volume decreases, relative surface area increases, and the effect can be demonstrated easily by noting the time taken to dissolve a variety of different sizes of sugar pieces in a fixed volume of water at a constant temperature. For example, four different grain 'sizes' could be derived from: a whole sugar cube, a cube broken into pieces, a cube crushed into granules and a cube ground into powder.

If the substance will not dissolve in a solvent, a *suspension* results. The best classroom example is muddy water – shake up some soil and water in a jar. Even after many hours (sometimes days), small particles will remain suspended in the water (a useful subjective test is how clearly small print can be read through the suspension).

Undissolved solid particles can be separated from the liquid by *filtering* (filtration). The mixture of solid particles in a liquid is poured into a funnel containing filter paper or other material that will 'trap' the larger particles (gravel is used in some parts of water filtration plants). As with sieving, the principle is that larger particles (the *residue*) are trapped by the 'mesh' of the filter paper, while the liquid (the *filtrate*) passes through. Everyday examples of this process would include the making of filter coffee (where the filtrate is the required product) and the 'straining' of peas or cabbage from the water in which cooking has taken place – in this case, the residue is the required material.

A useful classroom example would be the separation of milk solids from liquid, using muslin or similar cloths, during the making of cream cheese. Similarly, sand or soil can be separated from water by filtering the mixture through filter or blotting paper, or kitchen roll.

Solid-in-gas

Solid-in-gas – for example, smoke particles in the air, technically an *aerosol* – can also be removed by *filtration*. This occurs commercially during the 'scrubbing' of air in industrial processes before its return to the atmosphere. An everyday example of this process in action would be the dirt that accumulates on curtains. The 'dirt' consists of small solid particles trapped by the weave of the cloth.

Liquid-in-solid

Liquid-in-solid – for example, butter, a *solid emulsion* – water droplets in a fat, can be separated by 'boiling off' the water (a process used in some types of cooking).

Liquid-in-liquid

Such a mixture is known as an *emulsion*, for example, a vinegar- and oil-based salad dressing. The constituents can most easily be separated by allowing the components of the emulsion to separate into 'layers' – the less dense component will 'float' on top of the denser component – and then by carefully pouring off the top layer.

   If the mixture of liquids is a solution, for example, alcohol and water, or petroleum, separation can be achieved by *distillation*. The basic process involves heating the mixture until one of the constituents reaches boiling point. The evaporated gas is drawn off the mixture, condensed and collected separately. This process is repeated a number of times during the 'fractional distillation' of crude oil, as the basic raw material consists of a mixture of a number of different products (fractions) with different boiling points.

Liquid-in-gas

An example of liquid-in-gas is mist or a cloud – fine water droplets suspended in the air, again, technically an *aerosol*. In Gibraltar, an outcrop of limestone rock with a serious water supply problem, water is collected from the damp easterly wind (the Levanter) that streams over the top of the rock, by means of large vertical screens of nylon fabric, down which the condensed droplets run into concrete catchments and reservoirs.

Gas-in-solid

An example of gas-in-solid is expanded polystyrene, a *solid foam*. Although the air does not mix with the plastic, a chemical reaction has occurred during the curing of the product, and separation of the components of the mixture is impossible in practical terms.

Gas-in-liquid

Gas-in-liquid may take the form of a solution – for example, oxygenated water in a fish tank – or a *foam* – for example, shaving foam – a mixture of soap products and a propellant gas.

Gas-in-gas

An example of gas-in-gas is air, which is a mixture of gases (see Key Idea 3.2: Natural materials from the physical environment). The separation of the individual gases is an industrial process that involves the liquefaction of air (which occurs at about –200°C), followed by fractional distillation.

WORKING SCIENTIFICALLY

Retrieving the ingredients from alien soup

Children should get the opportunity to choose the appropriate equipment for an experiment. Providing them with a mixture of water, paper clips, sand, salt, marbles and rice can provide them with an effective problem-solving activity. Not only do they have to think about the equipment needed to separate different items, but they also need to consider the best sequence in which to separate them.

Changing materials

The processes that cause changes in substances or materials can include physical and chemical reactions.

Physical changes

Physical changes include those that cause a change in shape (*mechanical* changes), a change in state (*heating* and *cooling*) or a physical *mixing* of substances or materials.

Mechanical changes

The squashing, bending, twisting, stretching and so on of solid materials (see above, Change in shape) occur as the materials respond to applied force. The resulting change will reflect the properties of the materials concerned. If the material is deformed within its elastic limit (a function of its stiffness; see Key Idea 3.2: Stiffness), the mechanical change will be reversible. If the elastic limit is exceeded by the applied load, plastic deformation will take place, and the change will be irreversible.

The *heating* and *cooling* of many simple materials can cause reversible changes in state. These include melting, boiling, evaporation, condensing and freezing (or solidifying) and they have already been described in detail above (see Key Idea 3.1: Changes of state). The heating and cooling of water can be used to demonstrate the conservation of mass – that is, that the mass of water will remain the same after a change of state. The careful freezing of a known *mass* (not volume) of water should result in an equal mass of ice, and melting of that ice should restore the original mass of water.

The *mixing* of materials is a process that can often be reversed (see above, Separating mixtures), and simple mixtures can usually be separated by sieving, filtering or by the evaporation of the solvent from a solution to recover the solute.

The making of a solution is another good way to demonstrate the conservation of mass. If 30 g of salt are dissolved into 100 g of water, 130 g of salt solution will result. It is not easy to demonstrate the conservation of mass during the reversal of the process, because of the practical difficulty involved in collecting all the evaporated water vapour and condensing it.

Chemical reactions and heat energy

During many chemical reactions, the bonds that exist between particles (atoms or molecules) of the substances involved (elements or compounds) are broken and reformed as new compounds are produced. If the total energy of the product is less than that of the original constituents, a release of energy accompanies the reaction. This energy release is commonly in the form of heat (which can be felt, for example, when plaster of Paris is mixed with water and allowed to 'set'), and this type of reaction is known as *exothermic* (literally, heat out).

Conversely, in some reactions, energy is needed to form the resultant compound, and this energy may be absorbed from the surrounding medium. A good example of this type of *endothermic* (heat in) reaction occurs when lemonade (citric acid) and bicarbonate of soda (sodium bicarbonate) are mixed. If the temperature of the lemonade is noted before the sodium bicarbonate is added, it will be noticed that a drop in temperature of up to 5°C can occur, once the sodium bicarbonate is stirred into the solution. The drop in temperature of the solution represents the transfer of heat energy needed to cause the breakdown of the molecular bonding (and the release of carbon dioxide gas). The effervescence that occurs when these two compounds are mixed is the basis for the 'fizziness' of sherbet.

Most of these types of reaction are not easily reversible.

TEACHING IDEA

Provide children with a checklist to help them identify the difference between physical and chemical changes. A permanent chemical change will result in one or more of the following:

*   bubbles of gas being released;
*   a change in temperature;
*   a change in colour;
*   the production of light or a flame.

You could provide children with a carousel of examples, such as sugar dissolving, a candle burning, vinegar and bicarbonate of soda fizzing, and cakes baking, to see if they can identify which are physical and which are chemical changes.

Changes involving oxygen

Many chemical reactions that are important in everyday life involve the use of oxygen from the atmosphere in a process known as oxidation. Two common examples are burning and rusting.

The *burning* (or combustion) of a fuel in the presence of oxygen results in the production of carbon dioxide and water and the liberation of a large amount of energy. What has happened during this process is that the carbon from the fuel (usually a hydrocarbon) is oxidized to form carbon dioxide, and hydrogen from the fuel combines with oxygen to form water. The energy released by the breaking of the carbon bonds during the reaction is transferred in a number of ways.

TEACHING IDEA

The fire triangle

To put fire safety into context, fire extinguishers can be explained by identifying how they prevent the process of combustion. Burning is a chemical reaction that needs three things: fuel, oxygen and heat. If one of the three things is removed, the burning can no longer continue. Some fire extinguishers (such as carbon dioxide or foam) prevent the oxygen getting to the fire, whereas water extinguishers take away the heat. Ask children to identify which of the three elements are being removed to prevent/stop a fire – for example, a fire blanket removes the oxygen supply.

Imagine a car starting up. The fuel (petrol or diesel) is burnt in the cylinders, in the presence of oxygen. The reaction is so rapid as to be explosive, and the energy released in the reaction can be transferred in the following ways:

Productive energy is transferred:

*   through the gears and clutch to make the car move forward – mechanical energy;
*   through the dynamo to power the electrical circuits – electrical energy – hence:
    – light energy;
    – sound energy (horn);

– magnetic energy (central locking system);
– heat energy (heating system).

Unproductive energy is transferred in an unusable form as:

* heat;
* sound (engine noise).

The chemical reactions are also traceable to the production of carbon dioxide (and carbon monoxide) as a component of the exhaust gases, and the water produced during the combustion of fuel can often be seen dripping from the exhaust pipe of a recently started car, or as the 'steam' coming from an exhaust pipe on a cold morning.

The original materials burnt as fuels cannot be recovered after combustion. The process is not reversible in any practical sense at all (coal, oil and natural gas are examples of fossil fuels; wood, charcoal and peat are present-day examples).

CONCEPT CONFUSION

It is important to distinguish between the terms melting, dissolving and burning. Melting is a reversible, physical change by which a solid turns to a liquid. Dissolving is also a reversible, physical change, but differs from melting in that the solid particles break up and mix among the liquid particles; reversing the process can be done by separating the liquid through evaporation, leaving the solids behind. Burning, however, produces smoke and ash, which are new products, as well as carbon dioxide and water vapour escaping into the air.

Another form of oxidation occurs when *rusting* takes place. Iron is oxidized in the presence of water to form hydrated iron oxide (rust). The process is a slow, corrosive one that causes millions of pounds worth of damage every year. Although the process is reversible in chemical terms, it is not practicable to do so – a rusted iron component could not be reconstituted in its original form. The solution is to slow down or prevent rusting by excluding oxygen (air) and water from the metal. This can be done by coating the iron with paint, a layer of tin, or of zinc (a process known as galvanizing), or by alloying the iron with chromium to make stainless steel.

WORKING SCIENTIFICALLY

Rusting

Children may explore the rates and prevention of rusting by placing iron nails in containers as follows:
* nails alone (control);
* nails dampened with water;
* nails under water;
* nails under boiled water (some oxygen removed);
* as each of above, but with the nails smeared with vaseline, painted or oiled.

Recording and interpreting results will allow children to identify why rusting takes place.

Finally, it is worth remembering that *cellular respiration* is a form of oxidation. The 'fuel' in this case takes the form of energy-rich organic molecules (carbohydrates) stored in the tissues of living organisms, and the oxygen is delivered to the tissues by the process of breathing. As with the combustion of fossil fuels, the products of this oxidation process are carbon dioxide and water, with an accompanying release of energy. Details of the process are given in Section 2 (see Key Idea 2.2: The Cardio-vascular system and Respiration).

KEY IDEA 3.3 SUMMARY

Chemical changes happen in biological processes, such as respiration and photosynthesis. They are also useful to help make new products, such as plastics, or release energy from fuel to run our cars. Children should be aware of the opportunities for chemical change to make new and useful materials, but must also be aware that some changes are irreversible and may have a lasting negative impact on the environment.

Working scientifically

- *Scientific research*: Children can research how fireworks are made, thinking about how different chemicals react to make different colours. Original fireworks were made from gunpowder, a mixture of chemicals including potassium nitrate, sulphur and charcoal. Modern fireworks are made by expert pyrotechnicians, who add chemicals for special effects.
- *Fair testing*: 'What affects the rate at which a solid dissolves?' is a good global investigation question. Children can change the temperature or type of solvent, the type or size of the solute, or the speed at which the solution is stirred. They can present their findings in the form of a graph to share with other groups.
- *Observation over time*: Children can dissolve salt into warm water until they have a saturated solution. If they attach a piece of string to the middle of a pencil and suspend this in the water solution, the growth of salt crystals can be observed and recorded over a sequence of days. Children can explore factors that change the size of the crystals.

Discussion point

- Why are different fire extinguishers used for different types of fire? This is an interesting area for exploration, highlighting to the children that some fire extinguishers work by removing the heat (for example, by spraying water over the fire), whereas others stop oxygen getting to the fire (for example, by smothering it with foam or powder).

Application

Seventy-one per cent of our Earth's surface is covered by water. More than 97 per cent of all water is salt water, leaving only 3 per cent as freshwater (nearly 70 per cent of the freshwater is frozen in the icecaps of Greenland and Antarctica). As a result, we need to be able to remove impurities and reuse it. Boiling water and capturing and condensing the steam form an effective way to clean water, but it can be very expensive. With a lack of large-scale water cleaning systems in developing countries, obtaining safe drinking water is a challenge. We can raise awareness by challenging children to design and research water-purifying inventions. The Lifestraw, for example, is a tube for purifying water from potential pathogens, such as typhoid, cholera, dysentery and diarrhoea.

Cross-curricular links

- *Literacy*: Children can be encouraged to write poems about Bonfire Night or fireworks. They can research and write newspaper articles about Guy Fawkes and the Gunpowder Plot.
- *Mathematics*: Children can record how long it takes sugar or salt to dissolve at different temperatures, converting their results into a graph.
- *Geography*: Recycling involves many processes of separation. Different countries have different recycling systems, which pupils could explore, before making their own recycling invention. It is important that children gain an understanding of how materials can be separated and recycled, to prevent wastage of limited resources.

Health and safety

- When demonstrating chemical reactions such as burning, ensure the room is well ventilated, use a snuffer to extinguish candles, fix candles or night lights on a stable base and place in a sand tray, use safety matches, tie back long hair and wear goggles.
- Pupils should be taught not to sit down during heating activities, so they can move more quickly if there is an accident.

Assessment for learning

Reflecting on predictions: Exploration of material changes provides lots of opportunities for predicting, for example, predicting what happens when materials are heated and predicting which materials dissolve in water. After testing, children can reflect on whether their predictions were correct or not. This can be conducted in pairs, so that children can discuss what they thought before and what they understand as a result of conducting the experiment.

The rock cycle

The main classification of rocks – into *igneous*, *sedimentary* and *metamorphic* types – is based on the way in which the rocks are formed.

IGNEOUS ROCKS

Igneous rocks are formed by the cooling of molten magma, which wells up from deep beneath the Earth's surface. In some places, the magma remains below the surface and cools slowly (*intrusive* igneous rock); in others, it is forced to the surface and erupts as volcanic ash and lava (*extrusive* igneous rock).

The magma is a melted mixture of rock-forming minerals (mainly silicates), and, as cooling proceeds, the individual minerals crystallize out and become solid at different temperatures. The crystalline nature of igneous rocks is a characteristic feature, and a sample of such rock looks rather like a fully interlocking, three-dimensional jigsaw.

If cooling has been slow because the magma has solidified deep below the surface, the resulting intrusive rock will usually be dark in colour and fairly dense, and its crystals will be large and obvious, as in granite, for example. If, however, the magma has been thrown out of the Earth during a volcanic eruption, it will have cooled rapidly, and the resulting extrusive rock will usually be pale in colour and less dense, and its crystals will usually be too small to be seen with the naked eye, as in pumice or volcanic ash.

In addition to obvious surface features formed from extrusive igneous rocks (such as volcanoes, ash cones and lava flows), intrusive igneous rocks are occasionally visible in the landscape as a result of the removal of the original surface layers by erosion. Examples of intrusive features that have been excavated by erosion in the UK include the columnar basalt of the Giant's Causeway in County Antrim in Northern Ireland (the same outcrop, incidentally, as the columnar structures of Fingal's Cave on the island of Staffa in the Hebrides) and the outcrops of the Great Whin Sill in the north east of England – at Hadrian's Wall, High Force waterfall and the Farne Islands, for example. Figure 3.20 summarizes the main features formed from intrusive and extrusive igneous rocks.

SEDIMENTARY ROCKS

The rocks of the Earth's crust are continuously being eroded. That is to say, they are broken down into small fragments by the process of weathering (frost-shattering, mechanical or chemical weathering) and then removed from their original sites by the transport of the weathered debris (by rivers, glaciers, the wind or the sea). A useful 'formula' is that:

erosion = (is a result of) weathering + transport

Eventually, the eroded fragments of the original rocks are deposited, usually under water, in thick layers (or strata). These layers of sediment eventually become compressed into rocks

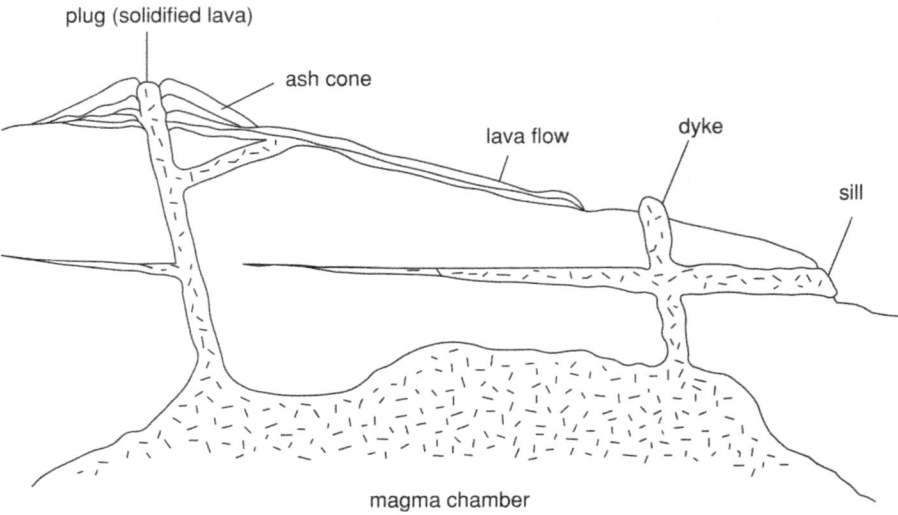

Figure 3.12 Features formed by igneous rocks

by the weight of water and other sediments above them. The resulting sedimentary rocks will, therefore, be characterized by the nature of the sediments from which they were formed.

Sedimentary rocks are, therefore, characteristically formed from small particles of weathered rocks and minerals that are bound together by a related matrix substance (rather like currants in a fruit cake). If the sediment is soft, it is often possible to scrape away the particles, and a look through a hand lens will usually confirm that the rock is not formed from interlocking crystals.

In sites where sediments may be deposited (where a fast-flowing river enters a lake, for example), the heaviest particles are usually deposited first, followed by a graded sequence of particle sizes, with the finest particles being deposited furthest out in the lake. This is summarized in the following table and in Figure 3.21.

FACT POINT

Chalk, like that found in the White Cliffs of Dover, is white because it is composed of the exoskeletons of millions of little sea creatures (sea plankton), compressed together under deep water, with no other sediments.

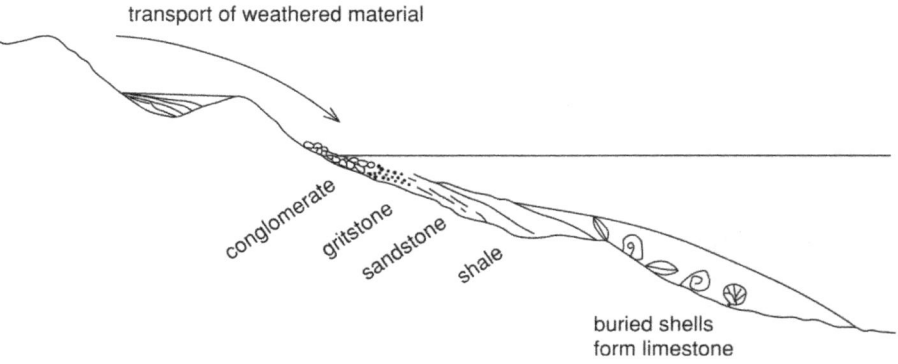

Figure 3.13 The deposition of sedimentary rocks

Sediment (becomes)	Sedimentary rock
Gravel	Conglomerate
Coarse sand	Gritstone
Sand	Sandstone
Mud	Mudstone
Silt	Shale
Calcium shells	Limestone
Silica shells	Flint, chert
Salts	Rock salt, gypsum
Plant fossils	Peat, coal, bitumen

METAMORPHIC ROCKS

Metamorphic (literally, 'change shape') rocks are formed when an original rock type (which may be igneous, sedimentary or metamorphic) is altered by the effect of heat or pressure, or both. This heat or pressure is easily generated in unstable areas of the Earth's crust where volcanic or earthquake activity is common.

Examples of *heat* metamorphism are as follows:

- *igneous rocks* become *gneiss* (broadly banded) or *schist* (narrowly banded);
- *limestone* becomes *marble*;
- *sandstone* becomes *quartzite*.

As an example of *pressure* metamorphism:

- *shale* becomes *slate*.

FACT POINT

Rocks' hardness can be measured on the Mohs scale, which measures the ability of minerals to scratch each other. Talc is measured at 1 on the Mohs scale, being very soft. However, diamond is 10, being the hardest known natural material.

FACT POINT

Diamonds vs graphite

Both diamonds and graphite are made up of carbon atoms, but they both have very different properties and uses. Most natural diamonds are formed at high temperature and pressure, in the Earth's mantle, from carbon-containing minerals brought to the Earth's surface by volcanic eruptions. Graphite, on the other hand, occurs mostly in metamorphic rocks as a result of carbon material changing into crystalline graphite.

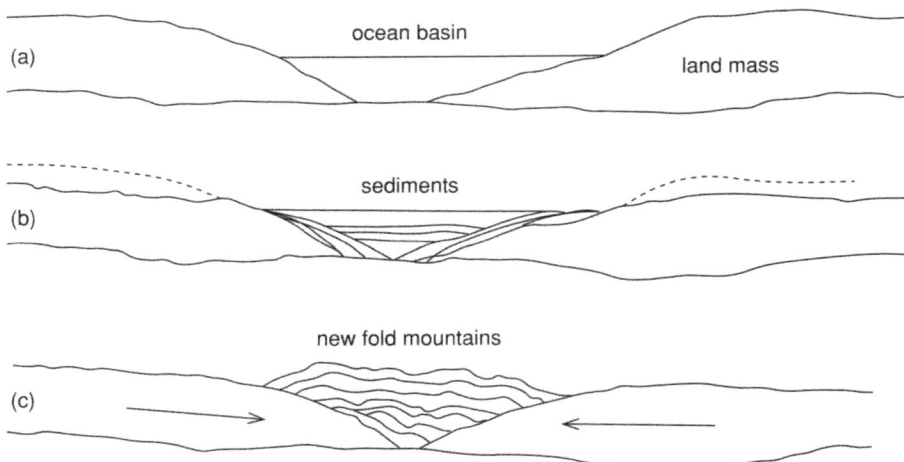

Figure 3.14 The rock cycle

It is possible to imagine a long-term rock cycle as follows: Following a *mountain-building* period, and the uplift of parts of the Earth's surface, possibly by buckling of the crust associated with the movement of continental plates, *erosion* begins, followed by the *deposition* under water of transported sediments. These sediments are compressed to form sedimentary rocks, which eventually fill the basins between former continental masses. When the continental masses move towards each other, again as a result of *crustal movement*, the folding and buckling of the sediments result in the formation of *new fold mountains*, and the process begins again.

Figure 3.22a represents two continental land masses separated by an ocean basin. Over many millions of years the surfaces of the land masses are lowered by erosion, and the weathered debris is transported into the ocean, eventually to become sedimentary rock strata (layers) of great thickness (Figure 3.22b).

Finally, when the two land masses are forced towards each other, the sediments in the ocean basin are buckled and uplifted to form fold mountains, as in Figure 3.22c. It is thought, for example, that the Mediterranean basin may be the remains of a large trench that filled with sediments transported from what are now Europe and Africa and then suffered uplift when the African plate moved against the Scandinavian shield, resulting in the formation of the present-day Alps.

CONCEPT CONFUSION

Bricks and cement are not rocks, as they are man-made, unlike naturally formed rocks. Children can use magnifying glasses to distinguish the difference between rocks and concrete.

SOIL FORMATION AND CHARACTERISTICS

The rocks that make up the foundations of the present-day landscape are often not visible as outcrops at all. This is because they lie beneath a layer of soil. As was pointed out in Key Idea 3.2, soil is the valuable natural material on which plant life (and therefore all animal life) depends.

Soil is a mixture of four main ingredients:

1   weathered particles of bedrock;
2   decaying organic matter (humus);
3   water;
4   air.

The larger particles of weathered rock tend to be at depth, and the largest concentration of humus is near the surface of the soil. It is the decay of organic matter that recycles the nutrients on which the plant cover depends. The gaps between the particles of soil will be filled with air near to the surface, and with water at a greater depth.

The nature of the soil in any particular place will be governed by a number of factors, including:

* the *type of bedrock* – a sandstone will tend to form a well-drained, gritty, *sandy* soil, usually light brown in colour. A shale or mudstone will cause a poorly drained, blue-grey, sticky *clay* soil to develop. A well-balanced mixture of sand and clay will give rise to a rich brown *loam* soil, and chalk or limestone will produce a thin, dark soil that tends to support grassland;
* the *climate* of the locality – areas with heavy rainfall will tend to develop waterlogged or poorly drained acid soils, whereas less rainfall will give rise to better-drained loams;
* the *flatness* or *steepness* of the slope – flat areas produce impeded drainage and waterlogged soils, whereas, on steep slopes, soil creep will cause the soils at the bottom of the slope to be thicker than those at the top;
* the *length of time* since the bedrock was exposed to weathering – the most mature soils are those that have been undisturbed for longest; those areas most recently exposed to weathering (such as areas of bare rock exposed by the melting of glacier ice) will give rise to the thinnest, 'skeletal' soils.

A useful and simple test of soil type is to take a small amount of soil in the hand and then try to roll it into a spindle. A clay soil will roll into thin spindles, a sandy soil will form poor or crumbly spindles, and a loam soil will be 'in between' these two types.

Similarly, if soils are placed in pots and 'watered', the speed at which the water disappears will be an indication of the permeability of the soil. A clay soil will be relatively impermeable – the water will take a long time to disappear. A sandy soil will have good permeability, and the water will 'drain away' quickly. Once again, a loam soil will be 'in between' the other two examples.

FACT POINT

Along with air and water, soil is one of the Earth's most important resources. Without it, we would not be able to grow food, support the diversity of plants and animals, or build houses, roads and infrastructure. In one teaspoon of garden soil, there are more than 6 billion organisms (more than the Earth's human population).

KEY IDEA 3.4 SUMMARY

The Earth's crust is made of rock made from different combinations of minerals. Rocks have many uses, from building materials to road construction. They are mined for minerals such as diamonds and metals (for example, platinum, copper and iron). Materials from rocks are also used for make-up production, toothpaste and even circuit boards. They are also a major component of soil, along with decaying plant and animal matter and minerals.

Rocks give us important information about how the Earth formed millions of years ago. The same strategies can be used to find out about other planets, such as Mars. For example, rocks from Mars may tell us if there was ever liquid water present.

Working scientifically

- *Sorting and grouping*: Children can group soils by different characteristics, including colour, texture and drainage.
- *Observing and researching*: Children can research and identify the rocks in the local area. Not only will this allow them to deduce what conditions were like long ago, but it may also indicate how rocks influenced local industries – for example, mining and production of building materials. Having a pretend rock museum will allow them to display their locally found rocks with some information on their history.
- *Pattern-seeking*: Children can sequence fossils according to how deep in the ground they were found, looking at clues for how preserved animals changed over time. This activity can support understanding of what fossils tell us about ancient living things.

Discussion point

- *How old are rocks?* Some rocks are as old as the Earth itself, but others are formed from recent volcano eruptions, such as those in Iceland and Hawaii. Scientists use something called relative age dating (i.e. newer rock layers will be found on top of older rocks) and absolute age dating (the real age of the rock, depending on fossils identified in it or radioactive decay in the rock!).

Application

Palaeontologists study rocks to find clues about the Earth's past, building a record of events that occurred millions of years ago. They use fossils to understand extinct and living organisms. Palaeontology does not only occur around the world: children may be inspired by astrogeology, looking at the structure and combination of planets and other bodies in the solar system.

Modelling fossil formation

- *Mineral replacement*: All the soft parts of an organism are decayed, leaving skeleton remains. These are buried, and, over time, the minerals are crystallized, hardening the skeleton remains and leaving fossils. A straw model can be submerged in jelly, and, once the jelly sets, the jelly can be squeezed out of the straws, representing the shape of the straw model.
- *Preservation*: The whole organism is preserved as a result of falling somewhere where there is no oxygen – for example, in resin, such as amber. This can be modelled by putting a plastic toy in jelly.
- *Impression*: The organism can be trapped in a rock and then it dissolves completely. Minerals enter the space and harden, forming a cast. This can be modelled by pouring plaster of Paris into a plasticine mould.

Cross-curricular links

- *Geography and history*: Studying volcanoes and earthquakes can give children a deeper understanding of rock formation. Looking at famous rock formations, buildings around the world and historical uses of stones will help children explore different rock types and their uses.
- *Computing*: Children can use and produce branching keys to identify different rocks. They can also use digital microscopes to make closer observations of rocks and soils.
- *Literacy*: Children can write fact files on different rocks, making their own rock museum. They can also create short story boards on how dinosaurs formed into fossils. They could be encouraged to use descriptive words when labelling rocks and soils.

Health and safety

- Ensure hands are washed following handling of soils and rocks. Children should be warned about the potential hazard of contaminated soils and not touching eyes and mouth when handling soils.
- Warn children to take care when observing rocks in case of any sharp edges.

Assessment for learning

PMI: When learning about rocks and soils, children approach the topic from many different angles, having had many different prior experiences. A useful retrospective activity to find out what they have learned in a rocks and soils topic is to complete a 'plus, minus, interesting' activity. Children record positive aspects of their learning (what they enjoyed, what they learned, what was useful), negative aspects (what they found challenging, what they didn't find useful) and interesting aspects (new questions, interesting facts). This could either be conducted independently or as a whole class, using post-it notes.

KEY IDEA 3.5

The water cycle

All living things depend on water for their survival. In addition to the part it plays in essential life processes, people also use water (among other things) for transport, industrial processes, sanitation and recreation.

There is a finite amount of water on the planet, and the small amount that is readily available is recycled over long periods of time. It is said that the water that today wells up in the Roman baths in the city of Bath fell as rain on the Mendip Hills 30,000 years ago. The proportion of the Earth's water supply that is available to living things is very small, as the following details show:

- 71 per cent of the Earth's surface is covered by water;
- 97 per cent of that water is salty, and 3 per cent is fresh;
- of the fresh water, up to 85 per cent exists in the form of ice;
- therefore, only 15 per cent of 3 per cent – that is, 0.45 per cent – of the Earth's water blanket is freely available at or near the Earth's surface, and it circulates in what is known as the water cycle.

In simple terms, the water cycle proceeds as follows:

- Fresh water from the atmosphere falls on to the Earth's land surface as *precipitation* (rain, hail, sleet, snow and, in some areas. fog and mist).
- Some of this water seeps into the ground, and some runs off the surface, eventually to collect in streams, rivers, lakes and the sea.
- Some groundwater is drawn up into plants and eventually returns to the atmosphere as water vapour (a gas) by a process known as *transpiration*. This involves the diffusion of water vapour out of the tissue of the plant leaves through small pores known as stomata. To see evidence of this process, seal a polythene bag over a growing plant for a short while – the inside of the bag will soon be covered with water droplets that have condensed from the water vapour transpired by the plant. Very large volumes of water are returned to the atmosphere by this process. It is said that a large oak tree transpires the equivalent of 360 litres of water per hour on a sunny day!
- Some surface water returns to the atmosphere by *evaporation* (see Key Idea 3.1: Changes of state) from the surface of rivers, ponds, lakes and the sea. This process can be rapid, even at normal atmospheric temperatures. To observe this, draw a chalk line round a shallow playground puddle and return to it regularly to compare the newly dried area as the puddle shrinks.
- The cycle is completed when water droplets, visible as clouds, form by the *condensation* of water vapour in the atmosphere. Eventually, coalescing droplets grow to a size large enough to fall from the sky as rain, hail, sleet or snow, depending on the prevailing weather conditions.

A diagram of the water cycle can be found at Figure 2.53.

CONCEPT CONFUSION

It is a common inaccuracy to think that clouds are made of gas. However, they are made from tiny droplets of water suspended in the air. The droplets can be held up by moving air because they are very small and do not weigh very much. Both mist and fog are a suspension of water droplets in the air, but the density of water droplets in mist is less than that in fog.

KEY IDEA 3.5 SUMMARY

Water is essential for life. Having an understanding of the processes involved in the water cycle allows us to appreciate how we obtain fresh drinking water and what affects our weather.

Our current understanding is that the Earth is the only planet in the solar system to have liquid water on its surface. The continuous recycling of water on Earth has happened for billions of years, meaning the water we drink has inevitably been on an exciting historical journey!

Working scientifically

- *Observation*: Children can observe the processes involved in the water cycle by putting water in a resealable bag and using tape to attach it to a sunny window. As the sun heats the water, the water will evaporate, and, when it gets colder, drops of water will run down the side of the bag, demonstrating condensation.
- *Comparative testing*: Children can compare the weight of water in liquid and solid forms by placing ice cubes in a Petri dish or jar on some digital scales and recording their weight before and after they have melted. Be careful to make sure any condensation has been wiped off the outside of the jar or Petri dish during the process.
- *Fair testing*: The speed at which water can evaporate can be investigated by putting equal-sized squares of damp cloth in different conditions to see which dries most quickly.

Application

It is important to appreciate water as a precious resource. Children should, therefore, be encouraged to consider water-saving methods, both at school and at home. They may even consider new water-collecting and -reusing systems that could be used in the future. They may also research and consider solutions to water shortages around the world.

Discussion point

- *Why does water expand when it freezes?* When water freezes, its volume increases. Water molecules as liquid are closer together than in the crystal structure of ice. As a result, water takes up less space as a liquid than it does as a solid. This is unusual, as most solids expand when they change into a liquid. Ice caps float because water expands on freezing, so that, on melting, the water will contract, causing no change to the water level.

Cross-curricular activities

- *Literacy*: Children can write a story of the journey of a water molecule, which they could present as a cartoon strip, to demonstrate their understanding of the processes involved. Children can also create poems describing water, snow and clouds.

- *Numeracy*: Children can investigate, record and compare how much water is used in different routine activities, such as using the washing machine, having a bath or shower or washing the car. They can use this information to compare how much water their families use. In geometry, children can investigate the symmetry in snowflakes before creating their own.
- *Drama*: Children could represent the water cycle (the journey of a water droplet) by acting and describing. Hot seating could be used, whereby children take on a part of the water cycle while others ask them questions – for example: How do you feel? Where are you going? Alternatively, children could act out the stages of the water cycle in mime.

Health and safety

- When experimenting with water, it is important to use absorbent material – for example, sheets of newspaper – to cover the area, to avoid slipping.
- If hot water is required, ensure adult supervision.

Assessment for learning

Self-assessment: When writing a story or cartoon about the journey of a water droplet, children could be asked to decide whether they have met the objective, by assessing their work against a success criterion. For example: have they used appropriate scientific vocabulary, have they included all of the main stages in the water cycle, have they identified what causes the water to change? They could record red, amber or green against each success criterion.

Chemistry: Schools National Curriculum coverage and progression

Below is listed each of the component parts of the relevant programme of study of science in the NC (DfE, 2013). The table demonstrates how each Key Idea is developed through progression of knowledge in the Key Stage 1 and 2 programmes of study.

Year group	Programme of study	Statutory requirements
Key Idea 3.1: The particulate nature of matter		
Year 4	States of matter	Compare and group materials together, according to whether they are solids, liquids or gases (*The states of matter*)
Year 4	States of matter	Observe that some materials change state when they are heated or cooled, and measure or research the temperature at which this happens in degrees Celsius (°C; *Changes of state*)
Key Idea 3.2: The classification of materials		
Year 1	Everyday materials	Distinguish between an object and the material from which it is made (*Questions about objects and materials*) Identify and name a variety of everyday materials, including wood, plastic, glass, metal, water and rock (*Natural and manufactured materials*) Describe the simple physical properties of a variety of everyday materials (*Properties and characteristics of materials*) Compare and group together a variety of everyday materials on the basis of their simple physical properties (*Properties and characteristics of materials*)
Year 2	Use of everyday materials	Identify and compare the suitability of a variety of everyday materials, including wood, metal, plastic, glass, brick, rock, paper and cardboard for particular uses (*The uses of materials*)

Year group	Programme of study	Statutory requirements
Year 5	Properties and changes of materials	Compare and group together everyday materials on the basis of their properties, including their hardness, solubility, transparency, conductivity (electrical and thermal) and response to magnets (*Properties and characteristics of materials*) Give reasons, based on evidence from comparative and fair tests, for the particular uses of everyday materials, including metals, wood and plastic (*Considerations for the choice of materials*)
Key Idea 3.3: Changing materials		
Year 2	Use of everyday materials	Find out how the shapes of solid objects made from some materials can be changed by squashing, bending, twisting and stretching (*Change in shape*)
Year 5	Properties and changes of materials	Know that some materials will dissolve in liquid to form a solution, and describe how to recover a substance from a solution (*Physical changes*) Use knowledge of solids, liquids and gases to decide how mixtures might be separated, including by filtering, sieving and evaporating (*Separating mixtures*) Demonstrate that dissolving, mixing and changes of state are reversible changes (*Physical changes, see also: The water cycle*) Explain that some changes result in the formation of new materials, and that this kind of change is not usually reversible, including changes associated with burning and the action of acid on bicarbonate of soda (*Chemical reactions and heat energy*)
Key Idea 3.4: The rock cycle		
Year 3	Rocks	Compare and group together different kinds of rock on the basis of their appearance and simple physical properties (*Igneous, sedimentary, metamorphic rocks*) Describe in simple terms how fossils are formed when things that have lived are trapped within rock (*The rock cycle*) Recognize that soils are made from rocks and organic matter (*Soil formation and characteristics*)
3.5 The water cycle		
Year 4	States of matter	Identify the part played by evaporation and condensation in the water cycle and associate the rate of evaporation with temperature (*The water cycle*)

REFERENCE

DfE. (2013) National curriculum in England: Primary curriculum. Department for Education. Available at: www.gov.uk/government/publications/national-curriculum-in-england-primary-curriculum (accessed 9 April 2017).

SECTION FOUR

Physics

SOME KEY IDEAS IN PHYSICS

4.1 *Sources and forms of energy: Energy is derived from a variety of sources, exists in a variety of forms, and can be stored, released and transferred*[1]

4.2 *Forces: Forces can make things start to move, can make moving things speed up, slow down, change direction or stop, and can make things change their shape*

4.3 *The Earth and beyond*

Figure 4.0 Energy

NOTE

1   Please note that Key Idea 4.1 has been subdivided into four sections for easy reference: The primary sources of energy, Forms of energy, Light, Sound.

Sources and forms of energy

Energy is derived from a variety of sources, exists in a variety of forms, and can be stored, released and transferred.

INTRODUCTION

Almost all of the physical interactions in the universe can be explained in terms of the transfer of energy. What follows is an attempt to describe, in a logical sequence, the sources and forms of energy that affect all our lives. Some of the concepts explored are not *directly* concerned with the Science NC at Key Stages 1 and 2. The hope, however, is that the knowledge and understanding implicit in the concepts outlined below may be seen by teachers as being of value, not as optional background information, but as basic to a deeper understanding of the processes of physical science. Where a concept directly supports an NC requirement, this is indicated in the text.

Some definitions

Terms such as energy, work, power, force (and forces) and pressure often cause confusion to people who may not have had the opportunity to study physics in any depth (and sometimes even if they have!).

Many of these terms describe interconnecting processes, and some of the confusion results from their interchangeable use in everyday speech. The next section will attempt to define some of these terms in scientific language, while at the same time setting them into everyday contexts in which they are more easily understandable.

To start with, *energy* is the *capacity to perform work*. To put it the other way round, for any work to be done – the boiling of a kettle, the moving of a pile of bricks, the synthesis of a protein molecule – energy is required. Energy is measured in terms of work done, and the unit of measurement is the *joule* (J).

Mechanical work is done when a force moves an object through a measured distance. *Work* (in joules) = *force* (in newtons) × *distance* moved in the direction of the force (in metres).

A possible cause of confusion here is the use of the same unit of measurement, the joule, for a number of apparently different processes. For instance, the joule is used to measure the quantity of energy produced during a chemical reaction that liberates heat – for example:

> 12 g of carbon burnt completely in the presence of oxygen will liberate 393.5 kJ of energy (kJ = kilojoule)

The joule can also be used to measure the amount of mechanical work done – for example:

> when a force of 1 N moves something through a distance of 1 m, 1 J of work is done

Although these examples may seem to refer to widely differing processes, what is being measured in both cases is the energy produced by, or causing, the particular effect.

Power is defined as the amount of *work done* or of *energy transformed* (joules) *per second* and is measured in watts (W). So, a 60-W light bulb, when lit, is transforming 60 J of energy (or doing 60 J of work) per second.

THE PRIMARY SOURCES OF ENERGY

Bonding within and between atoms and molecules

The ultimate source of energy in the universe is that which exists in the bonding between the particles in the atom, and in the bonds between the atoms and molecules of all matter. All of the known sources and forms of energy can eventually be traced back to the attraction and repulsion of atomic and molecular particles. These forces of attraction and repulsion are thought to be of four basic kinds: strong nuclear, weak nuclear, electromagnetic and gravitational forces.

A fundamental principle of science that relates to energy is the *law of conservation of energy*. Basically, this states that energy can be converted from one form to another, but cannot be created or destroyed. What is believed to happen is that energy is not 'used up' by a system, but is transferred or converted into other forms of energy. So, the energy released by the combustion of petrol fuel in a car is converted into heat, sound, mechanical movement, electricity (which is then used as a further energy supply) and so on. None of the original energy derived from the breaking of the hydrocarbon bonds in the fuel is 'lost', but it can all be accounted for, at least theoretically, in terms of energy transfer or conversion.

TEACHING IDEA

Using a money analogy, we can explain that energy does not simply disappear. Energy is moved from one place to another, in the same way that our money is moved from our savings to a supermarket cash register. Like energy, money can be saved until we want to use it!

Modern versions of this principle would extend the law to include mass as well as energy. Albert Einstein, with the famous equation $e = mc^2$, showed that mass and energy were theoretically interconvertible (e = energy; m = mass; c = the speed of light, a constant).

It is now known that, when matter releases its energy, a small loss of mass results. In normal chemical reactions, the rate of conversion of mass to energy is so small that it is difficult to measure accurately. In nuclear reactions, however, so much energy is released that the change in mass is large enough to be measurable.

The effects of the bonding forces within and between atoms and molecules can be classified in terms of a variety of primary energy sources, resulting in a range of further sources of transferable energy:

- *bonding within atoms* (strong nuclear force) gives rise to *nuclear energy*;
- *bonding and transfer between atoms and molecules* (*weak nuclear* and *electromagnetic forces*) gives rise directly to chemical, electromagnetic and strain energy;
- *gravity* (the *force of attraction between masses*) gives rise to *potential* and *kinetic energy*.

Famous scientist factbox

Name	Albert Einstein (1879–1955), German physicist
Link to NC	Year 5 – Forces
Famous for	He produced one of the most famous equations of all time: $E = mc^2$ (energy equals mass multiplied by the speed of light squared)
	He also developed the theory of relativity. Imagine it is raining, and the rain is blowing against your back. If you ran, the rain wouldn't hit your back as hard, travelling more slowly than you. Scientists would say the rain was travelling more slowly *relative* to you
Working scientifically	Einstein was a problem-solver. He had a strategy of breaking down problems and solving them in stages
Impact on society	For cars and phones to have accurate GPS (global positioning system), satellites have to take Einstein's relativity theory into account. Satellites are travelling quite fast and, as they are about 20,000 km above Earth, experiencing gravity that is weaker, so the relativistic effects need to be taken into account to maintain accuracy. Einstein's famous equation relating mass and energy was the basis for developing nuclear power, which may help us to develop clean, cheap and abundant energy in the future
Controversies	Einstein's Nobel Prize for his theory of relativity was subject to argument for years before it was honoured. Many other scientists argued that it was unproven and tried to reject it

Two further ideas are worth noting:

1   The *vibration of atoms and molecules of matter, intensified by the transfer of energy from other sources*, gives rise to *heat and light energy.*
2   Some of the energy derived from these sources can be transferred or transmitted by *waves.*

One such 'family' of waves is that which relates to the electromagnetic spectrum, where energy transferred from electrons is transmitted in wave form. Another example is that of *sound*, where the mechanical energy of a vibrating material is also transferred in wave form.

FORMS OF ENERGY

The following sections provide further detail on the nature and characteristics of the forms of energy listed above.

Nuclear energy

The bonds that hold together nuclear particles of matter involve very large amounts of energy. It is said, for example, that, if it were possible to convert (and conserve) all the nuclear energy in just 1 g of matter, it would keep a 1,000-W light bulb burning for 2,850 years!

In some cases, this energy is released slowly, and in small amounts, under natural conditions (as in radioactive decay). In others, very large amounts of energy are released rapidly by the deliberate splitting (or fission) of atomic nuclei.

Radioactive decay

Some elements have isotopes (see Key Idea 3.1: The periodic table) that are relatively unstable and that lose atomic particles at a given, measurable rate under natural conditions. Such isotopes are said to emit radiation and to be radioactive. In emitting the atomic particles, the radioactive isotopes are said to decay, and the rate of decay is measured as the half-life, that is, the time taken for half of a given mass of the isotope to decay.

In decaying, an isotope may:

- lose positively charged particles from the atomic nuclei (alpha particles). Because of the resulting loss of atomic mass, this has the effect of converting the original element into one that is placed earlier in the periodic table. An example of alpha decay is the natural decay of uranium, which, through a number of conversions, eventually decays to form lead;
- lose negatively charged electrons (beta particles). This occurs as the result of a nuclear neutron becoming a proton, and the effect is to move the element 'up' the periodic table. An example of beta decay is the decay of carbon-14 to nitrogen, a process that takes many thousands of years and that is used in the accurate dating of organic remains;
- emit, as high-energy electromagnetic waves, the highly penetrating (and, therefore, potentially damaging) gamma rays, which have no electric charge.

Nuclear fission

When an atom of the radioactive isotope uranium-235 is bombarded by neutrons, it is possible for the atomic nucleus to absorb one of the 'incoming' neutrons. The resultant, highly unstable, uranium-236 nucleus tends to split (hence, nuclear fission), forming the nuclei of two new elements – barium and krypton, for example – while, at the same time, releasing two or three high-energy neutrons and a large amount of energy (300 billion J). If this process is controlled so that one of the released neutrons itself bombards and is absorbed by another uranium-235 nucleus, a chain reaction results that can produce large amounts of energy, converted as heat.

This is exactly what happens inside a nuclear reactor. Naturally occurring uranium contains about 99.3 per cent stable uranium-238, and 0.7 per cent radioactive uranium-235, a mixture that will not sustain a chain reaction. U-235 can be enriched, however, so that the fuel rods in a nuclear reactor contain 97 per cent U-238 and 3 per cent U-235. These fuel rods are sheathed in graphite to slow down the movement of the bombarding neutrons, thereby increasing the chances of absorption of neutrons by the U-235 nuclei. In addition, rods of boron steel can be lowered into the reactor to absorb neutrons if the reaction is proceeding too fast.

In a conventional, gas-cooled nuclear reactor, the heat produced by the fission reaction is absorbed by carbon dioxide gas that is pumped through the reactor. This gas, at 400°C, is then passed through water boilers, producing steam, which is then used to turn turbines to generate electricity, as in a conventional fossil-fuel-fired power station.

If the neutron bombardment were unchecked, the rate of absorption of neutrons were not moderated by boron steel, and the uranium fuel were all of the U-235 type, then an uncontrolled nuclear explosion would occur, and this is the basis of the 'atom bomb'.

Nuclear fusion

When atomic nuclei join together (fusion), even more energy is liberated than during the fission process. In the natural universe this process is happening in the Sun (and, indeed, in all other stars). Nuclei of 'heavy' hydrogen (known as deuterium) collide and combine in conditions of high temperature and pressure, forming helium nuclei and releasing large amounts of energy. The burning of the Sun is, in effect, an uncontrolled nuclear explosion. It has been calculated that the Sun is converting 4.2 million tonnes of mass into energy *every second*. When considering that the conversion of *1 g* of mass results in the production of 300 billion J, the power of the Sun as a producer of energy is placed into clear focus.

A present-day scientific controversy concerns claims made in the late 1980s that nuclear fusion had been achieved under 'cold' conditions – that is, involving normal laboratory glassware. Researchers claimed that significant amounts of heat had been generated during the electrolysis of deuterium oxide (heavy water). Their claim was that this heat generation could not be explained simply in terms of an exothermic reaction (see Key Idea 3.3: Chemical reactions and heat energy) and may, therefore, have occurred as a result of nuclear fusion. The potential industrial and commercial significance of this claim is obvious, but other workers have refuted the claim, stating that the experiment has been unrepeatable to date, and the controversy continues.

Whether derived from fission or fusion, the energy contained in the atomic nucleus can be released and transferred into other forms. In peaceful applications, this usually involves the use of the heat from the reaction to generate electricity for industrial or domestic purposes. A more 'strategic' role for nuclear power is the use of the resultant electricity to drive surface ships and submarines, or to generate the massively destructive force of a nuclear explosion.

It is perhaps appropriate to use these latter examples in order to reflect on the ethical, moral, social and political implications of, and the dilemmas that almost always result from, the application of scientific knowledge. There are no easy answers, but surely we should all continue to ask questions of the decision-makers?

TEACHING IDEA

Debating the controversies of nuclear energy

Children could debate the pros and cons of using nuclear energy. Some may argue why it may provide a good solution to human energy demands. However, nuclear plants are expensive to build, and accidental leakage of radioactive chemicals poses extreme risks to health. Radioactive nuclear waste is also expensive to store safely, long term.

CONCEPTS TO SUPPORT KEY STAGE 2

Chemical energy

As outlined in Key Idea 3.3 (Chemical reactions and heat energy), energy is released when the bonds between the atoms and molecules of compounds are broken during chemical reactions, and the total energy of the products of the reaction is less than that of the original substances.

CONCEPT CONFUSION

It is useful to highlight that batteries store chemical energy. Through reactions with different metals and an acid, the chemical energy is converted into electrical energy. This could be demonstrated by using a potato- or fruit-powered clock.

This release of chemical energy is most commonly seen during reactions that involve oxidation (the burning, or combustion, of substances in the presence of oxygen). Those substances that readily give up their energy when burnt, and particularly those that contain carbon, can be used as fuels, that is, as convenient sources of energy. Examples would include:

- the burning of renewable natural fuels, such as wood and charcoal, to release energy in the form of heat and/or light (sound is also generated, but is, in the context of heat generation, a 'waste' of energy);
- the combustion of 'fossil fuels', such as coal, oil and natural gas, for the same purposes;
- the respiration by plants and animals of the energy-rich organic compounds derived from food in order to provide energy for life processes.

In any of the above examples, the basic 'chemistry' of the reaction is that compounds of carbon and hydrogen (hydrocarbons in the case of natural and fossil fuels, carbohydrates in the case of plant and animal tissues) react with oxygen from the air to produce carbon dioxide, water and energy. The chemical formula for the burning of natural gas (methane) is:

$$CH_4 \text{ methane} + 2O_2 \text{ oxygen} \longrightarrow \text{burning} \longrightarrow CO_2 \text{ carbon dioxide} + 2H_2O \text{ water} + \text{energy heat}$$

The formula for the cellular respiration of glucose is:

$$C_6H_{12}O_6 \text{ glucose} + 6O_2 \text{ oxygen} \longrightarrow \text{respiration} \longrightarrow 6CO_2 \text{ carbon dioxide} + 6H_2O \text{ water} + \text{energy (chemical energy bonding)}$$

The basic requirement of most fuels is that they should be efficient in the production of heat, which can be converted to other forms of energy. In some cases, this heat energy is transferred to light by the increased vibration of the molecules of the substances involved in the reaction. An example would be the burning of candles made of paraffin wax, where the heat produced is locally intense enough to cause the particles of carbon to glow white hot – hence, the light of the candle flame.

The heat produced by the burning of fuels may also be used:

- directly, to heat water for the production of steam for industrial processes, or to heat other substances, for example, in the smelting of metals, or for domestic use (for cooking in areas dependent on renewable fuel sources) or for central heating;
- for conversion into electricity for industrial and domestic use (see below).

FACT POINT

What is the greenhouse effect?

The greenhouse effect is a natural process in which greenhouse gases (carbon dioxide, methane, nitrous oxide, ozone and water vapour) in our atmosphere trap heat to insulate the Earth's surface. However, human activity (for example, burning fossil fuels and cattle farming) is increasing the amount of greenhouse gases in our atmosphere, trapping more heat and contributing to climate change.

In the case of some fuels, the speed of reaction is so rapid as to be explosive. This property has been used effectively (although not particularly efficiently) in the development of the internal combustion engine. The explosive power of the energy release that takes place inside the cylinders of a car engine when an air–petrol mixture burns is converted into the mechanical energy of movement, electromagnetic energy for the ignition system, windscreen wipers, central locking system and so on, heat, light and sound.

Long-term energy transfer

In terms of the Earth, the ultimate source of usable energy is the Sun, our nearest star. It is the Sun that provides us with radiant energy in the form of light and heat, and it has been doing so for a long time – modern estimates put the age of the Sun at 6 billion years, and that of the Earth at 4.6 billion years.

It is interesting to track the sequence of energy transfers that would have taken place during the geological formation of fossil fuels and their subsequent recovery and combustion in modern times.

- The nuclei of deuterium atoms in the Sun collided and combined to form helium nuclei, with an accompanying release of (nuclear) energy.
- Some of this energy would transfer to the Earth in the form of solar radiation of heat and light.
- Green plants would use the light (electromagnetic) energy from the Sun to synthesize carbohydrates (chemical energy).
- During the Carboniferous period of geological time (between 350 and 270 million years ago) some of the green plants were preserved without decaying in shallow marshes or lagoons (a modern-day equivalent would be a peat bog).
- Other plants (in particular, marine algae) would have been eaten by aquatic animals whose remains themselves were preserved by a covering of sediments on the ocean floor.
- Over spans of geological time, the preserved plants became coal, and the preserved animals turned into oil, with an accompanying production of natural gas (hence, *fossil fuels*). The original carbohydrates present in the preserved plant and animal tissues were fossilized as hydrocarbons.
- As the fossil fuels have been recovered and burnt in modern times, the chemical energy that has been 'locked' into the bonding of the hydrocarbon compounds for up to 350 million years has been released and transferred for the benefit of present-day people, but with the consequent problem of the disposal of waste products.

In the case of coal ash, disposal is often in landfill sites or out at sea. If nuclear waste products are considered also, the problem is twofold. First, there is the need to make highly radioactive materials safe, and second, there is the need to ensure the security of materials with obvious military significance – another example of the interface between science, society at large and the decision-makers.

With reference to the carbon dioxide produced as a result of the burning of fossil fuels, the commonest response of the industrialized nations has been simply to discharge it directly into the atmosphere.

In addition to the possibility of global warming as a result of this increase in the amount of carbon dioxide in the atmosphere (see Key Idea 2.6: The carbon cycle), one of the important points to remember about the consumption of fossil fuels is that they are non-renewable (at least in terms of human time spans). The modern-day consumption of fossil fuels represents a 'cashing-in' of energy that was 'banked' millions of years ago. It is, in effect, a once-and-for-all process and should, therefore, be a cause for concern. Although coal reserves are extensive (if unpopular), supplies of oil and natural gas may well run out over the next 50 years or so, and this will have a serious impact on transport systems and policies worldwide.

Renewable (i.e. non-chemical and non-nuclear) forms of energy may well assume increasing importance in future years, as supplies of fossil fuels decline. Those forms already in use include:

- solar energy, where the radiant heat energy from the Sun is converted directly into electricity in 'solar cells';
- tidal energy, where the kinetic energy of moving water is converted into electricity at tidal barrages;
- wind energy, where the kinetic energy of air moving from high- to low-pressure areas in the atmosphere is converted into electricity at 'wind farms';
- hydroelectricity, where the kinetic energy of falling water is converted into electric power.

In addition, the direct conversion of the motion of sea waves has been used experimentally to generate electricity, but it is unlikely that this will ever become fully commercially viable as an alternative energy source.

TEACHING IDEA

Pizza-box solar ovens

Children could develop an understanding of how to harness the Sun's heat energy by making pizza-box solar ovens. Simply by lining the inside of a pizza box with foil and cutting out a large window in the lid and covering it with cling film, you can make your basic solar oven. Leave it in direct sunlight, placing something that can easily melt inside (for example, a marshmallow or chocolate cube) and wait for about 20 minutes. You could even use data loggers to track the temperature change.

Electricity

As has been described above, much of the energy released from within and between atoms and molecules, as well as the kinetic energy derived from molecular motion (tidal, wind, wave and hydro-energy), is converted into electricity. This is because electricity is a convenient form of energy that can be transported relatively easily (along cables or power lines) and can itself be converted into other forms of energy, such as heat, light and sound.

The following sections will deal with the nature of electricity and its behaviour in simple circuits, the generation of electricity, and static electricity.

What is electricity?

At its simplest, an electric current is a flow of electrons. In order for an electric current to flow in a simple circuit, two requirements are necessary:

1   a source of chemical energy;
2   a continuous loop of a conducting material that will allow the transfer of that energy.

The source of chemical energy most commonly used in primary schools is the electric cell (a group of cells form a battery). Batteries are relatively safe, because they produce small

CONCEPT CONFUSION

Electrons do not come out of a battery or wall socket into a circuit and simply change to a form of energy such as light or heat. Electrons are already part of the circuit. The job of the power supply is to 'push' the electrons around the circuit.

amounts of electricity and cause a 'one-way' electron flow – they are said to produce a 'direct current' as opposed to the 'alternating current' and high power of the mains electricity supply. Modern batteries are 'dry' – that is, their chemical constituents are often in solid or gel forms and are commonly encased in metal or strong card. Each will have two terminals or connection points, a positive terminal (the anode) and a negative terminal (the cathode).

The chemical reaction that takes place in the battery produces an excess of electrons at one pole of the battery, and, as electrons have a negative electrical charge, this pole is the negative terminal or cathode. Similarly, there is a net positive charge at the other pole of the battery, and this is the positive terminal or anode. If the two terminals of the battery are connected to a continuous loop (or circuit) of materials that will allow the transfer of those electrons (electrical conductors), the difference in electrical potential between the two battery terminals will cause the electrons to 'flow' through the material, as a current of electricity, from the negative pole (the cathode) to the positive pole (the anode) of the battery.

Note: there is a possibility of confusion here. Although it is now known that the flow of electrons in an electric circuit is from the negative to the positive pole of a battery, the current is traditionally depicted in circuit diagrams as flowing from the positive to the negative pole, and this is termed the 'conventional' current.

The most effective electrical conductors are metals, in particular copper and silver (see Key Idea 3.2: Thermal and electrical conductivity) and graphite (an allotrope of carbon).

TEACHING IDEA

Modelling electricity

Many models and metaphors can be used to understand electricity. One activity involves getting children to sit in a circle with a loop of string that they all hold in the palms of their hands. As one child acts as the battery and starts to move the string, children allow it to pass through their hands. The string acts as the current, flowing around the circuit (which comprises the children allowing the string to move).

Electricity in simple circuits

There are three important variables that relate to electrical circuits: current, voltage and resistance.

The electric *current* in a circuit – the flow of electrons – can be measured as the quantity of charge passing any particular point in the circuit in a given time. The unit of electrical charge is known as the coulomb (which is the charge on 6×10^{18} electrons), and when 1 coulomb of charge flows in 1 second, the current is said to be *1 ampere* (or 1 amp or 1 A). In conventional form:

charge in coulombs (Q) = current in amperes (I) × time (t): $Q = It$

And:

current in amps (I) = charge flowing in coulombs (Q) per second (t): I = Q/t

A useful mental model for this effect is to imagine the *rate of flow* of water in a pipe. The current (of water) flowing through a pipe, in litres per second for example, could be measured by finding the total volume that passed a given point in a particular time, and then dividing that volume by the time of flow in seconds. This would be directly analogous to finding the current in an electrical circuit by dividing the total charge by the time over which the charge was measured – that is, I = Q/t. Similarly, the total volume of flow of water through a pipe could be calculated by multiplying the current in litres per second by the total time of flow in seconds. This would be analogous to Q = It.

What are the factors that affect the current – the rate of flow – of electrons in a simple electric circuit? First, for the current of electrons to flow at all, there must be a difference in electrical potential between different parts of the circuit. This *potential difference* is measured in volts, and a potential difference of *1 volt* (V) between two points will allow *1 J* of work to be done *per coulomb of electric charge* passing between the points. The voltage of a battery is, therefore, a measure of the amount of energy it can provide and is a function of the transfer of energy from the chemical constituents of the battery to the conducting materials of the circuit. A 12-V battery will therefore transfer twice as much energy (12 joules per coulomb) as a 6-V battery.

To continue the water analogy, if an electric current can be represented by the *rate of flow* of water in a pipe, the voltage would correspond to the water *pressure*. This, in a closed circuit such as a central heating system for example, would be governed by the size and power of the water pump (or, in an electrical circuit, by the battery).

The second factor affecting the rate of flow of electrons in a circuit is the *resistance* of the materials in the circuit. Some materials, even though they allow the passage of electrons – that is, they are conductors of electricity – nevertheless can slow down or impede electron transfer. Such materials are known as resistors, and their resistant properties are measured in ohms. A resistance of *1 ohm* will need a voltage of 1 V to drive a current of 1 A through it. Using the water analogy once more, the resistance of different materials (or components) in an electrical circuit can be compared to pipes of different *diameter* through which water must pass in a closed system – the smaller the diameter of the pipe, the greater the resistance to the flow of water.

So, the flow of electrons (the current) in an electrical circuit is related to the potential difference (the voltage) and the resistance of the circuit materials, just as the flow of water through pipes is related to the water pressure and the diameter of the pipes in the system.

These relationships have been summarized in the form of a law, known as Ohm's law, which states that the current flowing in a circuit is proportional to the potential difference (the voltage), providing the temperature of the conductor remains constant.

The formulae that derive from Ohm's law can be rewritten in three different ways, in order to isolate each of the variables in turn:

$$\text{current}(I) = \frac{\text{voltage}(V)}{\text{resistance}(R)} : I = \frac{V}{R}$$

$$\text{voltage}(V) = \text{current}(I) \times \text{resistance}(R): V = IR$$

$$\text{resistance}(R) = \frac{\text{voltage}(V)}{\text{current}(I)} : R = \frac{V}{I}$$

These can be used to begin to understand the behaviour of components in simple electrical circuits.

There are two types of simple circuit:

1   *series* circuits, where component parts are connected 'end to end', and there is only one possible route along which the electric current may flow;
2   *parallel* circuits, where one or more components may be connected 'side by side', so that there is more than one route along which the electric current may flow.

Series circuits

In a series circuit (Figure 4.1a) as there is only one possible route for the flow of electrons:

*   the current will be the same at any point in the circuit, and it can be measured by connecting an ammeter into the circuit, in series;
*   the voltage will vary at different points in the circuit, will be 'shared out' between the components in the circuit, depending on their resistance, and can be measured by connecting a voltmeter across any part of the circuit, in parallel;
*   the total resistance of the circuit will be the sum of the resistances of all the circuit components.

What does this mean in practice? Using a simple example, and referring to Figure 4.2a, if a battery is delivering 6 V, and a lamp has a resistance of 6 ohms, using Ohm's law (and ignoring the resistance of the connecting wires):

$$\text{current (in amps)} = \frac{\text{voltage (in volts)}}{\text{resistance (in ohms)}}$$

$$I = \frac{V}{R} = \frac{6}{6} = 1 \text{ amp}$$

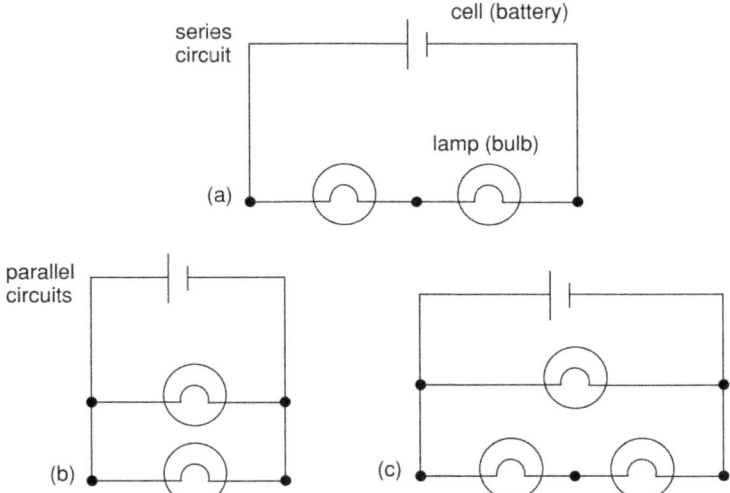

Figure 4.1 Series and parallel circuits

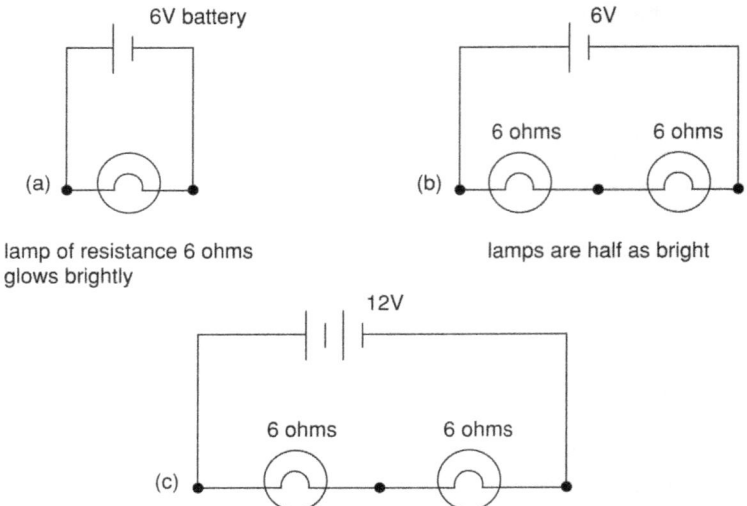

Figure 4.2 Changing effects in series circuits

And so, a current of 1 A is flowing in the circuit. If another lamp were added to the circuit, in series (as in Figure 4.2b), the voltage would remain at 6 V, but the resistance would have been increased to 12 ohms (sum of resistances = 6 + 6). The current would then be:

$$I = \frac{V}{R} = \frac{6}{12} = 0.5 \text{ amps}$$

As a result of the reduction in current to 0.5 A, the two lamps in this circuit would be glowing less brightly than the single one in the previous circuit. If the two lamps in Figure 4.2b were required to glow at the same brightness as the single one in 4.2a, the voltage in the circuit would need to be increased to 12 V, in order to return the current to 1 A (as in Figure 4.2c):

$$I = \frac{V}{R} = \frac{12}{12} = 1 \text{ amp}$$

The current in a series circuit can therefore be raised by increasing the voltage, or lowered by increasing the resistance (by adding more components).

Parallel circuits

In a simple parallel circuit, however (Figures 4.1b and c), there are alternative routes for the flow of electrons, and the current will flow along both. This results in a very different effect when two electric lamps are connected in parallel.

The total resistance in a parallel circuit is calculated from the reciprocal values of the individual resistances; for example:

$$\frac{1}{R(total)} = \frac{2}{R1} + \frac{1}{R2} \text{ etc.}$$

So, in Figure 4.3, the *total resistance of the circuit* is calculated from:

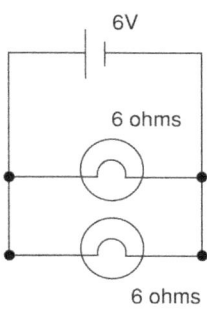

$$\frac{1}{R} = \frac{1}{6} + \frac{1}{6} = \frac{2}{6}$$

if $\dfrac{1}{R} = \dfrac{2}{6}$ then $R = \dfrac{6}{2} = 3$ **ohms**

Again, from Ohm's law: current (in amps) $= \dfrac{\text{voltage (in volts)}}{\text{resistance (in ohms)}} = \dfrac{6 \text{ volts}}{3 \text{ ohms}}$

Figure 4.3
The effect of resistance in a parallel circuit

Therefore, the current flowing in the parallel circuit in Figure 4.3 = 2 A.

As the current of 2 A divides equally between the two routes of the circuit in Figure 4.3 (because they both present the same resistance), it follows that 1 A is flowing along each route, and both lamps will be as bright as the single lamp in the series circuit in Figure 4.2a.

If the aim in designing a circuit was to be able to add extra lamps, while maintaining their brightness, then a parallel circuit would be ideal for the purpose. However, this approach is not without cost, of course, and, in this case, the life of the battery is greatly shortened by the connection of components in parallel.

If the resistances of the 'branch' routes in a parallel circuit are different, more current will flow along the 'easier' route. This means that, in a parallel circuit, the route that presents the lesser resistance to the flow of electrons – that is, the route containing the components with the lower resistance – will have a higher current passing along it than the route that presents the higher resistance. But, whichever way the current 'divides' at the junction in a parallel circuit, the sum of the currents that flow along the 'branches' of the circuit will always be equal to the current entering (or leaving) the junction. So, in the example in Figure 4.1c, if a 3-A current were flowing in the circuit, 2 A would flow through the branch with the single lamp, and 1 A would flow through the branch with two lamps. When the two routes join, the total current of 3 A is restored.

Switches

In some cases, the components (lamps, bells and buzzers, motors and so on) that are connected in an electrical circuit are not required to function continuously. Rather than disconnect the battery each time the current is to be cut off, an alternative is to use switches of various kinds. A switch is simply a device that will 'make and break' a circuit. Usually, when a switch is closed, the circuit is 'made', that is, there is a continuous loop of conducting material connected to the electricity supply, and current can flow. Conversely, when the switch is open, the circuit, and hence the supply, is interrupted.

In addition to normal switches that stay in a fixed position until deliberately changed, there are spring-loaded switches for bell pushes, pressure-sensitive switches for burglar

---

WORKING SCIENTIFICALLY

Children can identify which materials are electrical conductors by investigating which would make a good switch for a circuit. They can make a simple circuit with a gap and test different materials (for example, pens, paper clip, foil, spring, eraser, ruler) to see which complete the circuit. Once identified, children could use the conductive materials to design their own switch.

alarms, light-sensitive switches for street or security lighting, temperature-sensitive switches for heating (or cooling) systems, tilt switches that make a circuit when an object is moved, and so on!

Circuit diagrams

The layout of an electrical circuit can be drawn as a picture or, using conventional symbols, as a circuit diagram. The basic information needed when 'converting' a circuit into a diagram includes the *number and type of components* in the circuit, the *order* in which they are connected and the *number and voltage of the batteries* included in the circuit. Figure 4.4 shows a drawing of a simple circuit and its corresponding circuit diagram. The conventional symbols for components commonly used in simple circuits can be found in the Appendix.

Work and power in electrical circuits

The energy of the electrons flowing in a current in an electric circuit can be transferred to the electrical appliances in the circuit, and the outcomes can be measured in terms of the *work done*. In the element of an electric fire or kettle, the energy is largely transferred as heat. In an electric bell, the energy is transferred as mechanical energy, transported as wave energy and heard as sound. In the filament of an electric lamp, the high resistance of the material to the passage of the current causes the molecules to vibrate at such a rate that both heat and light energy are released.

Overall, the work done, in joules, is measured as voltage × charge, and, as the charge = current × time:

$$\text{work done} = \text{voltage} \times \text{current} \times \text{time} = V \times I \times t$$

As *power* is defined as work done per unit time (see Some definitions, above), power, in watts (W) in an electrical circuit, is defined as:

$$\text{potential difference (voltage)} \times \text{current} = VI$$

This simple equation allows us to discover some interesting insights into the running of electrical appliances. For example, what current would flow through a light bulb rated at 240 V, 60 W? And what would be the resistance of the filament?

As W = VI, that is, 60 = 240 × I (current):

$$\text{the \textbf{current} (I) taken by the lamp is } \frac{60}{240} = \textbf{0.25 amps}$$

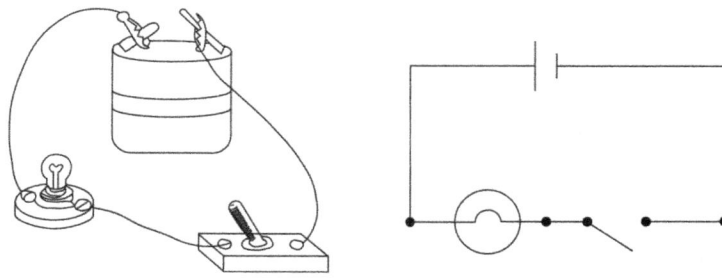

Figure 4.4 A simple circuit and its corresponding circuit diagram

And from ohm's law, resistance = $\dfrac{\text{voltage}}{\text{current}}$

so the **resistance** of the filament = $\dfrac{240}{0.25}$ = **960 ohms**

Using the same formulae for an electric iron rated at 240 V, 1,000 W, we find that the iron takes a current of 4.16 A and has a resistance of 57.69 ohms.

Finally, the 'unit' of electricity in terms of domestic supply is the kilowatt hour (kWh) – that is, the electrical energy that would do 1,000 joules of work per second, supplied for an hour. If we know the unit cost of electricity, and this information is usually included in electricity bills, we can calculate the running costs of our electrical appliances. How much does it cost to boil a kettle? How much to leave a light on overnight? How much to bake a fruit cake? And how much to watch a TV news bulletin? How much cheaper is it to cook a jacket potato in a microwave oven than in a conventional oven (leaving aside the issue of the difference in texture resulting from the two different cooking methods)? (The cost of 1 unit of electricity at the time of writing is 9.91 pence; 1 unit of electricity is 1 kWh, i.e. 1,000 W × 3,600 s = 3,600,000 J.)

- a *kettle* rated at 2,000 W takes *4 minutes to boil*, and so it does: 2,000 (W) × 4 (min) × 60 (s) = 480,000 joules of work;
- a *lamp* rated at 60 W, *left on overnight* (say *8 hours*), does: 60 (watts) × 8 (hours) × 60 (minutes) × 60 (seconds) = 1,728,000 joules of work;
- an *oven* rated at 3,000 W is used for *2 hours* to *bake a fruit cake*. It does: 3,000 × 2 × 60 × 60 = 21,600,000 joules of work:

Cost = $\dfrac{21,600,000}{3,600,000}$ × 9.91 = **46.56 pence**

- a *14-inch colour TV* rated at 60 W is *switched on for 30 minutes* during a news bulletin. It does 60 × 30 × 60 = 108,000 joules of work:

Cost = $\dfrac{108,000}{3,600,000}$ × 7.76 = **0.23 pence**

- a *microwave oven*, rated at 600 W, takes *6 minutes* to *cook a jacket potato*. It does 600 × 6 × 60 = 216,000 joules of work:

Cost = $\dfrac{216,000}{3,600,000}$ × 7.76 = **0.46 pence**

- a *conventional oven*, rated at 3,000 W, takes *1 hour* to *bake* the same potato. It does 3,000 × 60 × 60 = 10,800,000 joules of work:

Cost = $\dfrac{10,800,000}{3,600,000}$ × 7.76 = **23.28 pence**

(Although it is unlikely that an oven would be used to bake a single potato, the simple cost comparison is a convincing demonstration of the effect of the lower power output of microwave ovens!)

TEACHING IDEA

Children may be tasked to survey all electrical appliances around the school or their home. Not only could they identify which devices are mains- and battery-powered, they could also be challenged to calculate how much different devices cost to run. The next challenge would be for children to identify ways in which they could reduce their electricity consumption.

The generation of electricity

Electricity supply from batteries has advantages and drawbacks. The advantages, particularly from a primary school perspective, include:

- the relative safety of low voltages and direct current;
- the convenience and portability of small units;
- the 'storage' of electricity in battery form;
- the ready availability of batteries.

FACT POINT

Edison and Westinghouse – War of currents

In the 1880s, Thomas Edison (who was the inventor of the electrical light bulb) devised a system of supplying electricity using low-voltage direct current (DC). However, in 1886, George Westinghouse began building a system for generating and distributing electricity using alternating current (AC). Edison's company made claims that AC was hazardous and not as good as the DC system. However, it is the AC system we still use today!

The earliest batteries were produced in 1800 by the Italian physicist Allesandro Volta. He stacked alternating discs of copper, zinc and cardboard soaked in salt water to form a 'Voltaic pile' from which an electric current could be drawn. Such batteries were large and cumbersome and, above all, expensive.

Even today, the major disadvantages of battery electricity are the costs involved (compare the price of the cheapest battery with the cost of boiling a kettle (see above) using mains supply) and the very factors that make it safest for primary school use – the availability of low voltages and direct current. For large-scale industrial and domestic use, other ways of generating electricity are needed, and these depend on converting the kinetic energy of motion into electricity.

As long ago as the 1830s, Michael Faraday had discovered that an electromotive force (in effect, a voltage) was induced in a conductor that was moved across the lines of force of a magnet. Faraday's first 'dynamo' featured a large copper disc that could be rotated between the poles of a horseshoe magnet. When the disc was turning, electricity was 'generated' and could be drawn off by means of contact points. Eventually, this process was refined so that a coil of insulated wire wound round an armature was made to spin rapidly inside a ring of powerful magnets, or, as in the case of modern electricity generating stations, the magnets are made to spin inside fixed coils.

This process of electromagnetic induction is the basis of all modern electricity generation. The differences in each of the systems relate mainly to the means by which the magnets fixed to the armatures are made to spin inside the coils in the generators, and these different methods are now summarized.

In *nuclear power stations*, the heat energy released by the fission of nuclear fuel (enriched uranium) is transferred to carbon dioxide gas that circulates in the reactor. The hot gas is piped from the reactors to water boilers, where it is used to produce 'superheated' steam at 400°C. At this stage, the process becomes similar to that of a 'conventional' or thermal power station, as the steam is used to drive steam turbines, turning heat energy into rotary mechanical energy – the kinetic energy of motion. The turbines are linked to the generators, whose rotating shafts 'produce' electricity by electromagnetic induction (see above, Nuclear energy).

Conventional or *thermal power stations* generate heat by the combustion of fossil fuels (coal, oil and natural gas). This heat energy is used to turn water into steam, which is used to turn turbines that are linked to the generators, as before (see Figure 4.5).

FUTURE APPLICATION

Fossil fuels

The burning of fossil fuels (which provides the main source of electricity for our technology-rich lifestyles) produces carbon dioxide, contributing to climate change. Understanding and discovering new ways to generate electricity that are cleaner and more efficient are important for the global future.

Hydroelectric power stations use the kinetic energy of falling water to drive turbines directly, and the generator magnets are attached to the drive shaft of the turbines.

Steam turbines (and, hence, the connected generators) rotate at high speeds – about 3,000 revolutions per minute (rpm) – generating electricity at 11,000–25,000 V. Hydroelectric turbines spin more slowly – at about 400 rpm, but the outcome is similar to that of steam turbines, because larger numbers of magnets are fixed to the hydrogenerator shafts. The generated voltage is then 'stepped up' by transformers to 275,000 or 400,000 V before transmission from the generating station via the grid or supergrid system of overhead cables. Transmission at high voltage (and low current) minimizes the power loss caused by the heating of the cables. At or near the point of use, the voltage is 'stepped down' to whatever value is needed for industrial use (10,000–40,000 V), or to the 240 V used in domestic supply in the UK.

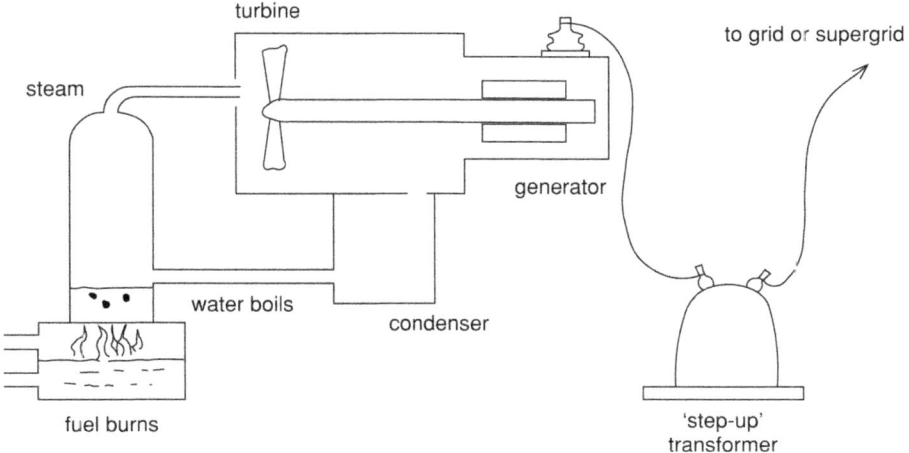

Figure 4.5 Stages in the generation of electricity

Electricity, as a form of energy, exemplifies Key Idea 4.1. It can be:

- stored (in battery form) and, hence, transported in small amounts and released at will;
- released during generation by the conversion of other forms of energy, or controlled and released by switching in circuits;
- transferred geographically by transmission lines to its point of use, or converted into other forms of energy as required.

In terms of convenience, availability, control and application, and cleanliness (at least at the point of use), it is easy to understand the widespread use of electricity in the modern world. The implications of the costs of electricity generation, in terms of consumption of non-renewable resources and pollution of the biophysical environment, should not, and ultimately cannot, be ignored.

TEACHING IDEA

Electrical safety with children

- Children should be warned never to touch exposed wires.
- They should be warned never to leave liquids next to electrical appliances.
- They should be warned never to operate electrical devices with wet hands.
- Batteries of 1.5 V or less are safe for classroom usage.

Static electricity

Perhaps the easiest (and cheapest) way to see the effects of electricity in the classroom is to investigate the accumulation of charged particles on materials with insulating properties. The charged particles result from the displacement of electrons from the atoms of the insulating material, and this displacement is often achieved by the collision of atoms brought about by friction – when the insulating material is rubbed against another insulator, for example. Because the materials are not conductors, the accumulated charges cannot 'flow' in the form of current electricity, but are 'static' and remain in place on the charged object until they either leak away to the air or the earth, or are deliberately discharged by contact with a conducting material. Some examples of the effects of static electricity are as follows:

- Vinyl records can become charged with static electricity. The excess of negatively charged particles on the vinyl attracts small, positively charged items such as dust particles and small fabric fibres ('fluff') to the record, and these particles will need to be removed if sound quality is not to be affected.
- An inflated balloon can be charged with static electricity by being rubbed against woollen cloth – a sweater or cardigan, for example. The 'charged' balloon can then be placed carefully against a wall, and the attraction between the charged particles on the balloon and the oppositely charged particles on the wall will allow the balloon to 'hang' against the wall for a short time, until the static charge 'leaks' away.
- Clothing made from synthetic fibres – nylon or terylene, for example – can become charged with static electricity, particularly in dry conditions (when there is less chance of the charge 'leaking' away through a damp atmosphere). The removal of such clothing sometimes results in the discharge of the static electricity, with accompanying sparks

(visible if the clothing is removed in the dark) and crackling sounds. The sparks occur because collision between electrons and air molecules during the discharge causes light to be emitted as a form of radiation, and the crackling sounds are heard when air is expanded by the heat of the discharge and then is rapidly replaced by cooler air rushing to fill the partial vacuum thus caused.

- The same process is at work during a thunderstorm. Static electricity builds up in the clouds when air and water molecules are brought into violent collision by pressure differences in the atmosphere. The electric charge, often at very high voltage, discharges to earth, or from cloud to cloud, as lightning. The energy of the discharge is converted to light as a 'flash' of lightning, and the heat of the discharge expands the air in its immediate vicinity so rapidly that the warmed air is replaced at supersonic speed – a thunderclap is caused by air breaking the sound barrier!

- If a tap is turned on so that the flow of water is controlled as a thin, but constant, 'thread', and a suitably charged object (such as a plastic pen that has been rubbed against a woollen garment sleeve, for example) is brought close to, but not touching, the stream of water, the stream of water will 'bend' towards the charged object. This is because the charged particles on the plastic pen attract the oppositely charged poles of the water molecules, 'pulling' them towards the pen.

- Finally, a moving car collects charged particles by friction with the air through which it passes, and, in dry conditions, these remain as a static charge on the vehicle. Under these conditions, the particles may be discharged by a person touching the outside of the car once it has stopped moving. The static electricity is, in effect, 'earthed' through the person, and the discharge is felt as an uncomfortable 'shock'.

TEACHING IDEA

Conductive ink pens are now available from education suppliers and can be used to draw circuits. Children could design circuits, along with LED bulbs and pin batteries, to make greetings cards with flashing lights! Pencil graphite is also a conductor of electricity. Try adding a thick pencil trail on a piece of paper to a simple circuit to see if a small bulb lights.

The electromagnetic spectrum

The energy derived from the bonding within and between atoms and molecules can be transferred in a number of ways – by chain reaction, by transfer through a material without the material moving (as in heat conduction), or by transfer through a moving medium (as in heat convection or wind energy).

In some cases, however, the vibration of electrons in materials causes the formation of rapidly vibrating electrical and magnetic fields, and the energy present in these electromagnetic fields is transmitted in wave form, without the presence of a material medium. In other words, electromagnetic energy can travel in wave form through a vacuum (such as space) – a process known as electromagnetic radiation.

The 'family' of waves by which such energy is transmitted is known as the electromagnetic spectrum and includes radio waves, microwaves, infrared rays, visible light, UV rays, X-rays and gamma rays. All of the waves in the electromagnetic spectrum travel at the same velocity through space – 300,000 kilometres per second – that is, 3×10^8 m/s. What causes the variations in the properties of the different waves is their wavelength – the distance between successive wave crests – and their frequency – the number of waves passing a fixed point per second.

As the velocity is the same for each of the wave types, and velocity = wavelength × frequency, it follows that the wavelengths and frequencies will be related. The longer the

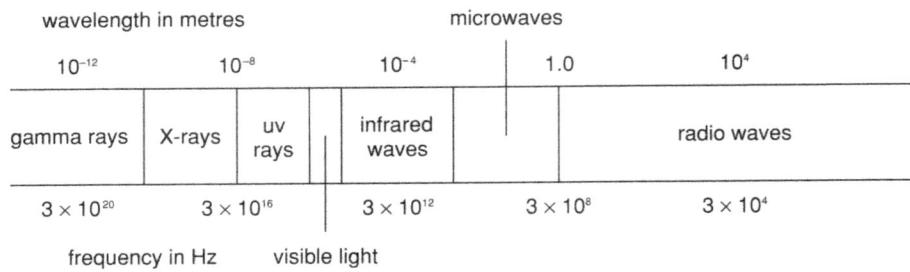

Figure 4.6 The electromagnetic spectrum

wavelength, the lower the frequency, and the shorter the wavelength, the higher the frequency. This is shown in Figure 4.6. Note that, in each case, the product of wavelength and frequency is equal to 3×10^8 m/s.

Radio waves are the longest of the electromagnetic waves, ranging from 10,000 m to less than 10 m in length. They 'carry' electrical impulses generated from sound energy that can be superimposed on the waveforms and then be decoded at a receiving station to reproduce the original signal.

Microwaves, at a wavelength of 1 m, are absorbed by water molecules, which themselves vibrate at an increased rate, and, hence, their temperature rises, and this effect is the basis of microwave cookery.

It is *infrared radiation* that accounts for the transfer of heat energy from the Sun, across the intervening 93 million miles of space, to the Earth's surface (60 per cent of solar radiation is in the form of heat). The heat absorbed by the Earth's surface is then transferred to the atmosphere, and it is this heat that causes temperature (and, hence, pressure) differences in the atmosphere and, therefore, drives the 'weather machine'. Infrared rays have wavelengths between 1 mm (10^{-3} m) and 1 micron (1 thousandth of a millimetre – 10^{-6} m).

Visible light is also a form of electromagnetic radiation. It ranges in frequency from red light (at about 0.8 microns – 8×10^{-7} m) to violet light (at about 0.4 microns – 4×10^{-7} m). An interesting thought is that there are actually only *six* colours in the well-known 'rainbow' of light. Sir Isaac Newton, who investigated the splitting of a source of white light by using a prism, in addition to being a brilliant scientist, was also an alchemist, and seven was a lucky number. It is tempting to imagine that the great man 'saw' seven colours in his rainbow, even though it is a matter of judgement as to how far the blue end of the spectrum divides into the three colours of blue, indigo and violet.

A glance at a colour wheel confirms the six-colour theory (in my opinion!). The three primary colours mix in pairs to form three secondary colours, and these are the six that are present in the rainbow – red, orange, yellow, green, blue and purple (see Figure 4.7).

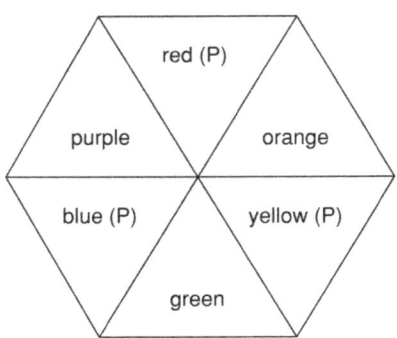

Figure 4.7 The six colours of the rainbow

UV light, at wavelengths from 0.4 microns (4×10^{-7} m) down to 0.01 microns (10^{-8} m), is a significant component of sunlight and one that stimulates the production of vitamin D in humans and causes 'tanning' by the production of the pigment melanin in the skin. It may also be a cause of the increasing incidence of reported cases of melanoma (skin cancer), as humans are exposed to increasing levels of UV light at the Earth's surface, as a result of the thinning of the upper-atmosphere ozone layer.

X-rays, with wavelengths from 0.01 microns (10^{-8} m) down to 0.00001 micron (10^{-12} m), are absorbed by solid matter, but can penetrate soft tissue. Their application in medical science is well known, as they allow practitioners to 'see' the state of the bones and teeth 'inside' a living person. If a radioactive tracer is used, as in a 'barium meal' or by the injection of an isotope into the bloodstream, the outline of soft tissues can also be photographed and monitored. The absorption of X-rays displaces electrons in the absorbing tissue, so prolonged exposure to X-rays can cause tissue damage.

Gamma rays range in wavelength from 0.00001 micron (10^{-12} m) down to less than 1 thousand millionth of a micron (10^{-16} m), (dimensions on so small a scale are inconceivable in real terms). These rays are associated with radioactivity. They are known to be emitted by radioactive substances and they are able to penetrate materials, including metals, to a considerable degree. They are difficult to screen and deflect, and their penetrative properties represent a serious hazard to human health.

Strain energy

Materials that have elastic properties (see Key Idea 3.2: Elasticity; and Stiffness (and flexibility)) are able to change their shape following the application of a load and recover their original shape when the load is removed. This property is essentially a result of the atomic and molecular bonding of the materials concerned, and of the behaviour of the molecules when loaded.

What happens with elastic materials is that the structure of the molecular bonding becomes distorted, but not destroyed, by the application of a load. When the load is removed, the molecular structures resume their original shape. In some cases, as in the 'uncurling' of a crumpled crisp packet or the 'unwinding' of a clock spring, this process of returning to original shape and size is a slow one. In other cases, as in the 'twanging' of a rubber band, the process is rapid and powerful.

The property of elasticity thus allows the energy of atomic and molecular bonding to be transferred as the kinetic energy of mechanical motion, and this in turn allows a force to be applied by the material during the process of returning to its original shape (for the effect of forces, see Key Idea 4.2, below).

The 'elastic' (or strain) energy inherent in elastic materials has been used in a wide variety of applications, some of which are listed below. Strain energy is available in:

- rubber: for 'bands', engine mountings, car tyres;
- metals: for springs – coil springs in force meters, suspension units and clockwork toys, leaf springs, lock mechanisms, bulldog clips;
- glassfibre: for archery bows, diving boards, vaulting poles;
- plastic foams: for soft furnishings;
- fabrics: for 'stretchy' clothing (for example, lycra), trampoline beds.

Potential and kinetic energy

All of the forms of energy described so far have their origins in the bonding within atoms (nuclear energy), or in the bonding and transfer between atoms and molecules (chemical, electromagnetic and strain energy).

In order to understand the concept of potential energy, it is necessary to have some understanding of the concept of gravity. This concept will be dealt with more fully in Key Idea 4.2 (Forces), but a brief introduction is appropriate here.

In simple terms, gravity is the force of attraction between masses. All objects are made up of matter, and the amount of matter in any given object is said to be its mass, measured in grams. Sir Isaac Newton was the first person to theorize that any two objects would be attracted towards each other by virtue of their masses, and that the strength of the force of attraction – the gravitational force – would depend on the masses of the two objects and their distance apart.

The (relatively) large mass of the Earth thus exerts an attraction – a 'pull' – on smaller objects in its near vicinity. Any object close to the Earth's surface will be 'pulled' towards the centre of the Earth – its centre of mass – by the gravitational force that exists between the Earth and the object. It is this tendency for objects to 'fall' to Earth under the 'pull' of gravity that gives rise to the linked concepts of potential and kinetic energy.

Potential energy

The energy that an object possesses by virtue of its position is known as its *potential energy*. If the object is not moving, no work is being done, nor is any energy being converted. However, if the object has been raised to its present position, work has been done on the object (work = force × distance moved in the direction of the force), and it has gained potential energy – that is, it has the potential to do work by virtue of its position. The greater the mass of the object and the height it has been raised above the surface, the greater the work that has been done on it, and, therefore, the greater its potential energy. Examples of 'objects' having potential energy would include the head of a piledriver that is poised for release, a skier at the top of a hill, a child (or adult!) at the top of a fairground helter-skelter, a glider at the top of a winch wire, or a 'head' of water in a hydroelectric-scheme reservoir. Each of these 'objects' has the potential for doing work, based on the position to which they have been raised above the surface of the Earth.

Kinetic energy

This is the energy that an object possesses by virtue of its motion. In each of the above examples, once the object is released and begins to move towards the Earth's surface, accelerated by the force of gravity, it possesses an increasing amount of kinetic energy. This energy, in the form of motion, would enable work to be done if any of the objects were involved in a collision (as in the piledriver, or the reservoir water 'hitting' the hydroelectric turbine blades). As the kinetic energy of the falling object increases, its potential energy decreases proportionally.

Not all kinetic energy is developed as a result of gravitational attraction. Any object in motion is said to possess kinetic energy. The motion may result from the conversion of other forms of energy; for example:

- Chemical energy derived from the combustion of a fossil fuel is converted into kinetic energy in a car engine. This kinetic energy is transferred through mechanical linkages – clutch, gears, drive-shafts – to the motion of the whole vehicle.
- Chemical energy from the respiration of food is transferred through a person's muscles and bones (levers) into kinetic energy when a supermarket trolley is pushed along or a bicycle is pedalled.
- Electrical energy is converted into kinetic energy in an electric motor, when a current passing through a coil of wire placed in a magnetic field causes the coil to rotate.

Kinetic energy is also important at the atomic and molecular level. It is the motion of molecules – for example, in a gas – that creates gas pressure (see Key Idea 3.1: The compression of gas). As more and more molecules of gas are forced into a fixed space, the number of collisions between molecules increases. These collisions result in a more intense 'bombardment' of the sides of the container by gas molecules. This, in turn, is measurable as an increase in gas pressure (pressure is force per unit area), as in the inflation of a balloon or a car tyre.

Finally, the kinetic energy (the motion) of atoms and molecules can be increased by the transfer of energy released from nuclear or chemical reactions. This increase in kinetic energy transfers as thermal (heat) energy, and this is the subject of the next section (see also Key Idea 3.1: Changes of state).

CONCEPT CONFUSION

The Sun doesn't just provide light and heat energy, but it provides most of the energy we need here on our planet. Heat and light energy from the Sun is converted into other forms. For example, the energy from our food comes indirectly from the Sun (plants capture the Sun's energy through the process of photosynthesis).

Heat and temperature

Heat energy is a function of the vibration of the atoms and molecules of which substances are made. As has already been described, the states of matter can be visualized in terms of the vibration of their constituent atoms or molecules, and changes of state in substances are brought about by the transfer, into and out of the substances, of heat energy in the form of atomic or molecular motion (see Key Idea 3.1: The states of matter; and Changes of state). Increases in motion, and therefore increases in the amount of thermal energy transferred into substances, give rise to:

- changes in state via melting, boiling and evaporation;
- the expansion of heated substances;
- the burning of fuels and the cellular respiration of carbohydrates in living cells.

All of these processes are described in Key Idea 3.3: Heating and cooling everyday materials; Changing materials; Chemical reactions and heat energy; and Changes involving oxygen.

The difference between heat and temperature

Heat is the total amount of thermal energy contained in a given amount of material and is measured in joules. Temperature is a measure of the intensity of heat – of how hot something is – and is measured in degrees Celsius (°C). On the Celsius scale, 0° is the freezing point, and 100° is the boiling point, of pure water. Some examples might make the distinction clearer:

- Two litres of water at 20°C will hold twice as much heat as 1 litre of water at 20°C. Although the water is at the same temperature in each case, there will be twice as many molecular collisions in 2 litres of water as in 1 litre (because there are twice as many molecules) – the total quantity of heat in 2 litres of water will therefore be double that which is present in 1 litre.
- There will be more heat in a bath full of tepid water than there will be in a match flame. Although the temperature of the match flame will be much higher than that of the

bathwater, the total molecular movement will be greater in the large volume of bathwater than in the small amount of fuel that burns to form the match flame.

- In some cases, it is possible to transfer heat into a substance without raising its temperature. Under conditions of atmospheric pressure, water heated to a temperature of 100°C will boil. If more heat is transferred into the water, it continues to boil (eventually boiling away as water vapour), without any rise in its temperature.

FACT POINT

Measuring temperature

Scientists in the past had different ways of measuring temperature. Daniel Fahrenheit (1686–1736) invented the Fahrenheit scale, with 0°F being the temperature of salt water freezing and 212°F being the temperature of water boiling. Anders Celsius (1701–44) designed a scale in which water freezes at 0°C and water boils at 100°C. The Kelvin scale, designed by Lord Kelvin (1824–1907), is the primary unit of temperature used by physicians. The Kelvin degree is the same size as the Celsius degree, but 0°C corresponds to 273.15°K, and 100°C is the same as 373.15°K, so that absolute zero is 0°K.

Heat transfer

In general, there is a tendency towards equilibrium in the physical world. Just as atmospheric pressure tends to 'even out', with high-pressure air flowing towards low pressure, and water 'seeks to find its own level', flowing from high to low ground, so heat will tend to flow from areas of higher temperature towards areas of lower temperature. In other words, there is a tendency for the energy of molecular vibration to disperse itself evenly through the materials of the physical environment.

Heat can be transferred in three ways – by conduction, convection and radiation.

Conduction is the transfer of heat energy through a solid material, either by the movement of free electrons, or by the collision of the molecules of which the material is made. 'Free electron' conduction is more rapid and is typical of those materials, such as metals, that have good thermal conductivity. 'Collision' conduction is slower and typical of poor conductors of heat. A simple demonstration of good and poor heat conductivity is to place metal and wooden spoons into a container of hot water. After a short time, the metal spoon handle is hot to the touch, because of the rapid conduction of heat along the handle. The wooden spoon, however, stays cool to the touch, as wood is a poor conductor of heat.

Convection is the transfer of heat by means of the movement of a locally heated fluid substance (usually air or water). As a fluid is heated in a particular locality, the heating causes expansion that, in turn, causes a lowering of density. The less dense, warm fluid begins to rise and is replaced by cooler, denser fluid from below. Eventually, convection currents are set up that allow for a continuous flow of heat upwards from the source. Examples of systems that use convection currents for heat transfer are as follows:

- Electric convector heaters warm the air at one place in a room, and the resulting convection currents transport the heat around the room.
- Domestic hot water systems depend on convection currents to transfer heat from an immersion heater (similar to the 'element' in an electric kettle) to the rest of the water in the hot tank.

It is easy to demonstrate the 'updraught' part of a convection current by hanging a piece of light material, or a cut-out spiral, above a convector heater. The movement of the hanging material will clearly provide evidence of the existence of rising currents of warm air.

Radiation is the transfer of heat without the presence of a material medium, by means of electromagnetic waves (see above: The electromagnetic spectrum). Heat radiation can be felt as the 'glow' from a fire or radiator, or as the heat from the Sun. It is interesting to remember that most domestic 'radiators', such as those found in central heating systems, in addition to *radiating* heat energy, will also warm a room by *convection*.

LIGHT

In some nuclear, atomic and molecular reactions, large amounts of energy are produced, and some of this energy is emitted by the vibrating particles in the form of light. As has already been described (see above, The electromagnetic spectrum), light energy is a form of radiation that is transmitted by electromagnetic waves. These waves are generated by changes in electrical and magnetic field strength and, as such, can travel through the vacuum of space. In this respect, light waves differ significantly from other forms of wave energy, such as sound or ocean waves, both of which need a medium or material to 'wave' in. Sound and ocean waves transmit energy through the oscillation of particles – of gases, liquids or solids in the case of sound, and of water in the case of ocean waves. Light energy, however, is transmitted by the oscillation of electromagnetic fields and, therefore, needs no material medium through which to travel.

For the purposes of this book, the behaviour of light *waves* can explain each of the concepts that will be explored (and certainly those of the Science NC). The story is not as simple as that, however, and it is important to note that not all of the effects of light can be explained in terms of wave behaviour. In some cases – photosynthesis for example – light behaves as if it were made of particles (photons), with different amounts of energy attached to each parcel (or quantum) of light of a particular wavelength. Suffice it to say that current explanations of the behaviour of light invoke a particle/wave theory that accepts the possibility that light conforms to wave theory on some occasions and to particle theory on others.

CONCEPTS TO SUPPORT LOWER KEY STAGE 2

Sources of light

There are a number of different sources of light, all of which have one thing in common – light sources transfer energy into the increased vibration of atoms and molecules such that the vibrating particles (which may be electrons, atoms or molecules) first emit heat by radiation, followed by light, as energy levels increase and particles vibrate even faster. Some examples of light sources and their energy conversions include the following:

- The Sun: The energy released by nuclear fusion (see above) is converted into radiant heat and (sun)light. The light from the Sun supplies us with our 'daylight' and the light energy that enables the process of photosynthesis to take place in green plants (see Key Idea 2.2: Plant nutrition – photosynthesis).
- Electric lamps (bulbs): Electrical energy is passed as a current through the thin wire filament (often made from tungsten) of a light bulb. The electrical resistance of the filament is high, and this resistivity increases the collisions between molecules in the material, causing both heat and light to be emitted. Most light bulbs contain an inert gas (usually argon), because, if air were used, the hot filament would react with the oxygen in the air and would 'burn' away.
- Fluorescent tubes: Electrical energy is used to excite the molecules of mercury vapour (mixed with an inert gas) inside a glass tube, producing UV radiation. The UV radiation causes a 'phosphor' coating on the inside of the tube to emit a fluorescent glow.

Fluorescent tube lights produce less heat, and therefore consume less power, than incandescent bulbs (a 40-W tube will produce the same light intensity as a 150-W bulb).

- A candle: Chemical energy released by the burning of a fuel (paraffin wax, a hydrocarbon) causes heating, and the particles of carbon from the fuel become 'white hot' – hence, the light of the candle flame.

The 'heat then light' sequence is related to the energy levels of the materials involved. As energy levels increase, causing particles to vibrate at ever-increasing speeds, the light produced has a colour that matches the frequency of vibration relative to the electromagnetic spectrum. As red light has the lowest frequency of visible light, and blue light has the highest, we would expect that the light emitted by a material that was experiencing increasing energy transfer – was heating up – would appear to change in a pattern that worked through the spectrum of visible light from red to blue. This is, in effect, what happens. Imagine a blacksmith heating a bar of steel. First, it glows a dull red, then orange, then yellow, and eventually it appears to be blue-white and white hot. A similar effect, deliberately restricted by design to the red end of the spectrum, is demonstrated by an electric fire that has just been switched on. Radiant heat from the electric element is felt before the fire begins to 'glow' red, then orange – the 'glow' of the electric element is, of course, a light source.

It is important to remember that all light sources *emit* light – they 'give it out' as a form of radiant energy. There is sometimes confusion in the minds of young children who think that any bright light, such as that *reflected* from a pale-coloured wall or a mirror, is a light source, and care is needed to distinguish the differences in such cases.

Light and seeing

At a simple level, and without going into explanations involving light rays entering the eye, it is possible to show that we need light in order to see. A simple device (a 'light and dark' box) can be used, or the process can be investigated as a 'thought experiment' (although the real experience is always more convincing!).

If a box is constructed as in Figure 4.8 (a shoebox is ideal as a basis), it can be used to compare the two experiences of looking at a picture or an object with and without light.

If an observer looks through the small 'peephole' when the shutter is closed, it will be difficult, if not impossible, to see anything of the picture at the end of the box. If the shutter is opened, allowing light to fall on the picture, it immediately becomes visible through the peephole. The without/with light difference is obvious and should be a convincing demonstration that light needs to fall on objects in order for us to be able to see them.

Light and dark

From the simple experiment described above, it should be possible to extend understanding into other, similar situations in the real world:

- What is it like inside the box when there is no light getting in? It is dark in the box.
- What happens when the daylight is poor or very dim? We cannot see very well.
- What happens when the daylight goes altogether? It is dark, and we cannot see at all (or, we have to switch on other lights to be able to see).
- What happens when we close our eyes so that no light can get into them? We cannot see anything at all.

From these and similar questions, based initially on the light and dark box, it is possible to progress towards an awareness that, when there is no light, it will be dark, and we will not be able to see anything.

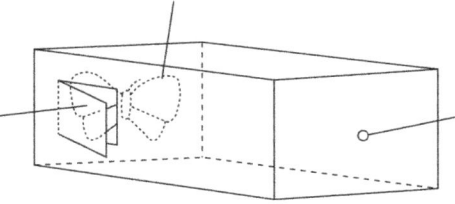

Figure 4.8 A 'light and dark' box

CONCEPT CONFUSION

In order for us to see, light hits an object and bounces into our eyes, not the other way around. Sometimes, we think that, when it is dark, there is no light, but, if it is possible to see things, then there must be some light sources allowing light to bounce off the things we can see.

CONCEPTS TO SUPPORT KEY STAGE 2

The behaviour of waves

If a piece of rope (such as a skipping rope) is fixed at one end and held loosely at the other, and the 'held' end is moved sharply up and down, a 'waveform' develops and seems to move along the rope towards the fixed end (see Figure 4.9). The same effect can be seen if one end of a coiled spring, such as a Slinky, is waved from side to side on a table.

What is happening in this process is that energy from the moving hand and arm is transmitted along the rope through the waveform. This energy can be felt as a jerk if the fixed end is held in a hand and a single 'wave' is imparted to the rope. It is important to notice that the rope does not go anywhere – what happens is that the *waveform* moves along the rope, at right angles to the vibrations of the rope, carrying its energy with it. Because the wavefront advances at right angles to the direction of vibration, these waves are known as 'transverse' waves. This transfer of energy by means of a waveform is also the process that causes a whip to 'crack'. Energy imparted to the whip handle travels in wave form along the whip until it reaches the end. It is said that the whip end moves faster than the speed of

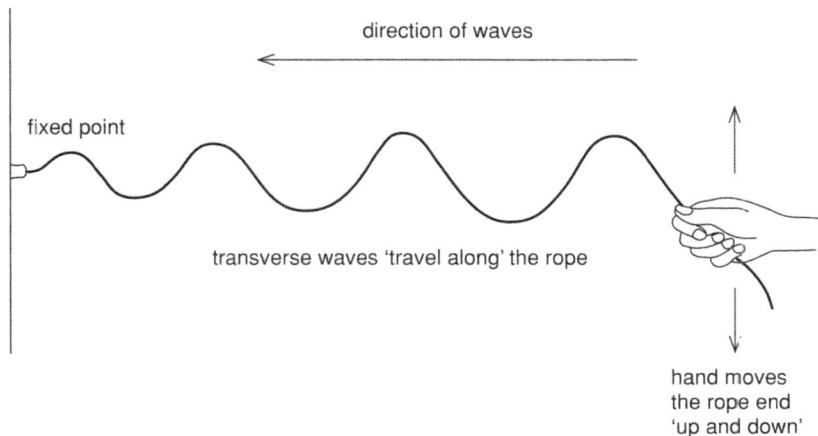

direction of waves

fixed point

transverse waves 'travel along' the rope

hand moves
the rope end
'up and down'

Figure 4.9 Making waveforms with a skipping rope

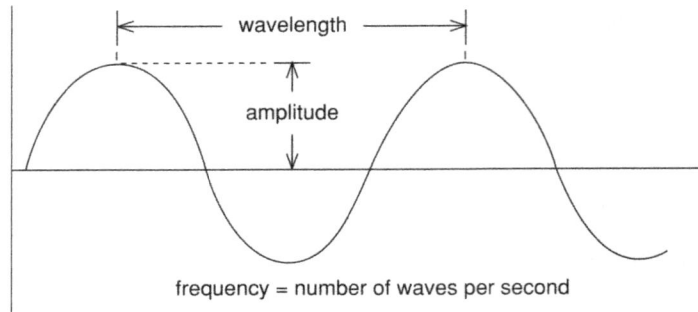

frequency = number of waves per second

Figure 4.10 The main features of waveforms

sound, and that the crack heard is the sound barrier being broken! The main features of waves are outlined in Figure 4.10.

The speed at which a wave travels is a product of its wavelength (the distance in metres between two successive wave crests) and its frequency (the number of 'waves' passing a point per second, measured as Hertz, or Hz), hence:

speed (in metres per second) = wavelength × frequency

The amplitude, or size, of a wave (the height from its crest to its undisturbed position) is a measure of its energy – the larger the amplitude, the greater the energy contained by the wave.

Light waves

Light waves, along with all the other waves represented in the electromagnetic spectrum (see above), travel at a constant speed of 3×10^8 metres (300,000 km) per second in a vacuum (and at almost the same speed in air). As can be seen from Figure 4.6, the constant speed is maintained because the wavelengths of light shorten as the frequency increases.

Red light, with the longest wavelength of about 0.75 of one-millionth of a metre (0.75 microns, or 0.75×10^{-6} m), has a frequency of 4×10^{14} Hz, and so its speed will be:

$$(0.75 \times 10^{-6}) \times (4 \times 10^{14}) \text{ m/s} = 3 \times 10^8 \text{ m/s}$$

Blue light, with the shortest wavelength of about 0.4 of one-millionth of a metre (0.4 microns, or 0.4×10^{-6} m), has the correspondingly higher frequency of 7.5×10^{14} Hz, and its speed will be:

$$(0.4 \times 10^{-6}) \times (7.5 \times 10^{14}) \text{ m/s} = 3 \times 10^8 \text{ m/s}$$

(Note: speed is measured as distance travelled per unit time, for example, 30 metres per second:

$$\text{and } \textbf{average (mean) speed} \text{ is: } \frac{\text{total distance travelled}}{\text{total time taken}}$$

Velocity is speed in a particular direction, and, when an object is travelling at uniform velocity, both its speed and direction remain unchanged.)

Light *waves*, along with other transverse waves such as ocean waves, behave in certain predictable ways, and this behaviour gives rise to certain effects. Light emitted from a radiating source (such as the Sun) travels away from it in straight lines in all directions and may, on reaching an object, be *absorbed* or *reflected* by, or *transmitted* through, the material of which the object is made.

FACT POINT

A light year

As will be elaborated in Key Idea 4.2, a light year is a measure of the distance that light would travel in 1 Earth year: approximately 10 million, million kilometres. As a result of the high speed at which light travels, we see nearby sources of light almost instantaneously. Light takes 8 minutes to travel from the Sun to the Earth, and even longer for distant stars. In other words, when we see stars, we see them as they were when the light set off, which could have been years ago!

Straight-line travel

Light (often produced as narrow 'beams' or 'rays' by the appropriate masking of a light source) can easily be shown to travel in straight lines. If light rays were 'curved', we would be able to see round corners! A more convincing practical investigation is to set up the simple experiment shown in Figure 4.11. When the holes in all three cards are in line, the light from the torch, travelling in a straight line, is visible. As soon as one card is displaced, so that the holes are no longer in a straight line, the light cannot be seen.

The reflection and absorption of light

When light reaches an object, some of it 'bounces off' (is reflected away from) the surface of the object. Almost all objects that are not themselves light sources reflect some of the light that falls on them, and the reflected light is 'scattered' in all directions from the reflecting surface. Some of this reflected light enters our eyes, enabling us to see the reflecting objects. Nerve endings in our eyes are stimulated by the light reflected by the surfaces of objects and people that surround us, and the received messages are transmitted to the brain, which interprets the information and 'sees' the objects concerned (see Key Idea 2.2: The nervous system).

If the reflecting object is flat – that is, if it has a plane surface – and is particularly shiny, almost all of the light falling on it will be reflected, producing clear images of the objects nearby. This effect provides the basis for mirrors. If the reflecting surface is not flat, as in a metal dish or a spoon bowl, the resulting images will have distorted shapes.

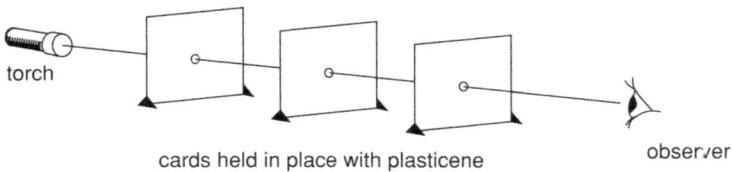

Figure 4.11 The straight-line experiment

FACT POINT

Cat's eyes

Cat's eyes were invented by Percy Shaw in the 1930s to help drivers see more clearly in the dark. Shaw realized that the headlights of his car were reflected from cats' eyes. He therefore used the same principle, by putting glass balls with a shiny surface on the back and positioning them at the edges and centre of the road. As a result, cat's eyes reflect the light from a car's headlights, allowing the driver to see the edge of the road more easily.

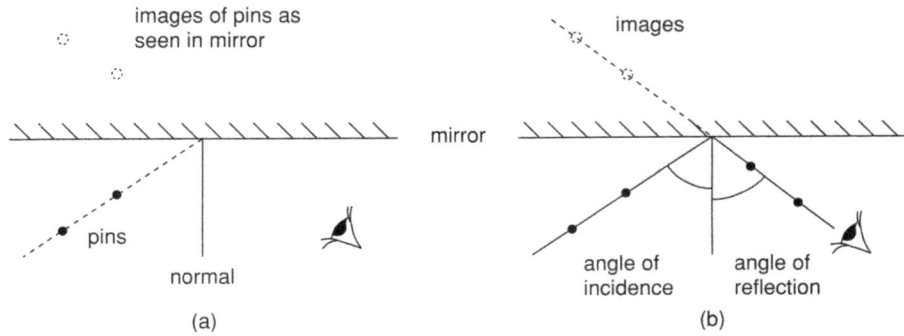

Figure 4.12 Angles of incidence and reflection

Light that falls on to a flat surface at a particular angle will be reflected from it at an equal angle, and it is this effect that causes the accurate (and 'reversed') reflection of the mirror image. This effect can be shown clearly with a mirror and four pins. Set up a mirror on a pinboard, as shown in Figure 4.12. Draw a line at right angles to the mirror surface (the 'normal' line) and position two pins so that they line up with the point where the normal line meets the mirror (Figure 4.12a). Now, place two more pins so that they appear to line up with the images of the first two pins, as seen in the mirror (Figure 4.12b). When the pin holes (representing the track of the light rays reflected from the pins) are later joined up with a pencil line, it will be discovered that the angle of incidence is equal to the angle of reflection.

CONCEPT CONFUSION

Shiny objects that reflect light can be confused with light sources – for example, mirrors, reflectors and even the Moon. Only objects that emit their own light can be seen in complete darkness.

The reversing of an image can easily be investigated by looking at familiar objects, or the written word, in a mirror. The image appears to be the 'wrong way round' (lateral inversion), but not upside down.

It is important to remember that, during the day, light from the Sun 'bathes' the objects on which it falls. There is sometimes a tendency for children to visualize sunlight as existing as single lines (possibly because of the frequent representation of light as 'rays'), and this can cause confusion.

TEACHING IDEA

Children may experiment with different shiny surfaces to explore how light is reflected in different ways. Looking at both sides of a shiny spoon can allow children to discover how light reflects from convex and concave surfaces. Children could also create their own mirror mazes to help them gain an understanding of reflection angles, deciding where mirrors need to be placed around a maze, so that a light ray can bounce off them to avoid obstacles.

We see the objects around us because they reflect light from their surfaces, and some of this reflected light enters our eyes. We see them *in colour* because objects and surfaces absorb some wavelengths of light and reflect other wavelengths, and it is these reflected wavelengths that give objects their colour. For example, when sunlight falls on the leaves of plants, the blue and red wavelengths are absorbed by the chlorophyll pigments (and are used in the process of photosynthesis), and the green wavelengths are reflected, which is why we see plant leaves as being a green colour. Objects that absorb all the light that falls on them, and therefore do not reflect light of any colour, are seen as black objects.

An interesting thought experiment relating to this concept is as follows: If you were in a completely dark, totally enclosed room, the walls of which consisted of 100 per cent non-reflecting black surfaces, and the atmosphere of which was completely pure and dust-free, what would you see if you switched on a torch in the room? (The answer is given at the end of the section.)

FACT POINT

What affects the colour of the sky?

Two of the main gases in our atmosphere are nitrogen and oxygen. These gases are able to scatter blue light when sunlight passes through the atmosphere. This is the reason why we usually see a blue sky. However, when the sun begins to set, the light has to travel through much more of the atmosphere, and so most of the blue light has already scattered, leaving the red light that makes a beautiful sunset.

TEACHING IDEA

Demonstrating why the sky is blue

Fill a glass with water, adding a little bit of soap to get a cloudy solution. In a dark room, shine a torch at the cloudy solution. The solution should look blue, as the small particles in suspension, just like the particles of nitrogen and oxygen, scatter blue light more than other colours.

Shadows

Objects or surfaces that reflect or absorb all of the light that falls on them (in other words, will not allow light to pass through them) are said to be opaque. If light falls on to an object directly, and from a bright source, and all of the light is reflected from or absorbed by the object, there will be an area 'behind' the object (relative to the light source) where less light is falling, and this area will be seen as a darker outline – a shadow of the object. This can easily be shown by bringing any object close to the wall of a brightly lit room. The shadow of the object will be obvious and will be sharper edged and darker, the closer the object is to the wall. As the object is moved away from the wall and is no longer 'shading' it so closely, more reflected light can reach the wall from other surfaces, and the shadowed area appears to go 'fuzzy', is less distinct and becomes less dark.

The shadows that are darkest and have the 'sharpest' edges are those 'cast' by objects that are in direct sunlight, or in the light emitted from a powerful source, such as an overhead projector (which is actually designed to focus and project on to a screen the shadows cast by areas of darker pigment – the writing or print – on overhead-projector slides).

On a cloudy day, when light from the Sun is diffused and scattered by the water droplets in the clouds, shadows are far less pronounced or are absent, because the light appears to be coming 'from everywhere' rather than directly from a single source. Indoors, however, where less light is available, even the scattered light of a cloudy day may be bright enough to produce shadows – daylight coming through the windows acts as a bright source in a relatively dark room.

WORKING SCIENTIFICALLY

Children could make shadow puppets and investigate how distances between a light source, the shadow puppet and a white screen can affect the size of the shadow.

Transmission

Some of the light that reaches an object may not be reflected or absorbed, but may be transmitted through the object, and objects that will allow the passage of light are said to be either translucent or transparent. A translucent material will allow the passage of some light, but the light is so scattered that no clear images are transmitted through the material. Tissue paper and 'frosted' glass are examples of translucent materials. A transparent material is one that transmits most of the light that reaches it, allowing more or less clear visibility of objects that are viewed through it. Glass, polythene and water are all materials that can be transparent in their 'clear' forms, although it is possible to turn any potentially transparent material opaque by the addition of pigments, which will reflect and absorb light of different wavelengths. This concept is a deliberate design feature of 'sunglasses', for example, where glass or plastic lenses are deliberately pigmented so that the amount of light entering the eyes is reduced.

It is important to remember that no material will allow the transmission of all available light, as some of the light energy will be absorbed during its passage through the material. It is said that window glass transmits about 80 per cent of incident light, and anyone who

TEACHING IDEA

Testing sunglasses

Children can be asked to bring a pair of sunglasses from home, so that they can test and compare which are the best for blocking light. Using the light sensor of a data logger to measure the amount of light passing through will allow children to make comparisons between the sunglasses. Remember to remind children that they should never look directly at the Sun, even through a pair of sunglasses.

has used increasing powers of microscope or telescope lenses will be aware of the dimness of image provided by higher-power lenses – a dimness caused by the absorption of much of the light by the lens material itself.

Refraction

When light, travelling through air, enters a denser material such as water or glass, it slows down (fractionally), and its direction is changed by its passage through such material, a process known as refraction. The investigation of this property led Sir Isaac Newton to conduct what is seen as one of the most famous experiments in the history of science. In a darkened room, Newton allowed sunlight, restricted to a narrow beam by a gap in the curtain, to fall on a triangular glass prism. The 'white' sunlight was broken up into its constituent components of coloured light – the spectrum – as the light was refracted through the glass of the prism (see above, The electromagnetic spectrum).

Light that is travelling between transparent materials of different densities will usually behave as follows:

- light falling at right angles on to the surface of a denser (transparent) material will pass straight through the material;
- light falling at an angle, and travelling into a denser material, will be refracted towards the normal – that is, a line at a right angle to the surface of the material;
- light leaving a dense material will be refracted away from the normal.

These effects are summarized diagrammatically in Figure 4.13.

An understanding of the behaviour of light, and of its refraction during its passage through glass, has allowed for the development of the branch of science known as optics. Using lenses of appropriate shapes, light can be bent so that images of objects can be focused and magnified (a highly beneficial outcome for all those people who need reading glasses, or who use binoculars or telescopes to 'bring distant objects closer').

In another everyday context, the refraction of light at a water surface causes an apparent shallowing, such that underwater objects appear to be in a different position from their actual location. An excellent demonstration of this effect is provided by a washing-up bowl (or other suitable opaque container), a coin and some water. Place a coin in an empty washing-up bowl so that it is just out of sight below the rim of the bowl. Without moving the viewing position, slowly add water to the bowl, and the coin will begin to appear above the rim. Figure 4.14 shows what is happening. Light reflected from the surface of the coin is refracted at the water surface, so that the previously invisible coin can be seen (although the image of the coin appears at a shallower depth than its actual position).

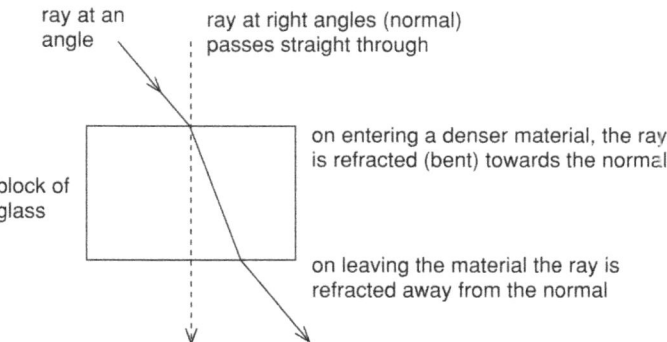

Figure 4.13 The refraction of light

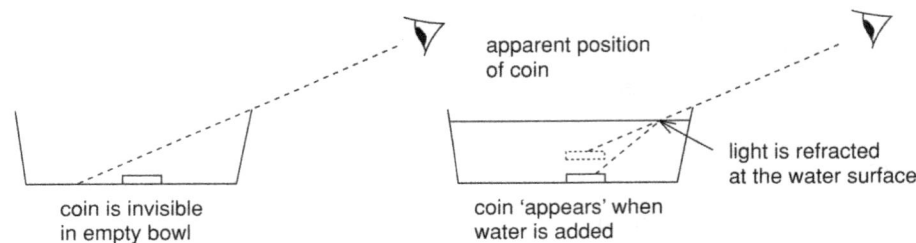

apparent position
of coin

coin is invisible
in empty bowl

coin 'appears' when
water is added

light is refracted
at the water surface

Figure 4.14 The appearing coin 'trick'

Thought experiment answer

The answer to the 'torch in the black room' thought experiment is: *you would see nothing*. The black walls would absorb all the light that fell on them, and there would be no 'beam' of torchlight visible, because there would be no particles in the atmosphere to reflect the torchlight back to your eyes.

SOUND

CONCEPTS TO SUPPORT KEY STAGE 2

Sound waves

Sound, like light, is a form of energy that is transmitted by waves, but sound differs from light in a number of fundamental ways.

First, sound is generated as a result of mechanical vibration. Any object that is emitting a sound will be vibrating. Sound can be made, therefore, by any means that will cause an object (or objects) to vibrate mechanically – by striking, plucking or blowing, for example.

Obvious (and visible) examples of objects that vibrate and produce a sound include a cymbal, the rim of which can be seen to be vibrating when struck, or a guitar string, which can be seen to vibrate when plucked and felt to vibrate when touched lightly with a finger. Other sounds that can be 'felt' as well as heard include the sounds emitted by a loudspeaker (the 'cone' of the loudspeaker or its fabric covering can be felt to vibrate), or the human voice box (the larynx), which can be felt vibrating if fingers are lightly placed against the throat while the person is talking or singing.

CONCEPT CONFUSION

Unlike light, sound does not travel in straight lines, but by vibrations that are made by an object and are carried through the air to our ears. Unlike rays of light, vibrations travel out in all directions from the source, like ripples when you drop a pebble in water.

An interesting activity is to consider exactly *what* is vibrating when musical instruments make a sound. Here are some examples:

*   stringed instruments: violin, viola, cello, bass; guitar, mandolin, lute, harp; piano, harpsichord, spinet; dulcimer, where the vibrating components are plucked, strummed, bowed or hammered strings.

Woodwind instruments include:

- 'blown' tubes: flute, piccolo, fife, recorder family, ocarina, where the vibration is started by air that is blown over a sharp edge at or near the mouthpiece;
- single-reed instruments: clarinet, saxophone family, where a single reed is made to vibrate by air blown across it 'end on';
- double-reed instruments: oboe, cor anglais, bassoon; bagpipes, where a double reed vibrates in the same manner;
- brass instruments: trumpet, trombone, euphonium, tuba, where the vibrating components are the player's pursed lips (children find great enjoyment in learning that, basically, brass players are blowing 'raspberries' into their instruments!);
- percussion instruments: drum family, where a membrane (the drum skin) is vibrating;
- pitched percussion instruments: xylophone, glockenspiel, marimba; chime bars, tubular bells, where the vibrating component is the material of which the instrument is made.

In many cases, it is the nature of the original vibration (plucked string, blown tube, double reed, etc.) that gives the instrument its own characteristic sound quality. The sound of an oboe is unmistakably different from that of a clarinet, and the difference is partly to do with the use of a double as opposed to a single reed as the vibrating sound source. The original sound can then be amplified by the shape and size of the instrument – by the sound box of a guitar or by the size of tubing and shape of the bell of a trombone or a tuba, for example.

FUTURE APPLICATION

There are a wide range of instruments from different countries and cultures. Not only can children bring in instruments to play and share with their class from their own culture, but they could invent new instruments using their knowledge of how sound is created.

Second, the waves that transmit sound energy need a material medium through which to travel – there must be some form of matter between the source of the vibration and the recipient. Sound can, therefore, travel through air and other gases, through water and other liquids, through solid materials, but *not* through a vacuum. The loudest explosion imaginable in space would be inaudible on Earth, as there is no intervening material medium through which the sound of the explosion could travel.

Third, and unlike light and ocean (transverse) waves, where the direction of the vibration or oscillation is at right angles to the direction of wave travel, the vibrations in *sound waves* are forwards and backwards in the direction of wave travel, and the waves are, therefore, said to be *longitudinal*. What happens is that the vibrating sound source causes alternate compressions and rarefactions (decompressions) in the molecules of the transmitting material, and these travel outwards from the sound source as waves. Once again, a Slinky can provide a good visual simulation of how a sound wave travels. Each neighbouring loop of the Slinky represents a molecule of air, or water, or some solid material, and, if the Slinky is laid on a table with one end fixed, and the other end is moved sharply towards the fixed point, a local compression 'wave' will pass along the spring. If the sharp movement is repeated so as to simulate a vibrating sound source, the transmission of the waves along the spring becomes clearly visible. Figure 4.15 gives an impression of the nature of a sound wave passing through a material.

Note: there is a possible cause of confusion here. As has been described, sound waves are formed from alternate compressions and rarefactions of molecules in the transmission

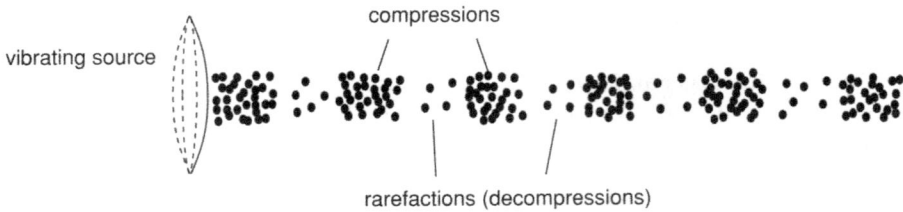

Figure 4.15 The movement of molecules in a sound wave

material, and the resultant vibration is forwards and backwards in the direction of wave travel. Sound waves are usually drawn, however, using the typical 'sine curve' waveform used to describe light and ocean waves (see Figures 4.10 and 4.18), where the vibration is at right angles to the direction of movement of the wavefront. Although such diagrams allow us to understand the relationships between wavelength, frequency, amplitude and so on, it is important to remember that the waveform depicted does not simulate the appearance or travel of a sound wave.

The speed of sound

As the materials of the transmission media vary in density – that is, in the 'closeness together' of their constituent molecules – sound travels at different speeds, and at different energy levels, through different materials. In general terms, the denser the material, the faster and more effectively sound will travel through it. As an example, sound travels at 331 m/s in air at 0°C (nearly 1 million times slower than light!), and at 1,400 m/s through water. Similarly, sound is transmitted more effectively by a liquid or a solid, than by a gas. The old 'tracking' device of listening for approaching footfalls by placing an ear to the ground worked because of the more effective transmission of sound through solid ground than through the air. This can be demonstrated easily in a classroom by asking someone to place an ear against a wall, while someone a distance away gently scratches the same wall with a fingernail. The 'scratching' sound will be clearly heard when listening with an ear against the wall, but may well be inaudible through the air.

In order for sound to be heard, some form of 'receiver' is necessary that can pick up the vibrations of the sound waves and translate them into understandable signals. In humans, this receiver is the eardrum, or tympanic membrane (see also Key Idea 2.2: The ear). Sound waves are gathered by the outer ear and funnelled down the ear canal to the eardrum, which then vibrates 'in phase' (resonates) at the same frequency as the incoming waves. The sound energy is then transferred, via the eardrum and the ear ossicles (three small bones, see Figure 2.13), into waves in a liquid (the perilymph) in the inner ear, and these vibrations are 'sensed' by hair cells in the coiled tube (the cochlea) and sent as impulses via the auditory nerve, to the brain, which 'hears' the sound.

FACT POINT

Ultrasounds

An ultrasound scanner is a medical device that is used to measure distances using sound wave echoes and convert these into images. Ultrasounds are used to monitor babies in the womb, but can also be used to find gallstones or look at the heart.

FURTHER CONCEPTS TO SUPPORT KEY STAGE 2

The reflection of sound

As with light and ocean waves, sound waves, when reaching an object, may be reflected and/or absorbed by the object, or transmitted through it.

When sound waves reach a solid object made of dense, rigid material, such as a wall or a rock face, most of the waves are reflected away from the surface of the material. If the 'hearer' is in a position to receive these reflected waves, the waves will be heard as an echo of the original sound. The reflected waves behave in the same way as light waves in that their reflected angle is equal to their angle of incidence (their incoming angle). This effect can be investigated by speaking quietly into a tube (a kitchen roll inner is ideal) held at an angle close to a wall. The speech can be heard most clearly through a similar tube held at a similar 'reflected' angle close by (see Figure 4.16).

The absorption of sound

Some materials, notably those that are flexible and soft, such as fabrics, polystyrene and some soft, fibrous materials, absorb sound energy, so that it is neither reflected back into the medium through which it has travelled, nor transmitted through the medium at which it has arrived. The vibration of the sound waves is prevented from travelling further, and very little sound is therefore heard beyond the absorbing surface. The use of soft, energy-absorbent materials is the basis for soundproofing. Areas that need to be soundproofed are lined with such materials in order to prevent or restrict the transmission of sound waves beyond the specified area. A simple 'amateur' soundproofing effect can be achieved through the use of card fibre egg-boxes, which are effective for two reasons. First, the cardboard material absorbs sound energy, and, second, the design of the egg-boxes maximizes the surface area over which sound can be absorbed. Heavy curtains, thick carpets and soft furnishings all have similar effects.

> **WORKING SCIENTIFICALLY**
>
> Children can compare different materials to identify which ones are better sound insulators by wrapping them over a sound source and measuring which reduces the volume most effectively.

The transmission of sound

This has already been described above, but it is worth noting that sound waves, which can only be transmitted through some form of material, travel faster as they transfer to denser materials. This is exactly opposite to the behaviour of light waves, which are slowed down by passage through a denser medium.

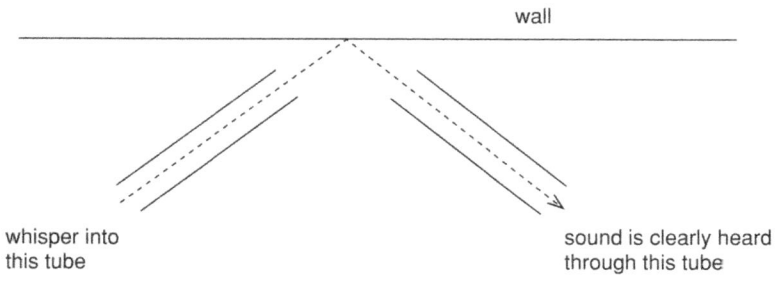

Figure 4.16 Investigating reflected sound

WORKING SCIENTIFICALLY

String telephones

Despite string telephones being quite old-fashioned, children can make them to explore how sound travels. The children can change different variables, such as length of string, size of cup or tension of string, to see how this affects the way sound travels.

Pitch

The pitch of a sound, in musical terms, relates to the frequency of vibration of the sound source. The higher the frequency, the higher the note heard, and vice versa. As a guide, humans can hear in a frequency range from about 20 Hz (twenty vibrations per second) up to about 18,000 Hz (the 'middle C' note on a piano is produced by a string vibrating 256 times per second, i.e. at a frequency of 256 Hz). It is well known that the range of audible frequencies decreases with a person's increasing age – high frequencies in particular become inaudible to older people. An experiment conducted recently showed that 40–50-year-old people were rarely able to hear frequencies above 13,000 Hz.

How can the pitch of a musical note be changed? By varying:

- the length of the vibrating column of air, as with the slide of a trombone, the valves of a trumpet or the holes in a clarinet or oboe;
- the thickness, length or tension of a string – the strings of a double bass are thicker and longer than those of a violin, and the notes produced are correspondingly lower. Increasing tension on strings of the same length and thickness will result in notes of higher pitch. Similarly, fretting or stopping a given string effectively shortens its length and increases the frequency (and therefore the pitch) of the resulting note;
- the mass of a struck object, as in the increasing size of xylophone or marimba bars, or of tuning forks. This can be seen clearly in the graph in Figure 4.17, which shows that the pitch of the note of a tuning fork is related to its mass – the higher the mass, the lower the note – an inversely proportional relationship.

In the cases described above, the shortening of the air column or the string, or the lowering of the mass of the struck object, will increase the frequency of vibration, and this

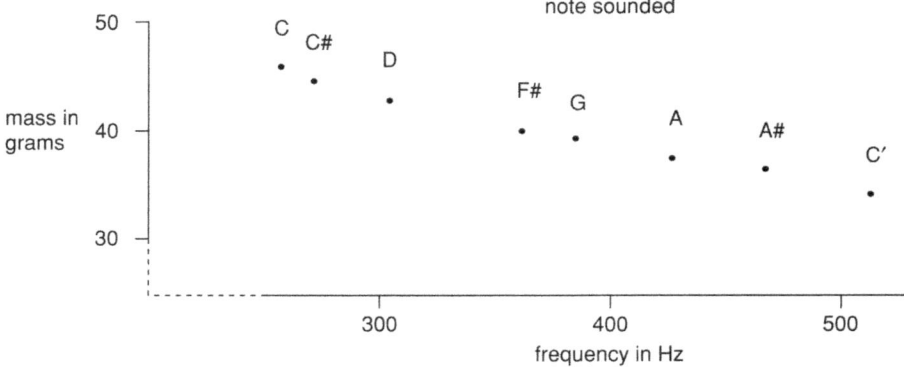

Figure 4.17 The relationship between the mass and frequency (pitch) of tuning forks

will cause a rise in pitch of the notes heard. Conversely, longer air columns and strings, or more massive struck objects will decrease the frequency of vibration, and deeper notes will be heard.

In musical terms, a doubling of frequency results in the raising of the pitch of a note by one octave. So, the middle C note of the piano has a frequency of 256 Hz, the C note that is one octave above middle C has a frequency of 512 Hz, and the C note that is two octaves above middle C has a frequency of 1,024 Hz.

Loudness

The loudness of a sound is a function of the amplitude of the waveform. A wave's amplitude is the height from its crest to its undisturbed position, and the greater the amplitude, the more energy is carried by the wave. Sound waves of large amplitude will have been produced by vigorously vibrating sources, and so the greater the amplitude of the sound waves, the louder the sound will be. To use a previous orchestral example, a double bass will usually sound louder than a violin, because the vibrations produced by the strings of the bass have a greater amplitude (are larger) than those of the violin.

Figure 4.18a shows the waveform of a loud (large-amplitude), high-pitched (high-frequency) sound, and Figure 4.18b shows a soft (small-amplitude), low-pitched (low-frequency) sound.

WORKING SCIENTIFICALLY

A sound meter on a data logger or tablet can be used to measure the loudness of different sounds. Children could record the sounds of different places at different times of the day, analysing and interpreting their findings.

TEACHING IDEA

Learning about hearing loss and technology that supports people with a hearing impairment will help children appreciate differing needs. Children can create posters conveying how to prevent hearing loss by protecting ears from loud noises – for example, concerts, machinery, head phones.

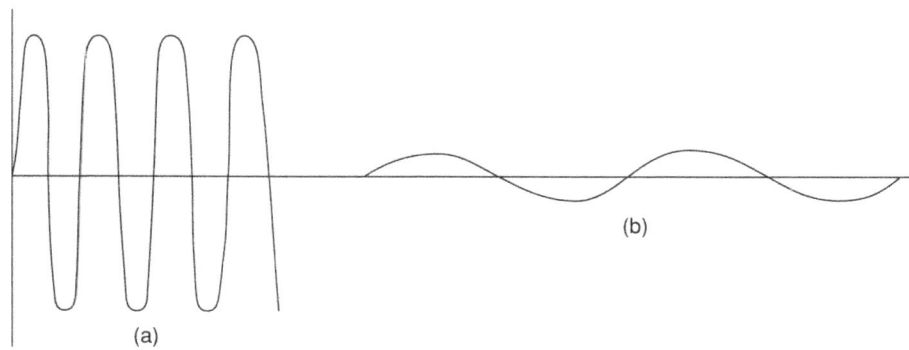

Figure 4.18 Sound waves – pitch and loudness

KEY IDEA 4.1 SUMMARY

Without energy, nothing would happen. Although energy in the universe remains the same, it is often transformed into a form that is no longer useful. It is important for children to become aware of the importance of energy in our lives and the ways in which it can be conserved.

Working scientifically

- *Pattern-seeking*: Children could be encouraged to make an energy diary, recording how they use energy during the day, comparing it with their peers and perhaps considering how they could reduce the amount of energy they use.
- *Observing over time*: Following health and safety procedures, children could carry out a daily meter-reading of the school's electricity over a week. They can consider how much energy the school uses and brainstorm ways in which energy consumption could be reduced. They can also look at how the sound levels change over the week, using data-logging equipment.
- *Research*: Children can research different ways of saving energy. They can compare electric cars to fossil-fuel-burning cars, or they can look at how technology (for example, LED televisions or energy-saving light bulbs) or simple strategies could reduce our energy consumption.

Cross-curricular activities

- *Mathematics*:
  - Children can record how much energy different foods have by looking at their labels. This could be presented as a graph showing which foods contain the most energy.
  - Children can measure and record the length of a shadow outside at different times of the day. Plotting this on a graph will help children to see the pattern between the sun's position and the shadow size.
- *Literacy*:
  - Children can create information leaflets or persuasive advertisements on ways in which we can save energy. Energy-saving strategies, such as not leaving appliances on standby, or turning the lights off when not in use, can be explained persuasively. Researching the pros and cons of different energy sources could also provide an excellent topic for a class debate, developing children's debating skills.
  - Designing, making and using shadow puppets to write and perform stories is a good way both to develop speaking skills and to show understanding simultaneously.
- *Art and design*:
  - Children can design and build boats powered by elastic bands. They can also design and make eco-friendly cars using solar panels.
  - The topic of light provides a range of art-related activities, from looking at and creating optical illusions, to colour-mixing activities.

Discussion point

- *Why do different countries around the world use different amounts and different sources of energy?* It is important to consider that our energy consumption has a global impact, and that, despite different needs and different sources, we all need to work together to reduce our consumption of fossil fuels and conserve our global environment. Do we need to use our cars to go to the shops just because we have them? Do we need to have three televisions on in the same house? These questions are worth discussing with an awareness of the bigger picture.

Future application

We are continually exploring new ways of harnessing energy from renewable sources. Solar panels can capture the Sun's light energy and convert it into electricity. Wind turbines are turned by wind energy, converting kinetic energy to electrical energy. Encouraging your school to invest in more renewable energy or trying to be more careful with the energy being used can help children appreciate the importance of energy conservation.

Health and safety

- Children should be advised never to look directly at the Sun, even when wearing sunglasses.
- Laser pointers should be used with care and never shone into people's eyes. Safe laser pointers have a power output of 1 mW.
- Children should be warned of the dangers of listening to music that is too loud. Listening to sounds above 85 dB for an extended period of time can damage the hair cells in the inner ear. These hair cells do not regrow, causing hearing loss.
- Children should be warned not to play with sockets or touch switches with wet hands. They should also be taught about the dangers of mains electricity: never to touch exposed wires, never to fly kites near power lines and to stay away from electrical substations.

Assessment for learning

Target cards / next steps: After conducting topics on different areas of energy such as heat and light, children can put forward what they would like to learn next about these areas. The questions and queries about light or sound or other energy could be displayed on a class wonder wall. It is important that children understand that there is always more to discover!

KEY IDEA 4.2

Forces

Forces can make things start to move, can make moving things speed up, slow down, change direction or stop, and can make things change their shape.

INTRODUCTION

Some of the difficulties that children (and adults) have with understanding forces and their effects are because:

- Forces themselves cannot be seen (although their effects can).
- Some forces cannot be felt.
- Some of the explanations of forces and their effects appear to contradict a 'common-sense' view of the way in which the world works – for example, why should a small object fall to the ground at the same speed as a large object, when both are released from the same height at the same time? (See below!)
- We may have limited personal experience of some of the common effects of forces in everyday life – for example, we are all affected by gravity, but how many people can really say that they are *conscious* of the 'pull' of gravity – when we lose our balance, we fall over; we do not feel as if we were pulled.
- Any simple 'earthbound' consideration of the forces acting on moving objects is complicated by the effects of gravity, friction and air resistance (see below).

Key Idea 4.1, relating to energy, has hopefully demonstrated some of the interrelationships between such concepts as energy, work and power. The present section will introduce some of the concepts that relate to forces and their effects, and will show how and where they interact with energy, work and power.

CONCEPTS TO SUPPORT KEY STAGES 1 AND 2

Some definitions

Forces are interactions between objects. In everyday terms, these interactions result in pushes and pulls, and it is sometimes helpful to make a mental substitution of the words 'push' or 'pull' whenever the term 'force' is encountered. This will be done in the text in the early part of the present section, so that readers can decide on its usefulness (or otherwise).

To revise the definitions from Key Idea 4.1, energy is the capacity or ability to perform work, and work is done (in mechanical terms) when a force (a push or pull) is applied to (or acts on) an object, causing it to move – remember:

work done (or energy transformed) = force (a push or pull) × distance moved
in the direction of the force (push or pull)

So, forces (pushes and pulls) are involved whenever work is done or when any object moves, and two simple, but very important, ideas that help with an understanding of forces are that:

1 forces act on (or are applied to) objects – they do not exist 'in' or 'on' objects, nor do objects 'use up' or 'run out of' force;
2 forces cause objects to accelerate (change their velocity) – either from being stationary to moving, or from moving at a constant speed to moving at an increased or a lower speed (a deceleration is seen as negative acceleration), or by a change of direction (velocity is speed in a particular direction, and so, if that direction changes, the velocity has changed, and this constitutes an acceleration).

In the next section, the following definitions may also be useful:

- *speed*, in m/s, is the *distance travelled/time taken* – for example, the speed of sound in air is 331 m/s;
- *velocity*, in m/s or kph (kilometres per hour), is *speed* (distance travelled/time taken) *in a particular direction* – for example, the car was travelling westwards at 90 kilometres per hour;
- *acceleration*, in m/s², is *change in velocity/time taken for this change* – for example, a car is advertised as being capable of accelerating from 0 to 90 kilometres per hour in 7.5 seconds;
- *mass*, in grams (or kilograms), is the *amount of matter* in an object.

Famous scientist factbox

Name	Sir Isaac Newton (1642–1727), Lincolnshire, England Mathematician and physicist
Link to NC	Year 5 – Forces
Famous for	Newton is famous for various scientific and mathematical contributions to our understanding of the world, including the three laws of motion, law of gravity, calculus (a type of mathematics that helps find lengths, volumes and areas through calculation) and light The first law of motion states that an object will keep moving in the same direction, unless a force acts on it to make it change direction, speed up or slow down The second law of motion is that the bigger the mass of an object, the bigger the force needed to make it accelerate and move. He created a mathematical formula for the second law of motion: $F = ma$ (the force (F) needed is equal to the mass of the object multiplied by the rate of acceleration) His third law of motion says that, 'for every action there is an equal and opposite reaction'
Working scientifically	Newton used *pattern-seeking* enquiries to identify universal laws
Impact on society	Isaac Newton changed the way we understand the universe. He has helped us to understand gravity and motion, thus helping us to shape our rational worldview

The effects of forces: The laws of motion

Sir Isaac Newton was the first person to systematically study the effect of forces (pushes and pulls) on the movement of objects, and his three laws of motion still enable us to predict the behaviour of moving objects in the everyday world. An annotated version of Newton's laws of motion is as follows:

The first law of motion

> Every object continues in a state of rest (remains stationary) or of uniform motion (constant speed) in a straight line, unless acted on by a force or forces.

What are the implications of the first law of motion in everyday terms?

The first part of the law, relating to stationary objects, is not difficult to visualize. A stationary object will remain stationary, unless and until it is acted on by a force or forces. So, when a force is applied to, or acts on, a stationary object, the object will begin to move. For example, imagine a brick lying on the ground (there are forces acting on the brick, but these forces are 'balanced' – see below). The brick will remain motionless on the ground until someone picks it up. In picking it up, the person is applying a force, a 'pull', to the brick (they can also feel the 'pull' of gravity on the brick), and it begins to move as it is lifted off the ground. Similarly, a line of stationary railway trucks will begin to move when a locomotive applies a force by pushing or pulling them to a new location, or a ball can be made to move through the air by the force applied to it (the push) from the thrower's arm and hand.

CONCEPT CONFUSION

As Newton's third law of motion states, every action has an equal and opposite reaction. Because children cannot see these forces, they find them difficult to understand. For example, when we are sitting on a chair, our weight causes us to push down on the chair, while the chair pushes up with an identical force, preventing us from falling through the chair. This can be shown using a force diagram, as we are unable to feel the force of the chair pushing our weight!

In the time during which the force is applied, the object undergoes acceleration – a change in velocity – from zero velocity (stationary) to a final velocity that will depend on the size of the force applied to the object, the length of time during which the force is applied and the mass of the object. Once the force is no longer acting on the object – that is, the brick has been lifted to its required height, the trucks have attained their required speed, and the ball leaves the thrower's hand – acceleration (but not necessarily movement) stops.

The second part of the law, relating to objects that are moving at a constant speed in a straight line, is not so easy to imagine in everyday terms. According to Newton, objects that are moving in a straight line at a constant speed will continue in that state until forces act on them that will change that state. In practice, such continuous straight-line movement at a constant speed, without the application of other forces, is possible only in conditions of zero gravity in a vacuum – that is, in deep space. Under such conditions, Newton theorized, an object that is moving at a constant speed in a straight line will continue to do so forever, unless it is acted on by a force.

Perhaps the closest we can get to seeing this effect in action is to consider a space probe heading for a distant planet. Once the probe has been started on its journey and has escaped the gravitational 'pull' of the Earth, it will continue in straight-line motion at a constant speed until forces are applied to it (usually by the firing of rocket motors) to change its direction of travel, slow it down or speed it up.

The interiors of spacecraft have proved to be excellent laboratories for experimenting with the theory implicit in the first law of motion. Footage from the ISS has shown astronauts 'placing' objects such as pens, spanners and even globules of water in 'mid air' inside the spacecraft. The objects appear to 'hang suspended'. In fact, they are simply obeying Newton's first law and are remaining stationary – staying where they are put – because no forces are acting on them. Similarly, when pushed gently in a particular direction, the objects move in a straight line and at a constant speed (also obeying the first law, and with no forces acting on them), until another force – contact with a hand or collision with part of the spacecraft – changes their speed or direction of movement.

On Earth, it is practically impossible to study a moving object that has no forces acting on it, as all moving objects are affected by the forces of gravity and friction.

The best we can do is to consider systems where the effect of friction is minimized – an ice-hockey puck sliding across ice, for example, or where the forces acting on a moving object effectively cancel each other out, as in an object moving down an incline that has been designed so that the effect of gravity compensates for the effect of friction.

As an earthbound example of the latter case, imagine a cyclist freewheeling at a constant speed in a straight line, down a long, very gentle gradient (the gradient is necessary to allow the cyclist to freewheel, but is gentle enough for the speed to be constant rather than accelerating, so that the effect of friction is minimized). The constant straight-line movement would theoretically continue until a force is applied to the object – which in this case is the combined system of the freewheeling cycle and the cyclist. The cyclist can change the constant straight-line movement by applying different forces to the system – by starting to pedal, for example – which would cause an increase in speed (an acceleration), or by putting on the brakes, which would cause a deceleration. External forces could also change the constant straight-line movement – the cyclist could be 'blown off course' by the force of the wind (the 'push' being provided by the kinetic energy of air molecules), causing a change of direction, or an extreme case would be the prevention of further forward movement by the contact force of a collision with a solid object – a crash, in other words!

Sometimes, the consideration of objects in constant straight-line motion on Earth can result in the apparent contradiction of the first of Newton's laws of motion. This is because, in practice, a number of forces will be acting on any object travelling in a straight line at a constant speed on or near the surface of the Earth. These will include:

- the 'pull' of the Earth's gravity;
- the force that tends to resist movement between objects – friction;
- air resistance (or drag) – a form of friction.

It is the combination of these forces acting on an object moving at constant speed in a straight line that will slow it down and may eventually cause it to stop. Imagine our cyclist again. If the cyclist was pedalling in a straight line along a horizontal road and was then to stop pedalling and begin to freewheel, the combined effects of gravity, friction and air resistance would eventually cause the cycle to slow down and stop. As another example, if a person in a supermarket was to stop pushing their shopping trolley, the trolley would also slow down and stop.

This 'slowing down and stopping' effect that happens to objects when 'pushing' or 'pulling' stops gives rise to one of the most plausible, common-sense contradictions to Newton's first law of motion – a contradiction that seems to be borne out by experience. Cyclists instinctively know that they need to keep pedalling steadily in order to maintain a constant speed on a horizontal road, and trolley pushers know that they must keep pushing steadily in order to keep trolleys moving at a constant speed around the store. Surely, then, experience shows that the maintenance of a constant speed needs the application of a constant force? According to Newton's first law, however, an object that has no forces (or balanced forces) acting on it will remain at rest or will continue travelling in constant straight-line motion, and so the cyclist should not need to pedal, nor the trolley pusher to push, in order to maintain the required constant speed!

There are two effects to bear in mind here. The first is that the slowing down and stopping of the cycle or the trolley *would* be predicted by the first law of motion – gravity, friction and air resistance are the forces that are acting on the moving objects in this case. Second, the constant 'push' supplied by the cyclist and the shopper is being used in each case to overcome the opposing forces – the combined effects of gravity, friction and air resistance – in order to maintain a constant speed. If it were possible to relocate the travellers to a hypothetical road or supermarket in deep space, where gravity, friction and air resistance were negligible, the movement of their separate vehicles would be, literally, effortless. Once the pedalling or pushing had accelerated the cycle or the trolley to the required speed, no further effort would be necessary, as constant straight-line motion would have been achieved.

Momentum

If, in Newtonian terms, there is no force acting on an object that is moving at a constant speed, what is it that keeps the object moving? It is the *momentum* of the object, which is a measure of the ease with which the object's motion can be changed. It is defined as:

momentum = mass × velocity

This is measured in kilogram metres per second (kg m/s).

An object with a small mass – for example, a cycle – moving at a constant speed will therefore have less momentum and will be easier to speed up, slow down, deflect (turn) or stop, than will an object of large mass – for example, a car or a lorry, travelling at the same speed.

An object will continue to accelerate as long as a force is applied to it. A ball, for example, is 'pushed' into the air by the thrower's hand. Once the force is removed – the ball leaves the thrower's hand – acceleration stops, and movement through the air continues because of the momentum imparted to the ball by its mass and velocity. Given that the forces of gravity and friction will eventually slow down and stop the ball, its momentum will keep it moving until another force acts on it to change its motion. That force may be the contact force applied when the ball hits the ground or a catcher's hand (or a pane of glass!).

The first law of motion describes the effect of forces on objects, and consideration of the law allows us to conclude that forces can start things moving (lifting a brick, throwing a ball), can make moving things speed up (pedalling a cycle that had been freewheeling), slow down or stop (putting on the brakes of a moving cycle), or change direction (being blown off course by the wind).

FACT POINT

Using momentum to make cars safer

As the result of a car crash, the car and its passengers decelerate rapidly, experiencing great forces owing to the change in momentum. Seat belts are designed cleverly, not only to stop you moving if there is a collision, but also to stretch a bit in order to increase the time taken for the body's momentum to get to zero, reducing the impact.

The second law of motion

The second law of motion describes the relationship between forces, acceleration and the mass of the objects on which the forces are acting:

> When a force acts on an object, the resulting acceleration is directly proportional to the force, and inversely proportional to the mass of (the amount of matter in) the object, and the acceleration changes in the direction in which the force acts.

Again, what does this mean in everyday terms? Put simply, when the force on an object increases, its resultant acceleration will increase proportionally. This can be shown by setting up an experiment as shown in Figure 4.19.

In a similar situation to that of the 'freewheeling cyclist' described above, the ramp is set up so that the pull of gravity on the trolley will just compensate for the effect of friction, and these two forces effectively cancel each other out.

Before the experiment is started, therefore, the ramp should be tilted so that the trolley will just roll down it at a constant speed – in other words, the effect of friction is overcome. It will then be found that, as the force pulling the trolley is increased (by the addition of weights to the end of the string), the acceleration of the trolley, measured as the increasing distance travelled each second, will increase proportionally. The table shows the (hypothetical) acceleration achieved when a trolley is pulled along the ramp by 100 g and 200 g masses.

	Distance travelled, m			
Weight 'pulling' the trolley	In 1st second	In 2nd second	In 3rd second	Total distance travelled in 3 s
100 g	1	2	3	6
200 g	2	4	6	12

It can be seen that, when pulled by a 100 g mass, the trolley accelerates – that is, it increases its velocity – at the rate of 1 metre per second, *every* second: 1 m in the first second, 1 + 1 m in the second second, 2 + 1 m in the third, and so on. Similarly, when pulled by a 200 g mass, the trolley accelerates at 2 metres per second every second (2 m in the first second, 2 + 2 m in the second second, 4 + 2 m in the 3rd and so on). Conventionally, these values would be written as 1 m/s² and 2 m/s². This effect can be summarized as:

$$\text{force is proportional to acceleration, or } \mathbf{F} \text{ (is proportional to) } \mathbf{a} \qquad (1)$$

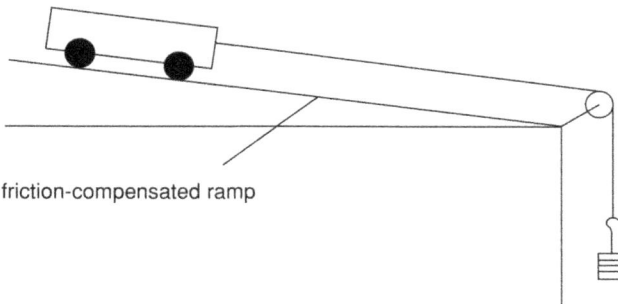

friction-compensated ramp

Figure 4.19 Investigating the second law of motion

It can be investigated easily by dropping a marble into a sand tray from different heights. The force of the impact of the marble in the sand will be proportional to the acceleration due to gravity and will, therefore, vary according to the length of time during which the marble falls – the longer the 'falling' time (i.e. the higher the release point), the greater the acceleration. A comparison of the size of the 'craters' left by the marble will confirm this.

Similarly, the force supplied or produced by a moving object will be proportional to its mass. Imagine the start of a snooker game. The cue ball is pushed towards the group of red balls and strikes them, scattering them around the table. What might the result be if the cue ball were to be replaced by a table-tennis ball or a sponge rubber ball accelerating at the same rate? In either case, the mass of the replacement cue ball is much smaller than that of the regular cue ball, and the correspondingly smaller force delivered by such small masses would have little impact (literally) on the triangular pack of red balls. This relationship can be summarized as:

$$\text{force is proportional to mass, or } \mathbf{F} \textbf{ (is proportional to) } \mathbf{m} \qquad (2)$$

This can also be investigated with a sand tray, but this time with spheres of similar size but different masses being dropped – for example, a pea, a marble, a ball bearing – into the sand, from the same height. Again, the larger 'craters' left by spheres of larger mass should confirm the effect.

The two effects described in equations (1) and (2) can be combined as:

$$\text{Force} = \text{mass} \times \text{acceleration, or } (\mathbf{F} = \mathbf{ma}) \qquad (3)$$

Conversely, if the force acting on an object remains constant, the acceleration of the object produced by the force will be *inversely* proportional to the mass of the object. In other words, if the mass of the object doubles, the acceleration will be halved, providing the force remains constant. In the trolley experiment shown above, the second law predicts that, if the mass of the trolley was 100 g, and it moved 1 m along the ramp in the first second of travel, an increase in the mass of the trolley to 200 g would result in it travelling only 0.5 m in the first second, under the effect of the same force: when the mass doubles, the acceleration is halved.

So, acceleration is inversely proportional to mass, or:

$$\mathbf{a} \textbf{ (is proportional to) } \frac{1}{\mathbf{m}} \qquad (4)$$

And, as F (is proportional to) a (from equation (1), above):

$$\mathbf{a} = \frac{\mathbf{F}}{\mathbf{m}} \text{ , a rewritten form of (3) above} \qquad (5)$$

CONCEPT CONFUSION

Children often think that, for something to be moving, one force has to be bigger than another. However, it is important to highlight that, when an object is moving steadily, or not at all, the forces are balanced. If forces are unbalanced (one force is bigger than the opposing force), acceleration or deceleration will occur.

Gravity

This last equation can also be exemplified by a consideration of objects falling – being pulled towards the Earth – under the effect of gravity. All finite objects are made of matter, and the amount of matter in an object is known as its mass, measured in grams. There is a force of attraction, known as the gravitational force, between all objects, and again it was Newton who realized that the force of attraction between two objects was a function of the mass and the distance apart of the two objects. The larger the masses of the two objects, and the closer together they are, the greater will be the gravitational attraction between them. Between objects of small mass, the gravitational force is so small as to be almost negligible. Objects of larger mass (such as the Earth), however, do exert a pull (a gravitational force) on small objects in their vicinity, and it is this pull, continuously exerted by the mass of the Earth, that tends to return any airborne objects to the Earth's surface. In practice, of course, this means that objects 'fall' to Earth under the effect of the gravitational force. Although we do not feel the 'pull' of gravity ourselves (partly because our systems have evolved under gravity, so that we tend not to notice it), we can feel the effect of gravity every time we lift an object – a heavy bag of shopping, for example. The force of gravity is 'pulling' the mass of the shopping back towards the centre of the Earth, and we need to apply a lifting force to overcome its effect. More force is needed to lift a heavy bag of shopping than a light one, because the heavy bag 'weighs' more. What is the difference between mass and weight?

TEACHING IDEA

Ask children to consider what it would be like if Earth had a fraction of the gravity that it currently has. They could record predictions of what would be easier and what would be more difficult: for example, the effect on sports, travelling, plant growth. It would allow you to assess what children understand about the effects of gravity.

The difference between mass and weight

In simple terms, mass is the amount of matter in an object and is measured in grams. Under normal circumstances, and as long as it remains intact, an object will always have the same mass – that is, there will always be the same amount of matter in it. A steel ball bearing will have the same amount of steel in it – its mass will be the same – whether it is on the Earth's surface or on the Moon.

The weight of an object is the force exerted by its mass as a result of the acceleration due to gravity. All objects are being accelerated towards the centre of the Earth by the planet's gravitational force, and the 'pull' of gravity on the mass of an object is known as its weight, measured in newtons (N). A newton is defined as that force that will give an acceleration of 1 m/s^2 to a mass of 1 kg:

$$\text{weight} = \text{mass} \times \text{acceleration due to gravity}$$

A useful idea is to imagine that mass is calculated by comparison of an object of unknown mass with standard masses (in grams) using a beam balance or scale (as in the statue of Justice on top of the Old Bailey). Weight is calculated by measuring the pull of gravity on the mass of an object – for example, by measuring the extension of a spring to which the mass has been attached, as in a spring balance or force meter (see Figure 4.20).

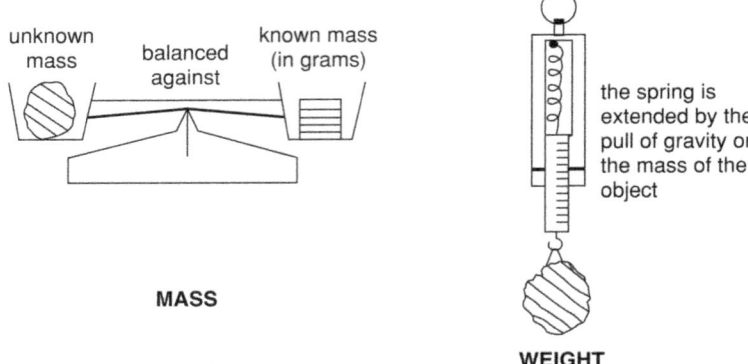

MASS   **WEIGHT**

Figure 4.20 Measuring mass and weight

A source of confusion here is that many spring balances are calibrated in grams, rather than newtons, and we talk about objects 'weighing' so many grams. Strictly speaking, objects have a *mass* of so many *grams*, and *weigh* so many *newtons*.

Repeating the commonly used moon analogy, if an object with a mass of 1 kg were weighed using a spring balance on Earth, it would weigh 9.8 N (as the acceleration due to the Earth's gravitational force is 9.8 m/s², and a newton is defined as that force that will give an acceleration of 1 m/s² to a mass of 1 kg). If the object was transferred to the Moon, its mass would not change (it would remain at 1 kg), but the object would weigh approximately 1.6 N, because the Moon, being smaller and less massive, has a gravitational pull that is about one-sixth of that on Earth. The weaker 'pull' of the Moon's gravity on the mass of 1 kg would result in a smaller extension of the spring balance, registering as a lower weight.

CONCEPT CONFUSION

Help children understand the difference between mass and weight by matching the correct units to each and discussing gravity. It is helpful to talk about weight on another planet, the Moon or an asteroid. It may not be appropriate to measure the mass of each child, but you could talk about how their weight would change if they were an astronaut, but their mass would stay the same.

DISCUSSION POINT

How does zero gravity affect astronauts?

Astronauts in space, living in weightless environments, are not using their bones and muscles to support their bodies in the same way as on Earth. As a result, they must do an extensive period of exercise each day to ensure they maintain their bone and muscle density. Children can research the exercise equipment and exercise regime astronauts on the ISS conduct.

Falling objects

The force – the 'pull' – of gravity varies – large masses are attracted towards the centre of the Earth with a larger force than are small masses, and that is why large masses weigh more than small ones. However, because, as mass increases, acceleration proportionally decreases, the overall effect on falling objects on Earth is that the *acceleration* due to gravity is constant. We can use the formulae derived from Newton's second law of motion to explain this behaviour.

$$\text{From } F = m \times a, \text{ we can derive } a = \frac{F}{m}$$

Imagine two objects, one of mass 50 kg and the other of mass 10 kg. At what rate will each of them accelerate if they are both released from the same height above the Earth, at the same time?

$$\text{Using } a = \frac{F}{m} \text{ we find that acceleration} = \frac{\text{Force (weight)}}{\text{mass}}$$

As a mass of 1 kg weighs 9.8 N, the 50-kg mass will weigh 490 N and will have an acceleration of:

$$\frac{490}{50} = 9.8 \text{m/s}^2$$

Similarly, the 10 kg mass will weigh 98 N and will have an acceleration of:

$$\frac{98}{10} = 9.8 \text{m/s}^2$$

As both objects have the same rate of acceleration, they will both fall at the same rate and will hit the ground at the same time.

This effect provides a good example of an area in which 'scientific' or 'school' knowledge is apparently contradicted by real-world experience or perception. Some children (and some adults) find it hard to understand, and even harder to accept, the constant acceleration due to gravity. There is often an intuitive belief that, 'heavier objects should hit the ground first', and, even when this is shown not to be the case, through theory or by practical demonstration, people often revert to their private 'belief systems', preferring to accept a common-sense view of the way in which the world works, rather than a scientific view that apparently does not 'stand to reason'.

FAMOUS SCIENTISTS

Contrary to the belief of Aristotle (Greek philosopher and scientist), Galileo (Italian scientist) proved that, in the absence of air resistance, all objects fall to the ground at the same rate. He tested this by dropping two balls, one light and the other heavy, to show they both hit the ground at the same time. This was further proved by astronauts on the Moon, who dropped a feather and hammer, simultaneously, that touched the surface at the same time.

An object falling through the Earth's atmosphere will not continue to accelerate indefinitely. At some stage, the force of air resistance, or drag, will equal the weight of the falling object. At this point, the forces on the object will balance, the object will stop accelerating and it will continue to fall at a constant speed, known as its terminal velocity. As an example, the terminal velocity of free-fall parachutists is about 120 mph (193 kph).

WORKING SCIENTIFICALLY

Paper helicopters

Children can investigate the factors affecting air resistance on paper helicopters. By changing the weight (adding paper clips), the size of the body or wings, or the shape of the wings, they can time how long it takes the spinner to land.

The third law of motion

The third law of motion states that every action has an equal and opposite reaction.

Imagine a 1-kg mass placed on a table. Because of the acceleration due to gravity, the 1-kg mass is exerting a downward force of 9.8 N on the table. The table is solid and rigid and is not moved by the force of the mass pushing down on it. Instead, it provides a reaction or contact force, exactly equal and opposite to the force applied by the 1-kg mass, and this reaction force supports the mass in a stationary position on the table surface. It is conventional, as in Figure 4.21, to represent the size and direction of the forces concerned by arrows of appropriate length and direction. The forces in this instance constitute a balanced pair, and the 1-kg mass remains stationary.

This is a difficult concept. Some accounts describe the table in the first example as 'pushing back' on the 1-kg mass, and many people find it hard to accept that the table actively 'pushes' the mass with exactly enough force to keep it in position. An easier concept, in my opinion, is the idea that the force provided by the 1-kg mass produces an equal and opposite reaction force on contact that *supports* the mass in position. If there were no reaction force, the 1-kg mass would 'sink' into the table surface!

Balanced forces can also affect moving objects, and this, too, seems difficult to understand. Surely, common sense would tell us that, if forces on an object were balanced, then it would not move? Newtonian physics suggests, however, that, if balanced forces are acting on a moving object, then the object will continue to move at a constant speed. For example, any object (such as a stone) dropping in 'free fall' towards the Earth will eventually be 'acted on' by a balanced pair of equal and opposite forces – the pull of gravity will be balanced by the force of friction supplied by the air resistance or drag on the object. The result will be constant motion towards the Earth, at a terminal velocity that reflects the mass and shape of the object concerned (see Figure 4.21).

A 'personal' experiment may help here. Stand facing a wall, at a distance of about 50 cm, and place your hands flat against the wall at about shoulder height. Gently bend your elbows so that you lean against the wall slightly and then push against the wall to recover your original position. You should have performed a 'standing-up' press-up against the wall. The wall has provided an equal and opposite reaction force to your push that has caused you to return to your starting position. Repeat the process, but this time push much harder against the wall. In this case, the equal and opposite reaction force provided by the wall enables you to 'push' yourself vigorously away from the wall – it is you, of course, who supplies the energy of the push. In similar fashion, a slow 'knees bend' followed by the straightening of your legs allows you to stand upright (the floor provides the equal and opposite reaction force), whereas a violent knees bend followed by a vigorous push with your legs results in

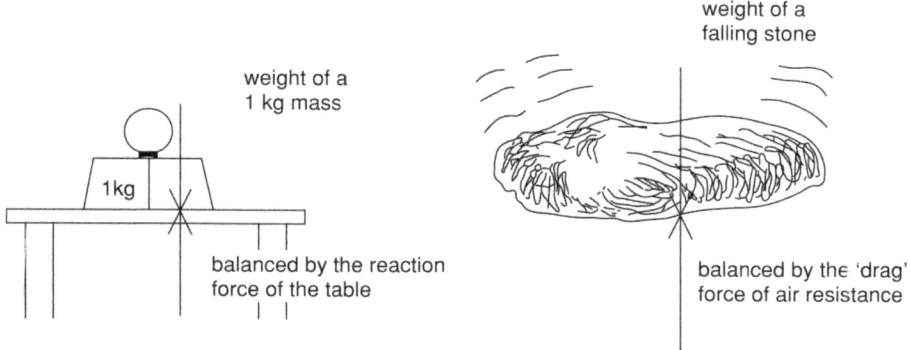

Figure 4.21 Equal and opposite reactions: Forces in balanced pairs

you leaving the ground in a vertical jump – again, the floor provides the reaction force that allows you to do this.

A combination of the first and third laws of motion shows us that, when objects are acted on by forces that have an equal and opposite effect – balanced forces – the result will be that stationary objects will remain stationary, and moving objects will continue to move at a constant speed. Hence, the 1-kg mass remains stationary on the table, and the stone continues to fall at terminal velocity.

Conversely, if the forces acting on an object are not balanced – that is, if one force is larger than another – acceleration of the object will occur. This may take the form of a stationary object beginning to move, a moving object beginning to speed up or slow down (and stop), or a moving object changing direction. It is important to keep in mind the distinction between objects moving at a constant speed (which may have balanced forces acting on them on Earth, or no forces acting on them in deep space) and objects that are accelerating, which will have unbalanced forces acting on them. These are examples of the effect of unbalanced forces:

- If a force (an upward pull) of more than 9.8 N is applied to the 1-kg mass, the mass will be lifted from the table.
- When a free-fall parachutist pulls the ripcord and the parachute opens, the force of friction is increased because of the air resistance of the large area of the canopy, and the parachutist is slowed down (decelerated) from terminal velocity (after a time, the forces will once again balance, and the parachutist will descend at a (slower) constant speed with the canopy open).
- A snooker ball, moving across a table, makes contact 'at an angle' with a stationary ball. The stationary ball (a) applies a reaction force to the moving ball, which is deflected from its original path, and (b) receives a 'push' from the moving ball and itself starts to move (see Figure 4.22).

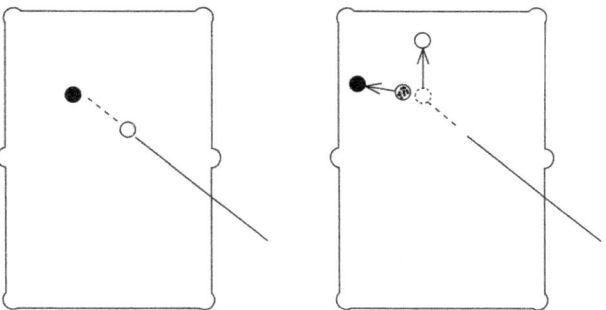

Figure 4.22 An example of the effect of unbalanced forces

The effects of forces: Change of shape

When forces act on materials, a number of effects may be noticed, depending on the properties of the materials concerned (see also Key Idea 3.2: The physical properties of materials).

If the material will sustain plastic deformation, the movement of the material caused by the application of a force may result in a change of shape. Imagine a piece of play dough being squeezed between finger and thumb. The opposite 'pushes' from the finger and thumb are large enough to move particles of the material relative to each other, and the play dough is flattened.

If the material is elastic (see Key Idea 3.2: Elasticity, and Key Idea 4.1: Strain energy), the forces acting on the material will cause the molecular bonds in the material to 'stretch', as in a rubber band, or to 'compress', as in the coil spring of a car's suspension system. When the material concerned is under such tension or compression, the forces of attraction between the molecules tend to restore the molecules to their original positions. This tendency in the material causes the application of a force, both within the material, and also to any objects attached to the material. So, a pile of papers is 'pulled together' by the force applied by a rubber band stretched around them, and the compression and resultant recoil of a car spring results in a smoother ride for the motorist.

Note: the elasticity of a material is not in itself a force; it is a property of the material. But, the molecules in an elastic material under tension or compression – that is, which have been moved out of place by the application of a tensile or compressive force – will themselves apply an opposing force as they tend to resume their original positions in the material.

FURTHER CONCEPTS TO SUPPORT KEY STAGE 2

Pressure

Pressure is defined as *force applied per unit area*, measured in newtons per square metre (N/m^2), a unit also known as a Pascal (Pa). Pressure is, therefore, a measure of the concentration of a force, and the concentration (or dissipation) of a force has a number of practical applications (and implications).

If, for any reason, a material is to be pierced, the concentration of an applied force through a very small area will have the greatest effect. This is exemplified by needles piercing fabrics, and nails and screws piercing wood and masonry. If the pushing force on a needle was to be 9.8 N (imagine the weight of a 1-kg bag of sugar), and assuming that the area of the point of a needle was one-thousandth of a square centimetre (0.001 cm²), the pressure produced at the needle point would be:

$$\frac{9.8}{0.001} = 9,800/m^2$$

This is equivalent to the weight of a 100-kg (15.7-stone) person!

This effect can also be seen (usually in the form of damage to the floor) when the pressure of a person's weight is applied through the small contact areas of stiletto-heeled shoes. Similarly, if water is flowing through a hosepipe, the pressure of the water leaving the pipe can be raised by reducing the diameter of the pipe (by placing a finger or thumb over the end of the pipe or by squeezing it). This will have the effect of reducing the area over which the force of the water is acting, and water will leave the pipe at an increased pressure (the same effect will result from placing a finger under a tap). This effect is immediately obvious when using a hosepipe with a 'variable' nozzle and can be seen when firefighters use a narrow hose nozzle in order to increase the pressure (and, therefore, the range) of the water used by their appliances.

Conversely, pressure can be lowered by 'spreading' the applied force over a larger area, and this effect can be seen in a number of applications. The spreading of weight over a large area of a suspect surface will minimize the likelihood of the surface giving way, and so, rescuers approach a hole in an ice-covered pond by crawling rather than standing on the ice and by spreading their weight on planks of wood or ladders. The effect of this action is to reduce the overall pressure by causing their weight to act over a larger area of the surface. Snow shoes produce a similar effect for people walking in deep snow, by increasing the surface area of the wearer's boot soles and, therefore, spreading their weight over a larger area of snow.

TEACHING IDEA

Compression and tension

Challenging the children to make towers using spaghetti and gum drops is an effective way for them to apply their understanding of forces to architectural structures. In preparation, they might research the structures of famous buildings around the world.

Forces in action

Key Idea 4.1 (The primary sources of energy) suggested that four forces – the strong and weak nuclear forces, electromagnetic and gravitational forces – are responsible for all the energy transfers in the universe. The effects of some of these forces have already been described elsewhere, including:

- the force of gravity (see above and Key Idea 4.1: Potential and kinetic energy);
- the forces of magnetic attraction and repulsion (see Key Idea 3.2: Magnetic properties);
- the forces of tension and compression in elastic materials (see above, Key Idea 3.2: Elasticity; Key Idea 3.3: Change in shape; and Key Idea 4.1: Strain energy).

Two further forces are now described, and these are the forces of friction and upthrust.

Friction

Friction is the force that opposes the motion of objects. When the molecules on the surface of an object come into contact with those of another surface, or with the molecules of a fluid (a liquid or a gas), forces of attraction between the molecules – the frictional forces – tend to 'stick' the surfaces of objects together, or to slow down the movement of a solid material through a fluid. When objects are slowed down by frictional forces in a fluid, the effect is known as drag – air resistance, for example, is a form of drag.

When friction is overcome, and movement results, two other effects can be noticed. First, the force applied in order to overcome the force of friction causes the conversion of energy as heat – moving surfaces heat up when they are rubbed together. Second, moving surfaces that are in contact tend to suffer from wear.

The force of friction, like the force of gravity, is always present on Earth. In everyday terms, it is practically impossible to produce a completely friction-free system, although, in industry and commerce, much time, money and effort are spent in the attempt to minimize the effects of frictional forces between materials. The effects of the force of friction can be both advantageous and disadvantageous.

WORKING SCIENTIFICALLY

Grippy shoes

Children can compare how much friction different shoes have by measuring the force it takes to move them across a surface. Once children have compared a range of shoes (from walking shoes to high-heel shoes to ballet shoes), they can then design their own pair of shoes, considering both their material and sole pattern.

Some advantages of friction are as follows:

- Frictional forces allow us to move. The soles of our shoes 'grip' the ground, and the tread of car tyres grips the road – if surfaces in contact simply slid apart, no movement would be possible.
- The braking systems in vehicles rely on the friction between brake pads and discs (or brake shoes and drums) to slow the vehicles down.
- The tuning pegs of violins and fastenings such as nails and screws rely on friction to remain in place.
- Friction allows us to warm our hands by rubbing them together on cold days.
- Air resistance slows down the descent to Earth of parachutists and space capsules (space capsules that return to Earth from beyond the atmosphere are slowed down to such an extent by the friction of the atmospheric air molecules that their surfaces glow red hot).

Some disadvantages of friction are as follows:

- Friction slows down vehicles and machinery. The effect of friction is counteracted by minimizing the area of surfaces in contact – perhaps the greatest discovery in this area was the wheel, which reduces the ground contact points on a vehicle to a minimum – and by 'streamlining' the design of the vehicle to minimize drag – the frictional effect of air resistance.
- Friction heats up and wears out machinery – these effects of friction are minimized by lubricating moving parts so that a thin film of oil or water is placed between the surfaces. Wear is minimized because the surfaces 'slide' over each other more easily, and the heat generated by friction is conducted away by the lubricant.

Obviously, different surfaces will have different frictional properties. Smooth, rigid and/ or polished surfaces will produce less friction than will rough and pliable surfaces. Surfaces that can 'mould' together are much more likely to 'stick' together. So, steep ice provides less friction, and is therefore harder to climb, than rough rock. Similarly, skates will slide smoothly on ice (too smoothly for beginners!), but will not slide at all easily on a wooden surface or a carpet. Riding a cycle on rough ground is harder work than riding on the road, because there is more friction between the rough ground surface and the 'chunky' tyres than there is between the tyres and the flat road.

The differences in friction between different surfaces can be investigated by finding out what force (using a force meter) is necessary to cause a block of wood covered with different fabrics to begin to slide on a 'standard' surface. Before you start, an interesting exercise is to predict what you think the 'rank order' of the fabrics and materials will be, from the 'slippiest' – that is, the one needing the smallest force to overcome the force of friction – to the 'grippiest' – that is, the one needing the largest force to produce the same effect. Figure 4.23 shows the set-up for the experiment, and the table gives some typical results for the forces needed to make a wood block covered with different materials begin to slide on a horizontal table top.

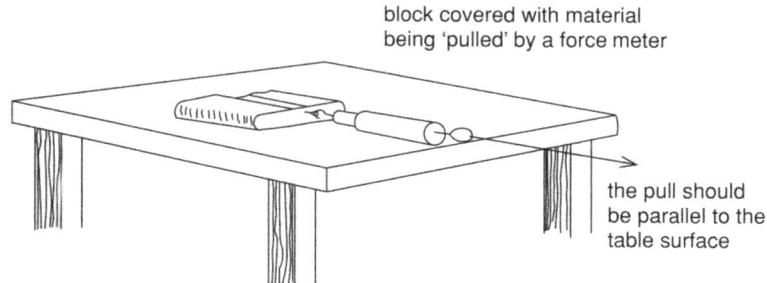

block covered with material
being 'pulled' by a force meter

the pull should
be parallel to the
table surface

Figure 4.23 Investigating the force of friction

Type of material covering the block	Force needed to start the block sliding (newtons)
Corduroy	1.0
Felt	0.90
Fine sandpaper	0.85
Coarse sandpaper	0.80
Satin	0.75
Lycra	0.65
Polycotton	0.50

The values for sandpaper seem at first to be anomalous. Surely sandpaper would provide a good grip – that is, need a large force to overcome the friction between itself and the table top? Consideration of the nature of the sandpaper surface may give us a clue here. The small sand grains, glued on to the paper, will act like roller bearings and will minimize the contact area between the sandpaper and the table top, so *less* force will be needed to overcome the friction of the sandpaper-covered block than for the felt or corduroy fabric, where the surface of the fabric can 'mould' to the table top with a consequently higher frictional force.

TEACHING IDEA

Ask children to list all of the things that would be difficult without friction. You could start by giving a few examples: you would not be able to rub out a mistake with an eraser, or pull a light cord, or even tie your shoe laces! This exercise will highlight lots of words associated with friction, such as grip, rub, grate and wear.

Upthrust

When a liquid is placed in a container, the weight of the liquid (its mass, which is being pulled downwards by the force of gravity), creates a pressure – a force per unit area – within the liquid. This pressure acts *in all directions* in the liquid, so that, in addition to the downward pressure on the bottom of the container and the sideways pressure on the sides of the container, there is an upwards pressure 'pushing' towards the surface of the liquid, and the force producing the upward pressure is known as *upthrust*.

It is easy to feel the upthrust produced in a container of liquid. Screw the cap tightly on to an empty plastic bottle and push it into a bowl or tank of water. You can feel the bottle being pushed back up to the surface, and the 'push' is the upthrust force provided by the water. If you hold the bottle stationary under water, the force that you need to apply to the bottle to keep it in position is equivalent to the upthrust force – the forces are balanced and in opposition.

The upthrust force in a liquid acts on the surface of any objects that are placed in the liquid, and one way to look at it is to imagine that the volume of liquid that has been 'pushed out of the way' – displaced – by the object is 'pushing back' in order to resume its original position in the body of the liquid (an example of the 'action and reaction' forces of Newton's third law).

TEACHING IDEA

Get children to experiment by pushing an inflated balloon under water. The water will exert an upward force on the balloon, making it difficult to push under the water. The more the balloon is inflated, the harder it will be to push under water, because the force of upthrust is greater.

Displacement

If you place a stone in a measuring cylinder of water, the water level will rise in the cylinder. The rise in level occurs because the stone has displaced (literally, taken the place of) a volume of water equal to its own volume (volume is sometimes seen as the amount of space taken up by an object, and is measured in cm³). The displacement method is often used to find the volume of irregularly shaped objects – simply note the volume indicated by the water levels in the measuring cylinder before and after immersion – the volume of the immersed object can then be calculated by subtracting the original volume from the volume after immersion.

FAMOUS SCIENTIST – ARCHIMEDES AND THE EUREKA MOMENT!

The idea of displacement can be shared with children by telling them the story of Archimedes, a Greek mathematician. Archimedes noticed that, as he sat further into the bath, the water level rose. He realized that an object immersed in water always displaced the volume of water equal to its own volume. As a result of his discovery, he was able to calculate the density of an object by dividing its weight by its volume.

Floating and sinking

What governs whether an object floats or sinks?

When any object is placed in water (or any other liquid), it will displace a volume of water (or other liquid). The weight of the volume of water displaced by the object is considered to be equal to the upthrust on the object in the water. When the weight of the volume of water displaced is equal to the weight of the object, the forces are balanced, and the object will float at the water's surface. If the total weight of the object is more than the weight of the water it displaces, the object will sink.

Some figures may help here. Three common objects were each placed into a measuring jug containing a known volume of water. In each case, the volume of water displaced by the objects was noted. The objects were then carefully lifted from the water and dried off, and their mass was measured on a kitchen scale (note the paradox – the mass, in grams, was 'weighed' on a spring-loaded scale). The table shows the results.

Object	Volume of water displaced (cm³)	Mass (g)	Floated/Sank
Apple	125	125	Floated
Orange	235	235	Floated
Egg	55	60	Sank

Using the knowledge that 1 cm³ of water has a mass of 1 g, it can be seen that the apple and the orange both displaced a volume of water the weight of which (equal to the upthrust) was equal to their own weight – hence, they floated. Conversely, the egg had a higher mass – that is, it weighed more than the mass of water that it displaced – and it sank.

How can we predict whether a solid object will float or sink? To be able to do this, we need to know something about the density – the mass per unit volume – of the object to be tested. If the object is less dense than the liquid into which it is placed, it will float on the surface; if the object is denser than the liquid, it will sink. In order to find the density of an object (expressed in g/cm³), we need to know both its mass and volume.

Returning to the objects in the table above (the masses of which had already been measured), each was replaced into the measuring jug so that its volume could be calculated. The egg presented no problem because it sank, of course, but the apple and orange were each held just below the water surface using the end of a teaspoon handle, to ensure that the total volume of each was measured. The results are given in the table.

Object	Mass (g)	Total volume (cm³)	Density (g/cm³)
Apple	125	170	0.73
Orange	235	290	0.81
Egg	60	55	1.09

As the density of water is 1.0 g/cm³ (1 g of water has a volume of 1 cm³), it is possible to predict, knowing the relative densities of the three objects, that the apple and orange would float, because their densities are lower than that of water, and that the egg will sink in water, because it has a higher density than water. It is interesting to make a similar comparison with the 'properties of materials' table in Key Idea 3.2 (p. 124). Those materials with densities greater than 1.0 g/cm³ will sink, whereas those with densities lower than 1.0 will float.

And yet, we know that ships made of steel and concrete will float. How does this happen? A solid block of steel, with a density of 7.86 g/cm³, would rapidly sink if it were placed in water. It is possible, however, to *shape* the steel so that it displaces a volume of water whose mass (and therefore weight) is larger than its own mass (see Figure 4.24). Under these conditions, the steel will float. What has happened is that the shaping of the steel (into a boat hull, for example) effectively increases the volume and, therefore, decreases the overall density of the structure. Obviously, under these circumstances, stability is important – if the boat tips too far sideways or is 'holed' below the waterline, water can enter the hull, and the 'increased volume' effect is lost, with potentially disastrous results.

The same principle is operating when lumps of plasticine (sinkers) are turned into 'boat' shapes (floaters), in a classroom. If the exercise is carried out using a suitable measuring

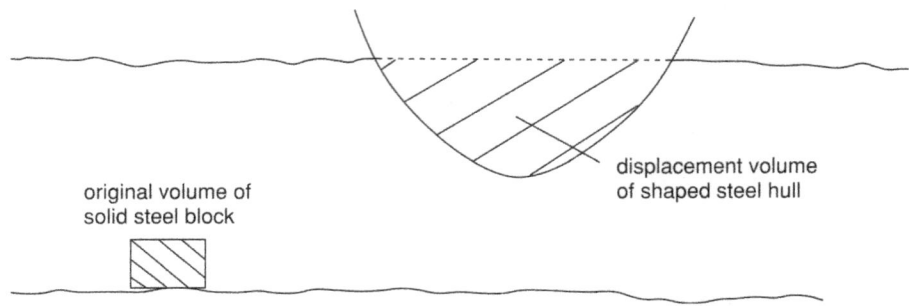

Figure 4.24 How the shaping of a hull effectively increases a vessel's volume

container, the volume (and hence the mass) of the water displaced by the 'successful' plasticine boats will be found to be larger than the volume of the lumps of plasticine from which the boats are made.

Objects weighed in air and water

If an object that is a 'sinker' (a 200-g mass, for example) is hung from a force meter and weighed in air, and then carefully immersed in water and weighed again, a weight loss will be found to have occurred, and this weight loss is equivalent to the upthrust of the water on the object.

If the weight loss is then converted into an 'apparent loss' in mass (this is easy with force meters, which are graduated both in newtons and grams), it should be the case that this apparent loss in mass is equal to the mass of water displaced by the sinking object (which can be found using the displacement method in a measuring cylinder).

The forces acting on a mass that was weighed in air and in water are illustrated in Figure 4.25.

In Figure 4.25a, the forces of gravity acting on a mass of 200 g and the tension in the spring of the force meter represent a balanced pair of forces, that is:

force of gravity (is balanced by) spring tension (2.0 N)

In Figure 4.25b, where the 200-g mass has been immersed in water, the balance occurs between gravity – the force acting downwards – and a combination of upthrust and spring

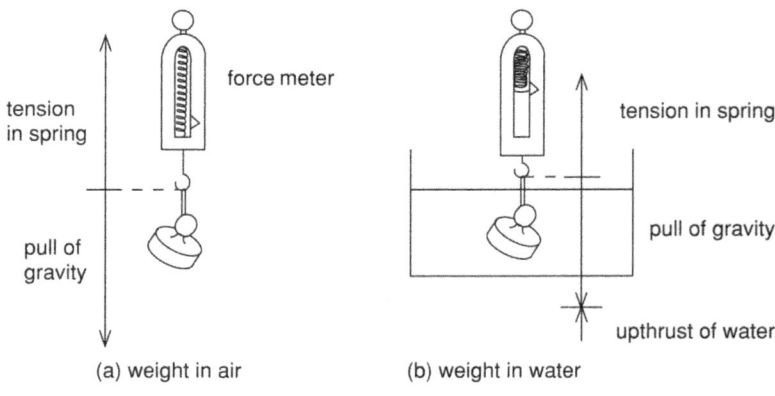

Figure 4.25 Forces acting on a mass being weighed in air and water

tension. As gravity is assumed to remain constant, the upthrust of the water 'pushing' against the 200-g mass reduces the effect of gravity on the extension of the spring. and, hence:

force of gravity (is balanced by) upthrust of water + spring tension (1.75 N)

The upthrust, equivalent to the weight loss, has therefore provided a force of 0.25 N, a force produced by a mass of 25 g. The displacement due to the immersion of the 200-g mass was 25 cm³, also equivalent to a mass of 25 g. The weight loss in water (expressed in grams) is, therefore, equivalent to the mass of water displaced by the immersed object.

We can use this piece of information to calculate the density of the object concerned. As density is mass per unit volume, and we know that the 200-g mass (weight = 2.0 N) displaced 25 cm³ of water (registering a weight loss in water of 0.25 N), the density of the material from which the 200-g mass is made is:

$$\frac{200 \text{ g}}{25 \text{ cm}^3} = 8.0\text{g/cm}^3$$

The 200-g mass used for the investigation was made of brass, and the value of 8.0 g/cm³ is close to the conventionally accepted value of 8.5 g/cm³ for the density of brass.

Mechanisms

The invention of levers, wheels, gears and pulleys has changed the way we live. Simple mechanisms make jobs easier: building, transporting heavy goods, travelling more efficiently are just a few examples. Simple mechanisms are used to change force or motion.

Levers are the simplest mechanism and include three types. The type of lever is dependent on the position of the load, effort and pivot:

- the *load* is the object you are trying to move;
- the *effort* is the force applied to move the load;
- the *pivot* is the point at which the load is pivoted.

The first type of lever has the load and the effort on opposite sides of the pivot, such as a see-saw or a pair of pliers (Figure 4.26). The second type of lever has the load and effort on the same side of the pivot, the load closer to the pivot, such as a wheelbarrow. The last type of lever has the effort and load on the same side of the pivot, but the effort is closer to the pivot, so that the effort is greater than the force applied to the load, such as tweezers.

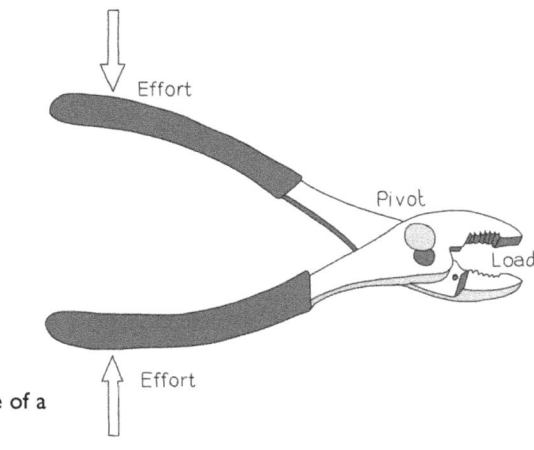

Figure 4.26 An example of a lever: Pliers

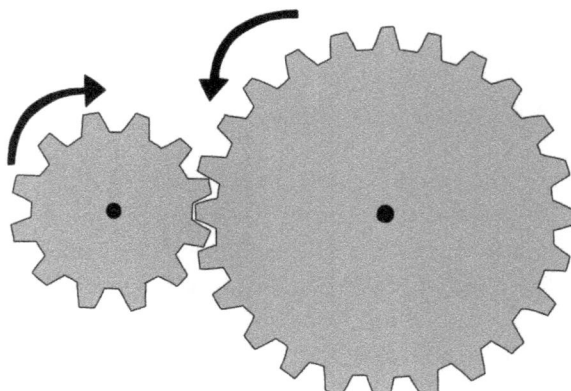

Figure 4.27 Gears

Gears are made of toothed wheels (cogs) fixed to shafts. The teeth interlock with each other, so that, as the first shaft rotates, it causes the second shaft to move (Figure 4.27). Gears have many uses in our lives: they are used to multiply or reduce speed and force, change direction of movement and spread force over a distance. Gear ratio is based on the number of rotations made by each gear – worked out by comparing the number of teeth. For example, if two gears with 6 and 18 teeth interlock, they will have a ratio of 1:3, where one cog will rotate once while the other will make three rotations. Common uses of gears are found in cars, bicycles, clocks and watches.

FACT POINT

Ancient computers

The Antikythera mechanism (designed by Greek scientists between 150 and 100 BC) is an ancient analogue computer that used at least thirty bronze gears to predict the position of stars and planets. The Analytical Engine (designed in Britain, 1837) was a mechanical computer designed by Charles Babbage to perform arithmetic. Modern computers, however, use digital signals instead of mechanisms.

Pulleys are mechanisms that change speed, direction of rotation or turning force. A pulley system includes two pulley wheels, each on a shaft, connected by a belt (Figure 4.28). If the wheels are different sizes, the smaller one will spin faster than the bigger one. They make lifting, lowering and some movements much easier. For example: lifting and lowering water buckets in a well, lifting sails on a boat, lifting elevators and lifting heavy items using cranes.

TEACHING IDEA

Fairground rides

Children can be tasked to design a fairground ride. They can begin by exploring the different mechanisms, drawing diagrams with direction arrows to explain how they work. They can then apply their understanding to their own fairground ride designs.

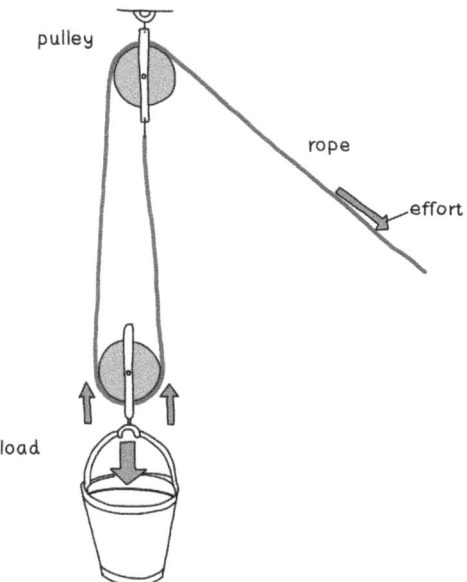

Figure 4.28 A pulley system

KEY IDEA 4.2 SUMMARY

Learning about forces allows children to understand their importance in everyday life. Pushes, pulls, magnetism, friction, air and water resistance, upthrust and gravity have allowed people to invent systems and devices that we use to make things easier.

Working scientifically

- *Comparative / fair testing*: Children can investigate factors that affect the strength of a model bridge. They can change the material, the shape or how it is connected, comparing the strength by recording how many different weights each bridge can hold.
- *Comparative testing*: Toy cars can be used to test the friction of different surfaces. Placing different materials on a ramp and measuring how far the cars can travel will allow children to compare the amount of friction.

Discussion point

- *How does a Maglev train work?* The idea of magnetism was used to invent the Maglev (magnetic levitation) train. The principle of two like poles repelling has been used to make the trains float above the track. As the trains are not moving along the track, the friction is reduced, allowing the train to reach much higher speeds.

Real-life application

Applying forces to real-world examples will help children to understand how they are applied. Whether the children are fans of motor racing, football or swimming, they can be tasked to identify all of the different forces acting on them/objects within these activities. They can also look at how forces can be useful or a nuisance in different situations – for example, icy roads make it more difficult to grip the roads, but putting chains on tyres can increase the amount of friction, making driving safer for drivers in extreme conditions.

Cross-curricular links

- *Design and technology*: Forces lend themselves to many technology and engineering activities. In making model bridges, model cars powered by elastic bands or model parachutes, children can apply their understanding of forces and motion. Children can design levers and pulleys to lift objects. They may be inspired by Leonardo da Vinci and his many inventions.
- *Mathematics*: When measuring and comparing forces, using Newton meters, stopwatches and metre sticks, children can record and present their data in tables and graphs.
- *History*: Researching inventions such as catapults, trebuchets, levers and pulleys provides an excellent link with the historical development of machinery.
- *PE*: The topic of forces can be applied to many sports, considering how a knowledge of forces can improve performance. From ice-skating, to football, to cycling, children can identify the different forces and how they can be changed to improve speed and functioning.

Health and safety

- When they are releasing objects from a height, make sure pupils stand on secure structures, such as PE boxes, rather than classroom furniture.
- Activities involving flying things, such as kites, hot-air balloons, catapults, water rockets, paper aeroplanes and so on, will require a large space and close supervision.
- Teach pupils to aim away from each other when testing flying objects and projectiles.
- Spring-based instruments, including home-made Newton meters, can be dangerous if suddenly released under tension.

Assessment for learning

True/false cards: To check understanding of key concepts related to forces, true or false cards could be used for statements that hold common misconceptions (such as those below):

1 Objects stop moving when their force runs out. (*False*)
2 There are no forces acting on a stationary object. (*False*)
3 An object moving at a steady speed has equal and opposite forces acting on it. (*True*)
4 An object accelerating must have a force acting on it. (*True*)
5 If an object runs out of force, it stops moving. (*False*)
6 The mass of an object is always equal to its weight. (*False*)
7 Heavy things fall faster than light things. (*False*)

Children can discuss with partners why they agree or disagree with each statement.

KEY IDEA 4.3

The Earth and beyond

INTRODUCTION

It is in astronomy, perhaps more so than in any other field, that those who study science are on the boundaries of knowledge and belief. For many centuries, people have looked into the night sky and wondered if there was anything (or anyone) 'out there', and the 'heavens' have been peopled with supernatural deities, the activities of whom have been used to explain the apparently inexplicable. There have been gods of thunder and of rain, and a god who drew the Sun across the sky each day in a fiery chariot.

As our understanding of the Earth's place in the universe has widened, many of the 'supernatural' explanations for natural events have been superseded by more rational accounts of the processes involved. It is not the place of science (and particularly of primary school science) to demolish sincerely held beliefs about the nature of the universe, but it is appropriate to consider alternative theories that may offer more convincing explanations of the processes of the natural world.

A religious account of the 'creation' constitutes one theory; the 'big bang' explanation of the origin of the universe is another. In the final analysis, people can (some might say should) make up their own mind about the nature of things in the light of the evidence presented to support the theory being advocated. Whatever seems to them to be a reasonable (or convenient) explanation will become incorporated into their own personal system of knowledge and belief. It is perhaps worth remembering that it is easy to offend religious sensibilities by offering theoretical explanations as 'facts'.

Without going too deeply into the philosophy of science, it is assumed that all teachers of science would acknowledge the provisional nature of science knowledge, and would endorse the view that what we offer in the way of scientific explanation represents the theory with the current best fit to the observable evidence. The following sections are presented with that thought in mind.

CONCEPTS TO SUPPORT KEY STAGES I AND 2

The solar system

The *Earth* is one of eight *planets* that orbit the Sun. The *Sun* is a *star* – a burning ball of gas – that emits light and heat energy as deuterium (heavy hydrogen) atoms fuse to form helium atoms (see Key Idea 4.1: Nuclear fusion). The planets do not emit light of their own and can be seen because they reflect the light of the Sun from their surfaces.

A useful mnemonic for remembering the names of the planets, from the innermost (nearest to the Sun) outwards, is:

My Very Energetic Mother Just Served Us Noodles

TEACHING IDEA

Children can create their own model solar system using fruit. There may not be a fruit big enough to represent the sun, and so you may have to use a ball.

Planet	Fruit
Mercury	Peppercorn
Venus	Blueberry
Earth	Grape
Mars	Pea
Jupiter	Watermelon
Saturn	Coconut
Uranus	Orange
Neptune	Lemon

The table shows data relating to the solar system.

	Distance from Sun (millions of kilometres)	Diameter (kilometres)	Axial rotation	Time for 1 orbit
Sun		1,384,000		
Mercury	57.9	4,840	59 days	88 days
Venus	108.1	12,400	243 days	225 days
Earth	**149.5**	**12,742**	**23 h 56 m**	**365.25 days**
Mars	227.8	6,800	24 h 37 m	687 days
Jupiter	777.8	142,800	9 h 50 m	11.86 years
Saturn	1,426.1	120,800	10 h 14 m	29.45 years
Uranus	2,869.1	47,600	10 h 49 m	84.01 years
Neptune	4,495.6	44,600	15 h 40 m	165.79 years

CONCEPT CONFUSION

It is important to highlight that Pluto is no longer considered a planet, as it does not fit the new criterion of being substantial enough to have cleared its orbit of other larger objects. Pluto is, therefore, considered a dwarf planet.

The Sun contains more than 99 per cent of all the matter in the solar system, and it is the mass of the Sun that provides the gravitational force that keeps the planets in their orbits. Each planet describes a more or less elliptical orbit round the Sun, and, with the exception of Pluto, these orbits are all roughly in the same plane. As can be seen from the table, the Earth completes an orbit round the Sun once every 365.25 days. This gives rise to our Earth year of 365 days, with the 0.25 days adding up to the extra day in the leap year, once every 4 years.

In addition to the major planets, the solar system also contains smaller planetary fragments or *asteroids*, some of which are concentrated in a belt between Mars and Jupiter, and *comets*, which are clusters of rock and ice (including ice formed from gases such as methane and carbon dioxide). Comets, in particular, travel in long, elliptical orbits that can carry them far beyond the orbit of Pluto before they eventually return towards the Sun again. When comets break up (sometimes owing to the melting of the ice that binds the fragments together), pieces of the resulting debris become visible from Earth as *meteors* or '*shooting stars*' as they 'burn up' owing to the heat generated by friction with the Earth's atmosphere.

TEACHING IDEA

Asteroids can be different sizes and are made of a mixture of rock, metal and carbon. Although they are mainly found in the asteroid belt between Jupiter and Mars, evidence from craters shows that they have hit Earth and the Moon. Children can recreate the impact of asteroids by throwing different-sized marbles into a tray of flour or sand. They can change the angle of movement, weight and size to observe the impact.

Day and night

At the same time as the Earth is travelling on its annual orbit round the Sun, it is also rotating on its own axis. A mental model sometimes used is that of a spinning top, and, although this may be helpful for imagining axial rotation, it is misleading when considering the relative speed of rotation. Similarly, the globe that can be seen rotating on the screen before the start of BBC TV programmes is also travelling far too fast – to get a scaled-down idea of the speed at which the Earth is spinning on its axis, imagine the speed at which the hour hand of a 24-hour clock would travel around the clock face – in relative terms, the Earth is turning slowly.

TEACHING IDEA

Right-hand rule

To memorize the direction of the Earth's rotation, children can do a thumbs-up sign with their right hand. If their thumb symbolizes the North Pole, the direction of the Earth's spin is shown by the direction their fingers curl in.

As the Earth is bathed in the light from the Sun, it is possible to imagine that one hemisphere will be in sunlight, while the other is in darkness, and that, because of the axial rotation, a fixed point on Earth will experience a period of light (daytime), followed by a period of darkness (night) in any given 24 hours (the period of axial rotation).

This process can easily be simulated by slowly rotating a globe on its axis in a beam of bright light – from a slide or overhead projector, for example (see Figure 4.29). The darker the room and the brighter the light source, the more pronounced the 'shadow' effect will be on the side of the globe away from the 'Sun'. As a point on the Earth's surface (or a small 'person' attached to the globe) rotates in the 'sunlight', sunrise, the apparent change in

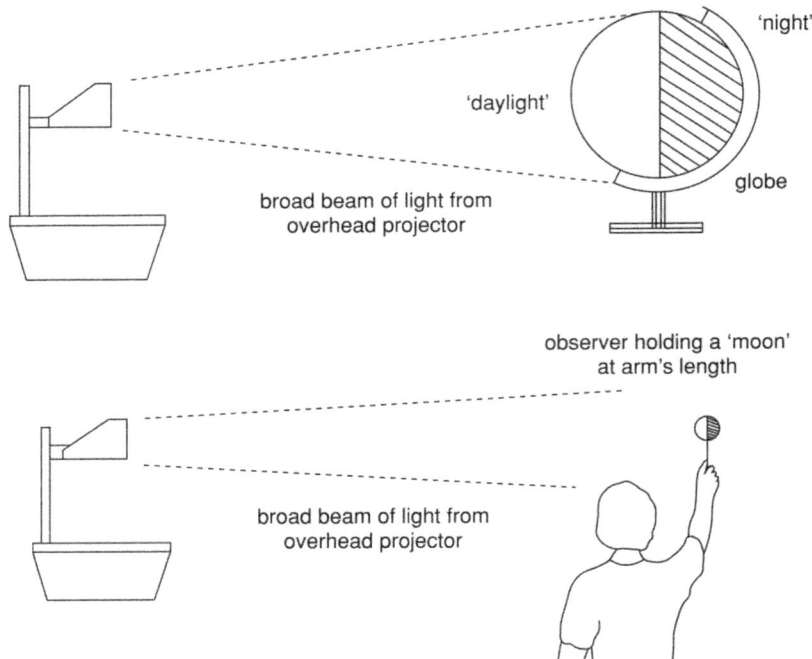

Figure 4.29 Simulating day and night

height and position of the Sun during the day, sunset and darkness can all be visualized. The Earth rotates on its axis from west to east, and so, in any simulation, the surface of the globe facing the observer should be moving from left to right. This ensures that the Sun 'rises' in the east and 'sets' in the west!

CONCEPT CONFUSION

Although the Earth seems flat, with the sun moving across the sky, a globe model of our planet can help children understand that the Earth is spherical, and that its movement on its axis is what gives us day and night, not the Sun's movement.

Seasons are not caused by moving closer and further away from the Sun, but are a result of the tilt of the Earth on its axis.

The seasons

We know from our own experience that, as the year progresses, the seasons change. The effects of these changes are seen and felt particularly in terms of daylight length and ambient temperatures. What causes this annual and predictable cycle of seasonal change? It occurs because the Earth's axis is tilted (at an angle of 23.5° from the vertical) relative to the direction of the light (and heat) from the Sun. Before considering the effect of this axial tilt, it is interesting to imagine what would be the case if the Earth's axis was not tilted, but was exactly perpendicular to the light from the Sun? In this case, *there would be no seasons*. Day and night would each be exactly 12 hours long, and, for any given place on Earth, the daily weather patterns would be predictable and identical, although the patterns would vary from place to place – the equatorial regions would still be warm, and the polar regions would still be cold.

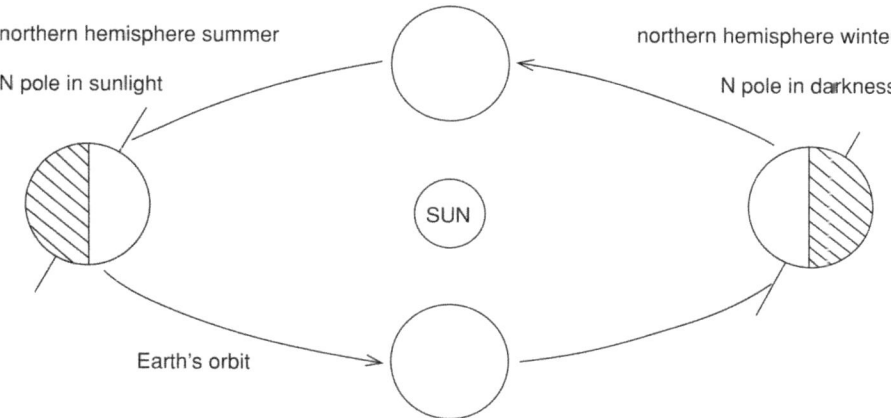

Figure 4.30 Summer and winter: The positions of the Earth and Sun

Figure 4.30 shows the effect of the axial tilt on the length of daylight experienced on Earth at different times of the year. During the northern hemisphere summer, when the northern hemisphere is, as it were, tilted towards the Sun, places in the northern hemisphere experience longer days than nights – that is, in a 24-hour period, they are 'in the sun' for longer periods than they are 'in the dark'. In June in the UK, for example, the summer days are about 18 hours long, and, at the 'extremity' of the northern hemisphere, places inside the Arctic circle experience 24-hour daylight in the 'land of the midnight Sun'.

Six months later, when the Earth has travelled halfway round its orbit, the northern hemisphere is now 'tilted away' from the Sun, northern-hemisphere winter nights are longer than days, and the Arctic circle is in darkness for 24 hours a day. At this time, the southern hemisphere is tilted towards the Sun, and it, in turn, experiences longer days than nights, with the Antarctic becoming the land of the midnight Sun.

At the intervening times between summer and winter (in March and September), the position of the Earth on its orbit round the Sun, coupled with the Earth's axial tilt, results in an even distribution of hours of daylight and darkness. This results, on or about 21 March and 21 September, in the vernal (spring) and autumnal equinoxes, respectively, each having 12 hours of daylight and 12 hours of darkness.

The Earth and the Moon

Just as the planets of the solar system are satellites of the Sun, some of the planets have orbiting satellites of their own. Jupiter has at least twelve satellites, four of which are visible through ordinary binoculars, and Saturn has ten satellites, in addition to its 'rings'.

The orbit and rotation of the Moon

The Moon is the Earth's satellite and is our closest celestial neighbour. It has a diameter of 3,456 km (2,160 miles), and it orbits the Earth at a distance of about 382,400 km (239,000 miles). A complete orbit takes just less than 28 days (a lunar month), and, during the orbit, the Moon itself rotates once on its axis. The effect of this axial rotation is that it is always the same hemisphere of the Moon that is visible from Earth.

Note: strictly speaking, the Moon does not simply 'go round' the Earth, but both bodies, held in position by gravitational attraction, rotate around a common centre of mass. As the Earth is about eighty times as massive as the Moon, however, the centre of mass of the Earth–Moon system lies inside the Earth, and so, effectively, the Moon is in a simple orbit round the Earth.

The phases of the Moon

As with the Earth, the Moon is also bathed in light from the Sun. During its 28-day orbit round the Earth, therefore, the appearance (not the shape!) of the Moon changes, as parts of the hemisphere that faces Earth move into and out of the sunlight. These changes in appearance are described as the phases of the Moon, and are summarized in the table.

Day of lunar orbit	Phase of Moon	Description of appearance
1	New moon	Moon invisible
8	First quarter	'Half moon', right side visible
15	Full moon	Complete disc visible
22	Last quarter	'Half moon', left side visible

The Moon's phases can be readily simulated by holding a suitable ball (the Moon) at arm's length and then rotating the person (arm, ball and all) in a bright beam of light (see Figure 4.31). The person (the viewer as from Earth) then sees the progression of the changing shadows on the 'Moon' (the phases) during a single orbit. If a suitable mark is placed on the ball, the effect of the Moon's single axial rotation can also be seen. In order to keep the same 'side' of the Moon facing the observer, the Moon will need to be turned once on its own axis during its travel round the orbit.

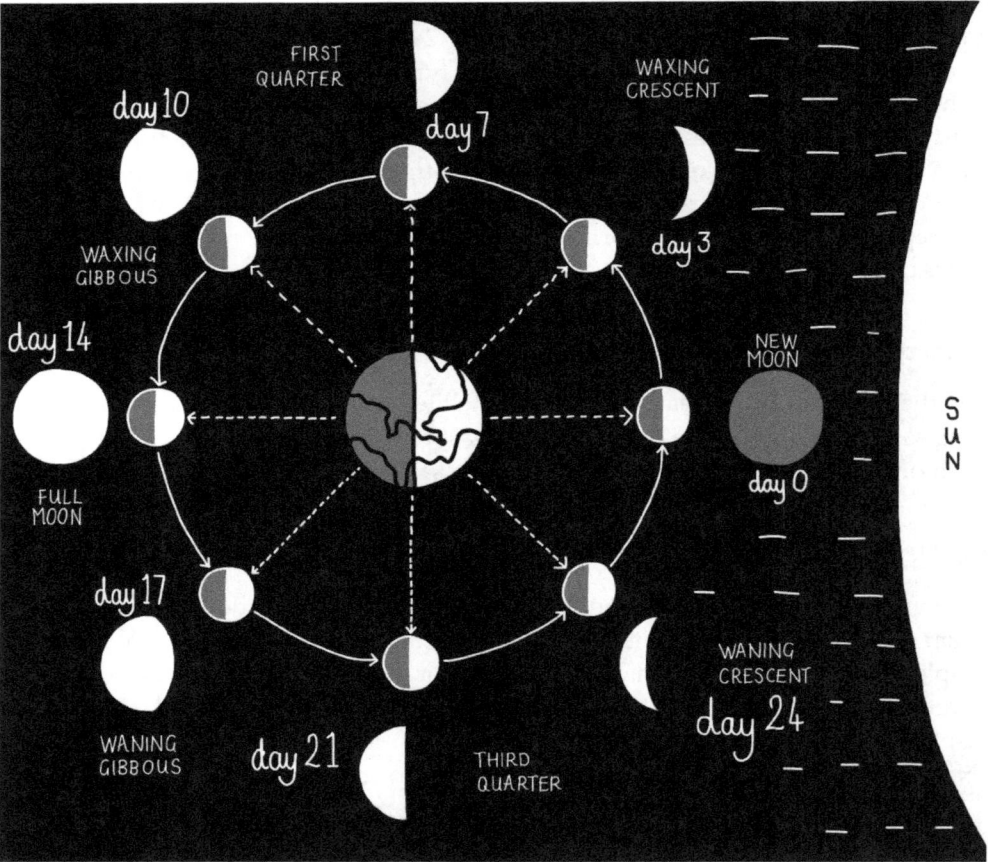

Figure 4.31 Simulating the phases of the Moon

CONCEPT CONFUSION

The phases of the Moon are not caused by the shadow of the Earth on the Moon's surface. They are caused by our view of the Moon as it orbits the Earth. As the Moon orbits the Earth, the same side always points towards the Earth, but different amounts of it are illuminated, depending on its position in relation to the sun.

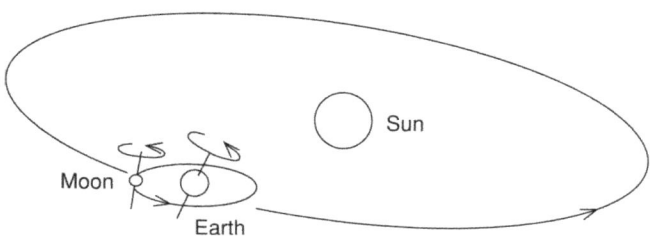

Figure 4.32 The orbits and axial rotation of the Earth and the Moon

TEACHING IDEA

The children can make a paper model demonstrating the movements of the Sun, Earth and Moon in relation to each other. Joining three discs (large, medium and small) with two strips of card and paper fasteners, the Moon should be able to rotate around the Earth, and the Earth (with the Moon) should be able to rotate around the Sun (see Figure 4.33).

To summarize the relative places and movements of the Earth and Moon in the solar system:

- The Sun, a star, is at the centre of the solar system.
- The Earth is one of nine planets in elliptical orbit round the Sun, with an orbiting period of 365.25 days.
- The Earth is also rotating on its own axis, with an axial rotation every 23 hours, 56 minutes.
- The Earth is orbited by the Moon, with an orbiting period of 27 days, 8 hours.
- The Moon is also rotating on its own axis, with an axial rotation time that is the same as its orbiting period; hence, the same hemisphere always faces Earth.

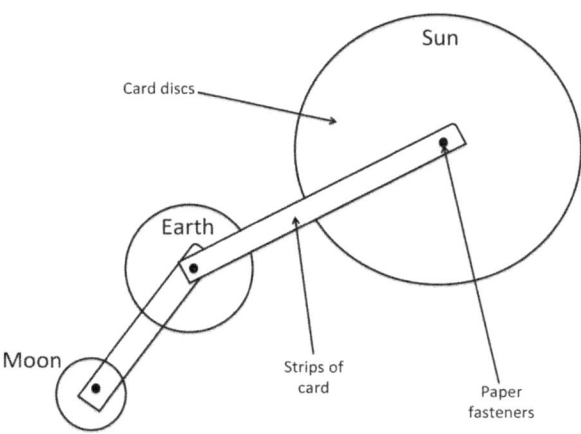

Figure 4.33 Paper model of Sun, Earth and Moon movement

TEACHING IDEA

Using a ball painted half white and half black can help the children understand why we have moon phases. By asking the children to observe the ball from different angles, they will be able to see the different moon phases and how they result from the Moon's orbit around the Earth.

The solar system and beyond

In the whole of science, perhaps one of the most difficult things to visualize and comprehend is the scale of the universe. This final section attempts to take us beyond the solar system, in order to gain some insight into the orders of magnitude involved when the component parts of the universe are considered.

In order to do this in any easily understandable way, it is necessary to use a variety of different scales and units. Figure 4.34 represents a composite diagram for use with a variety of 'celestial scales'. The line is drawn with a radius of 15 cm and a thickness of 0.5 mm.

- *Scale 1*: If the curved line were to represent the curved surface of the Earth, then all the physical features of the Earth's surface, from the top of Mount Everest to the bottom of the deepest ocean trench, would fall within the thickness of the drawn line.
- *Scale 2*: If the line were then to represent the curved surface of the Sun, then the arrowed circle (3 mm in diameter) would represent the size of the Earth, drawn to the same scale.
- *Scale 3*: If the line were to represent the surface of the star Betelgeuse (a red giant visible in the 'top left' corner of the constellation of Orion), then the arrowed dot (1 mm in diameter) would represent the Sun drawn to the same scale!

Betelgeuse is so large (with a diameter of 400 million km) that the entire orbit of the Earth round the Sun could be contained within its own diameter.

So much for size, but what about distance? On a universal scale, the solar system is so small and isolated that, once we leave its confines, our units of linear measurement are of limited value to us. In order to appreciate the distances involved if we were able to make a journey beyond the solar system, we need a different unit of measurement, and one that has been found convenient is the *light year*. A light year represents the distance travelled by light in a year, that is:

300,000 (the speed of light in kilometres per second) multiplied by
365 × 24 × 60 × 60 (the number of seconds in a year)
= 9.46×10^9 m, or 9.46 billion km

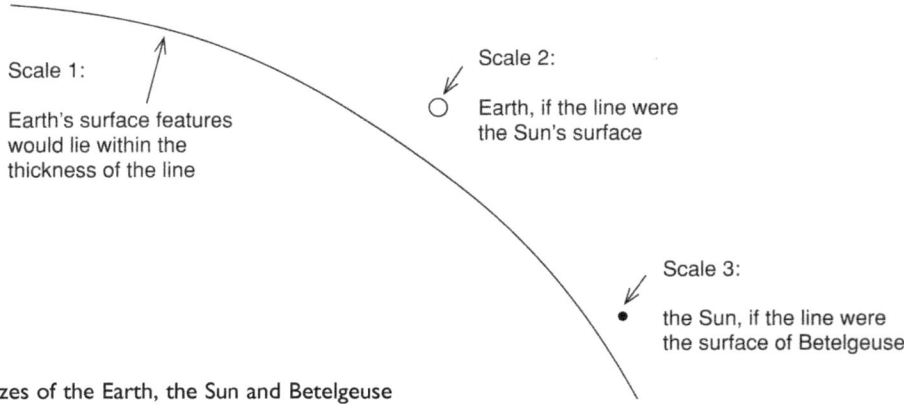

Figure 4.34 The relative sizes of the Earth, the Sun and Betelgeuse

In terms of the solar system, the light reflected from the Moon takes 1.25 seconds to reach the Earth, and the light from the Sun takes about 8.25 minutes. It is a measure of our isolation in the universe that our nearest stellar neighbour – the closest star – lies at a distance of four light years away!

FACT POINT

Yuri Gagarin, a Soviet cosmonaut, was the first person to orbit the Earth, in 1961. Neil Armstrong and Buzz Aldrin were the first humans to walk on the surface of the Moon, in 1969. In 1998, the ISS was launched, on which astronauts conduct a series of science experiments to benefit life on Earth and crews in space.

Galaxies

The Sun is a medium-sized star in a collection of stars – a star system known as a *galaxy*. The galaxy that contains the Sun – 'our' galaxy – is of a type known as a spiral nebula and has an estimated population of 100 billion stars, of which only some 6,000 are visible to the unaided eye, even though some stars are many times larger than the Sun. The size of Betelgeuse has already been described, and the star named Antares, in the constellation Scorpio, is large enough to contain the orbit of the planet Mars round the Sun.

CONCEPT CONFUSION

Stars do not disappear during the day, but we can no longer see them owing to the huge amount of light from the sun. Light pollution in urban areas can also make it difficult to spot certain stars at night.

The shape of 'our' galaxy has been described as a flattened disc of stars and star clusters. It has been estimated to be 100,000 light years in diameter, and up to 20,000 light years thick at its centre. The Sun is positioned along one of the spiral arms of the galaxy, about 32,000 light years from its centre. When we look at the 'Milky Way' in the night sky, we are looking through the galactic disc 'end on', hence the concentration of light in that area. Even the small magnification provided by binoculars can bring into range countless stars that are invisible to the unaided eye, and the Milky Way seen through a telescope is an awesome sight.

In terms of movement, the entire galaxy is itself rotating in space. It has been calculated that the Sun is moving at about 240 km/s about the galactic centre and will take about 200 million years to complete one galactic revolution.

Intergalactic space

Even the size of the galaxy pales into apparent insignificance when we realize that only three of our 'neighbouring' galaxies are visible to the unaided eye (the Large and Small Magellanic Clouds and the Andromeda nebula). However, the 200-inch reflecting telescope at the Mount Palomar observatory in California (one of the largest optical telescopes in the world) is capable of photographing *1 billion* galaxies. The most distant objects in the universe that can be located by astronomers are estimated to be of the order of 9 billion light years distant, and the light that we now detect from these objects was emitted by them nearly 4.5 billion years before the Earth came into existence!

Famous scientist factbox

Names	Galileo Galilei (1564–1642), Pisa, Italy Italian astronomer, physicist, engineer, philosopher and mathematician Claudius Ptolemy (AD 100–170), Alexandria, Egypt Astronomer and mathematician Ibn al-Haytham, or, to Europeans, Alhazen (965–1040) Cairo Muslim scientific thinker and polymath Nicolaus Copernicus (1473–1543) Royal Prussia, Poland Renaissance mathematician and astronomer
Link to NC	Year 5 – Forces Year 5 – Earth and space
Famous for	Galileo worked on a variety of experiments, including the speed at which different objects fall, mechanics and pendulums Ptolemy believed that the Earth was the centre of the universe. This idea is known as the 'geocentric' theory. He is also famous for his work in geography. He was the first person to use longitude and latitude lines to identify places on the face of the Earth Galileo heard about the invention of the telescope and, without having seen an example, he constructed a better version and made many astronomical discoveries. These included mountains and valleys on the surface of the Moon, sunspots, the four largest moons of the planet Jupiter and the phases of the planet Venus Alhazen studied the anomalies between Aristotelian and Ptolemaic models of the solar system and wrote his own thesis called, 'On the Structure of the World' Galileo is best known for gathering evidence that supported the Copernican theory that the Earth revolved around the Sun. At the time, Galileo's discoveries were controversial, because they challenged the Catholic Church's beliefs and caused him to be put on trial and imprisoned Copernicus identified that it was the Sun and not the Earth that was at the centre of the universe. This model is known as the heliocentric model (*helios* means Sun). It has the Sun motionless at the centre of the Universe
Working scientifically	Galileo's approach to science was unusual at the time – scientists didn't generally carry out experiments to test out their theories. Effectively, Galileo developed what we now know as 'the scientific method' of experimentation Observation over time and pattern-seeking, seeing how the sun and planets appeared to move across the sky, to ascertain their theories of the universe. Copernicus also used scientific research to develop his view of how the universe works
Impact on society	Galileo used evidence to prove that the Earth revolved around the sun. Together, they contributed to our understanding that we can always develop a better understanding of how the world works, and, even when a theory appears correct, it is always debatable, especially with new evidence Ptolemy's longitude and latitude work has helped us map places on Earth

One final idea relates to the 'big bang' theory of the origin of the universe. Evidence exists that all objects in the universe are receding from each other at great speed – the universe is expanding. 'Our' galaxy is rapidly moving away from all its neighbours, and from all other galaxies, further into the empty regions of deep space.

FACT POINT

What is the big bang theory?

Most scientists believe that our universe began very hot, small and dense. Space then expanded very quickly outwards (the big bang), forming tiny particles of matter. The big bang occurred more than 13.7 billion years ago, and the universe is still expanding. Evidence for the big bang theory includes:

- all galaxies are moving away from us;
- the further away a galaxy is, the faster it is moving away.

Scientists are continuing to work to solve the mystery of what may have caused the big bang in the first place.

To bring us back to Earth again, and to summarize what we know of the relative movements of the Earth and the Moon in relation to the Sun and the galaxy, let us consider how it is that all of us on Earth are moving in four different directions at the same time:

- The Earth is turning on its axis.
- The turning Earth is orbiting the Sun.
- The Sun is moving round the galactic centre, as the galaxy rotates in space.
- The galaxy is moving apart from all other galaxies.

A cosmic address

In terms of orders of magnitude, it is interesting to consider where an individual person may be placed in the context of the size of the known universe. So, what might our cosmic address be, in universal terms?

How about this?

Room	Year 3 classroom
Building	Lingmill Primary School
Town	Anytown
County	Barsetshire
Region	South-west England
Country	United Kingdom
Subcontinent	Europe
Continent	Eurasia
Planet	Earth
	The solar system
	'Our' galaxy
	'Our' galaxy cluster
	The currently observable universe

KEY IDEA 4.3 SUMMARY

The size and scale of the universe is hard to comprehend. As a result, it is important to teach about our place in space, developing an understanding of time and space. The topic of space should aim to capture the awe and wonder of science, encouraging children to ask questions about our Milky Way and the universe.

Working scientifically

- *Scientific research*: Carry out a project on one of the space expeditions, about the adventures of an astronaut or about one of the robotic probes that has been sent into space.
- *Observing over time*: Children can go outside to the playground to draw around each other's shadow. They can repeat this a few times at different times over the course of the day, to see how the shadow changes. This can be related to how sundials work to tell the time. They can even have a go at making their own sundials.
- *Observing over time*: Using a digital thermometer and a digital camera, children can pick an area of the school that has trees and plants and can record the temperature and take a photo once a month. The data and images could be used to create a wall display showing the changes in seasons over a year. The same could be done with observing the moon phases over a month.

Application

Artificial satellites allow global communication systems to work: telephones, TV transmissions and global positioning satellites (GPS) for navigation. Weather satellites also allow us to predict weather patterns and help us to warn populations of extreme weather conditions, such as storms and tsunamis.

Cross-curricular

- *Drama*: Children can role play space travel, considering what it might be like to travel to space and live in anti-gravity conditions. They might describe what the Earth looks like from space and articulate the challenges of living on a space station.
- *Literacy*: Creating space-themed stories can not only convey the children's ideas of Earth and space, but can provide inspiration for creative writing. Using space-themed books can also give children ideas to write their own stories. Researching different constellations and finding out about the stories and legends behind them can provide inspiration for children's own story writing.
- *History*: Children can research the names and stories behind star constellations and scientists who raised theories about the solar system and space.
- *Mathematics*: Information collected on day lengths and time zones can be interpreted by getting the children to draw graphs. The children can also investigate and compare information about different planets, such as day length, year length, size and gravitational pull.
- *Design and technology*: Children can construct bottle rockets filled with water and then use a bicycle pump to launch them. Alternatively, children could create model space stations using recycled materials.

Discussion points

- *Could we survive without the Moon?* The Moon provides us with a stable climate and regular seasons because of its gravitational force preventing the Earth from wobbling in space and keeping its axis stable. In proportion to other planets, we have the biggest moon in the solar system.
- *Could we live on the Moon?* Neil Armstrong was on the Moon for 21 hours. However, the Moon has harsh conditions, with no air to breathe and harmful solar radiation, and so, without oxygen supplies and a special space suit, it would be impossible. The Moon has extreme temperatures, with the coldest temperature of −233°C out of the sun and the hottest temperature of 123°C. It also has no accessible water, although a space probe has found frozen water, which means there may be water for drinking and growing plants.
- *Is it possible to travel to another planet?* By 2024, Bas Lansdorp (a Dutch entrepreneur) hopes to fly forty people to Mars on a one-way mission, but we still need lots of technological advancements before this becomes a reality.

Health and safety

Children should be warned not to look directly at the Sun, as it can be dangerous for our eyes. If observing a solar or lunar eclipse, children should be provided with protective glasses to do so.

Assessment for learning

Child-constructed success criteria: Learning about space provides many opportunities for self-directed projects. These could involve designing a space habitat, creating a presentation on a planet or researching an astronomer or astronaut. By asking the children to formulate their own success criteria, they will be able to help assess their own work once completed.

Physics: Schools National Curriculum coverage and progression

Below are listed all the component parts of the relevant programme of study of science in the NC (DfE, 2013). The table demonstrates how each Key Idea is developed through progression of knowledge in the Key Stage 1 and 2 programmes of study.

Year group	Programme of study	Statutory requirements
Key Idea 4.1: Sources of energy – electricity		
Year 4	Electricity	Identify common appliances that run on electricity Construct a simple series electrical circuit, identifying and naming its basic parts, including cells, wires, bulbs, switches and buzzers (*Electricity in simple circuits*) Identify whether or not a lamp will light in a simple series circuit, based on whether or not the lamp is part of a complete loop with a battery (*Series circuits*) Recognize that a switch opens and closes a circuit and associate this with whether or not a lamp lights in a simple series circuit (*Switches*) Recognize some common conductors and insulators, and associate metals with being good conductors. (*Electricity in simple circuits*)
Year 6	Electricity	Associate the brightness of a lamp or the volume of a buzzer with the number and voltage of cells used in the circuit (*Electricity in simple circuits*) Compare and give reasons for variations in how components function, including the brightness of bulbs, the loudness of buzzers and the on/off position of switches (*Switches; Series circuits; Work and power in electrical circuits*) Use recognized symbols when representing a simple circuit in a diagram (*Circuit diagrams*)

Year group	Programme of study	Statutory requirements
Key Idea 4.1: Sources of energy – light		
Year 3	Light	Recognize that they need light in order to see things and that dark is the absence of light (*Light and dark*) Notice that light is reflected from surfaces (*The reflection and absorption of light*) Recognize that light from the sun can be dangerous, and that there are ways to protect their eyes (*Light and seeing*) Recognize that shadows are formed when the light from a light source is blocked by an opaque object (*Sources of light; Shadows*) Find patterns in the way that the size of shadows changes (*Shadows*)
Year 6	Light	Recognize that light appears to travel in straight lines (*Straight-line travel*) Use the idea that light travels in straight lines to explain that objects are seen because they give out or reflect light into the eye (*The reflection and absorption of light*) Explain that we see things because light travels from light sources to our eyes or from light sources to objects and then to our eyes (*The reflection and absorption of light*) Use the idea that light travels in straight lines to explain why shadows have the same shape as the objects that cast them (*Shadows*)
Key Idea 4.1: Sources of energy – sound		
Year 4	Sound	Identify how sounds are made, associating some of them with something vibrating (*Sound waves*) Recognize that vibrations from sounds travel through a medium to the ear (*Sound waves; The absorption of sound*) Find patterns between the pitch of a sound and features of the object that produced it (*Pitch*) Find patterns between the volume of a sound and the strength of the vibrations that produced it (*Loudness*) Recognize that sounds get fainter as the distance from the sound source increases (*Loudness*)

Year group	Programme of study	Statutory requirements
Key Idea 4.2: Forces		
Year 3	Forces and magnets	Compare how things move on different surfaces (*The effects of forces; The first law of motion*) Notice that some forces need contact between two objects, but magnetic forces can act at a distance (*Key Idea 3.2: Magnetic properties*) Observe how magnets attract or repel each other and attract some materials and not others (*Key Idea 3.2: Magnetic properties*) Compare and group together a variety of everyday materials on the basis of whether they are attracted to a magnet, and identify some magnetic materials (*Key Idea 3.2: Magnetic properties*) Describe magnets as having two poles (*Key Idea 3.2: Magnetic properties*) Predict whether two magnets will attract or repel each other, depending on which poles are facing (*Key Idea 3.2: Magnetic properties*)
Year 5	Forces	Explain that unsupported objects fall towards the Earth because of the force of gravity acting between the Earth and the falling object (*The effects of forces; Gravity; The difference between mass and weight*) Identify the effects of air resistance, water resistance and friction that act between moving surfaces (*The effect of forces; Forces in action; Friction*) Recognize that some mechanisms, including levers, pulleys and gears, allow a smaller force to have a greater effect (*Mechanisms: Levers, pulleys and gears*)
Key Idea 4.3: The Earth and beyond		
Year 1	Seasonal changes	Observe changes across the four seasons (*The seasons*) Observe and describe weather associated with the seasons and how day length varies (*The seasons*)
Year 5	Earth and space	Describe the movement of the Earth, and other planets, relative to the Sun in the solar system (*The solar system; Day and night; The seasons*) Describe the movement of the Moon relative to the Earth (*The Earth and the Moon*) Describe the Sun, Earth and Moon as approximately spherical bodies (*The Earth and the Moon, The solar system*) Use the idea of the Earth's rotation to explain day and night and the apparent movement of the sun across the sky (*Day and night*)

REFERENCES

DfE. (2013) National curriculum in England: Primary curriculum. Department for Education. Available at: www.gov.uk/government/publications/national-curriculum-in-england-primary-curriculum (accessed 9 April 2017).

APPENDIX

Symbols used in drawing circuit diagrams

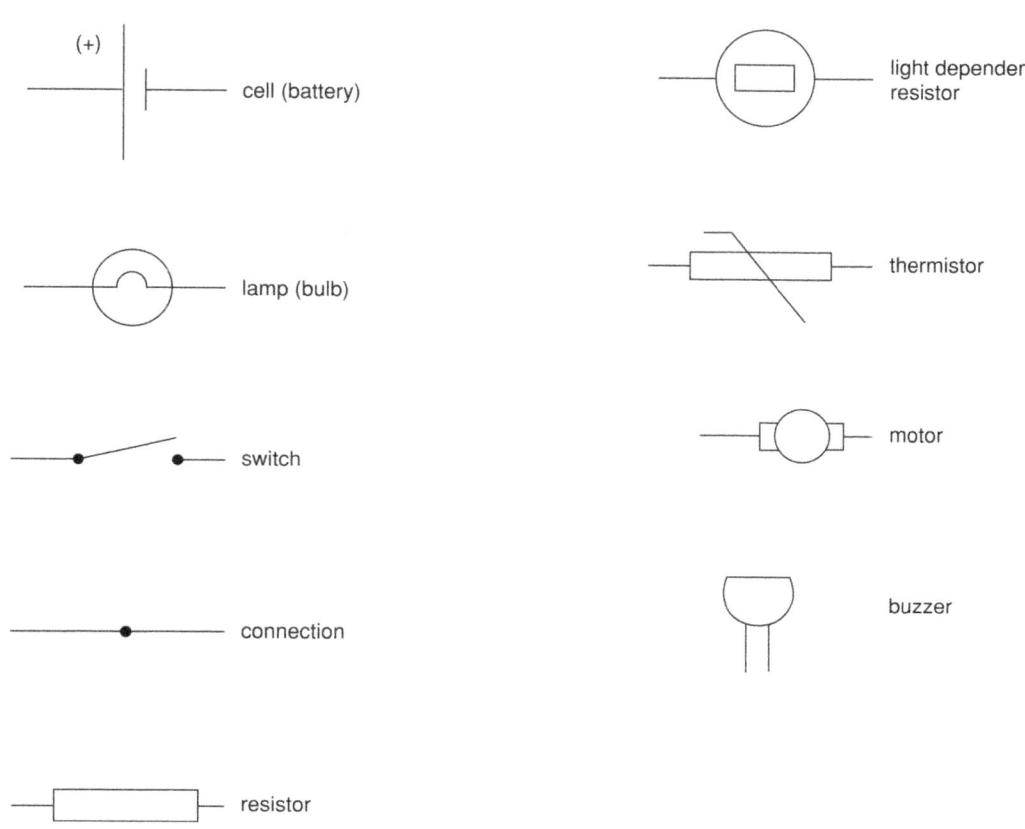

(+) cell (battery)

lamp (bulb)

switch

connection

resistor

light dependent resistor

thermistor

motor

buzzer

Index